W9-BSC-783

SECURED TRANSACTIONS

IN A NUTSHELL

FOURTH EDITION

By

HENRY J. BAILEY III
Professor of Law Emeritus
College of Law, Willamette University

and

RICHARD B. HAGEDORN
Professor of Law
College of Law, Willamette University

WEST
GROUP

ST. PAUL, MINN.
2000

COPYRIGHT © 1976, 1981, 1988 WEST PUBLISHING CO.
COPYRIGHT © 2000 By WEST GROUP
     610 Opperman Drive
     P.O. Box 64526
     St. Paul, MN 55164–0526
     1–800–328–9352

ISBN 0–314–23817–4

 TEXT IS PRINTED ON 10% POST CONSUMER RECYCLED PAPER

2nd Reprint — 2002

Dedicated
To
The Students and Our Colleagues
at the College of Law
Willamette University

*

PREFACE

Perhaps a fitting student reaction to a course in Secured Transactions may be found in the following, which was supplied to one of these writers several years ago by an anonymous (presumed) student:

> Yea thru the valley of the debts he has led us
> > Tho I fear no evil
>
> Because the debtor pays filing fees
> > And file I must when the cause is almost just.

The purpose of this Nutshell is to discuss the law embodied in Article 9 of the Uniform Commercial Code on Secured Transactions, as set forth in the revised versions of 1972 and 1999. Of necessity, the discussion covers both the old, or 1972 version, of Article 9 and the new, or 1999 version, since only a few states as of the writing of this edition of this Nutshell have enacted the 1999 version. The 1999 version was actually approved in 1998 by the co-sponsoring bodies of the Uniform Commercial Code, the American Law Institute and the National Conference of Commissioners on Uniform State

PREFACE

Laws. However, it is known as the 1999 version and shall be referred to as such throughout this Nutshell.

The discussion is comprehensive in scope, but necessarily limited in coverage of particular features of the law of secured transactions as embodied in Article 9 because this Nutshell is presented for use by students who seek a discussion of the basic elements of secured transactions law under the Code. The book should also be of aid to practicing attorneys who face problems in this area but lack experience in handling this particular area of law.

Both authors gratefully acknowledge the countless hours spent by Kathleen E. Marbut in preparing the text.

Henry J. Bailey, III
Richard B. Hagedorn

Salem, Oregon
April, 2000

OUTLINE

CHAPTER 2.
THE SECURITY AGREEMENT

OUTLINE

CHAPTER 3. RELATIONSHIP OF THE
PARTIES PRIOR TO DEFAULT

CHAPTER 4. PERFECTION OF SECURITY INTEREST

CHAPTER 5. PERFECTION OF SECURITY INTEREST BY FILING

OUTLINE

CHAPTER 6. CHOICE OF LAW AND PERFECTION IN MULTIPLE STATE TRANSACTIONS

CHAPTER 7. PRIORITIES OF
SECURED PARTIES AND OTHERS

OUTLINE

CHAPTER 8. BANKRUPTCY OR INSOLVENCY OF DEBTOR

CHAPTER 9. DEFAULT AND ENFORCEMENT OF SECURITY INTEREST

OUTLINE

RESEARCH REFERENCES

Am Jur 2d, Alteration of Instruments §§ 56, 57; Bailments §§ 274, 275, 299; Banks and Financial Institutions §§ 715-718, 859-864; Commercial Code §§ 1 et seq.; Fraudulent Conveyances §§ 246, 270; Letters of Credit § 2; Products Liability §§ 535, 550, 659, 673, 674, 706, 723, 741-773, 779-793, 1535, 1536; Sales §§ 1-27, 70-79; Secured Transactions §§ 737-741.

Corpus Juris Secundum, Accord and Satisfaction § 57; Bailments § 40; Banks and Banking §§ 446, 447; Bills and Notes, Letters of Credit §§ 3, 343; Evidence §1228; Sales §§5,7; Secured Transactions § 2

ALR Index: Uniform Commercial Code

ALR Digest: Sale § 1.5; Uniform Commercial Code §§ 1 et seq.

Am Jur Legal Forms 2d, Uniform Commercial Code §§ 253:1 et seq.

Am Jur Pleading and Practice (Rev), Commercial Code Articles 1-9

RESEARCH REFERENCES

46 Am Jur Trials 687, Failure of Performance in Computer Sales and Leases

17 POF3d 541, Banking Negligence-Improper Dishonor of Letter of Credit

27 POF2d 243, Sales: Implied Warranty of Fitness for Particular Purpose; 26 POF2d 1,

Sales: Implied Warranty of Merchantability; 14 POF2d 693, Commercial paper: Negligence Contributing to Alteration or Unauthorized Signature under UCC § 3-406; 13 POF2d 411, Failure to Act in Commercially Reasonable Manner in Resale of Goods; 12 POF2d 179, Commercial Reasonableness of Aggrieved Party's Acts Following anticipatory Repudiation of Sales Contract; 11POF2d 131, Reduction or Mitigation of Damages-Sales Contract

24 POF 201, Buyer's Defenses under Article 2 of Uniform Commercial Code to Actions by Seller

RESEARCH REFERENCES

Use Westlaw® to Research Commercial Law

Access Westlaw, the computer-assisted legal research service of West Group, to search a broad array of legal resources, including case law, statutes, practice guides, current developments and various other types of information. Consult the online Westlaw Directory to determine databases specific to your needs.

Searching on Westlaw

With Westlaw, you can use the Natural Language search method, which allows you to describe your commercial law issue in plain English. For example, to retrieve documents discussing the priority of a secured party in commingled goods or proceeds, access the Uniform Commercial Code Cases Plus database (UCC-CS+) and type the following Natural Language description:
Priority of secured party in commingled goods (proceeds).

You can also use the Terms and Connectors search method, which allows you to enter a query consisting of key terms from your issue and connectors specifying the relationship between those terms. For example, to search for the phrase consignment interest in the same paragraph as the term inventory, type the following Terms and Connectors query: "consignment interest" /p inventory.

Use KeyCite® to Check Your Research

KeyCite is the citation research service available exclusively on Westlaw. Use KeyCite to see if your cases or statutes are good law and to retrieve cases, legislation or articles that cite your cases and statutes.

For more information regarding searching on Westlaw, call the West Group Reference Attorneys at 1-800-REF-ATTY (1-800-733-2889).

TABLE OF CITATIONS
to the
UNIFORM COMMERCIAL CODE

References are to Chapters (Ch.)
and Sections (§)

UCC ARTICLE 1

UCC CITATIONS

UCC ARTICLE 2

UCC ARTICLE 2A

UCC ARTICLE 3

UCC CITATIONS

UCC ARTICLE 4

UCC ARTICLE 5

UCC ARTICLE 7

UCC ARTICLE 8

1972 UCC ARTICLE 9

UCC CITATIONS

UCC CITATIONS

UCC CITATIONS

UCC CITATIONS

UCC CITATIONS

UCC CITATIONS

UCC CITATIONS

1999 UCC ARTICLE 9

UCC CITATIONS

UCC CITATIONS

UCC CITATIONS

UCC CITATIONS

UCC CITATIONS

UCC CITATIONS

UCC CITATIONS

UCC CITATIONS

UCC CITATIONS

CHAPTER 1

INTRODUCTION

§ 1. Scope of Coverage; Uniform Commercial Code

a. *The Revised 1972 and 1999 Versions of Article 9.*

This Nutshell discusses *secured transactions* under Article 9 of the Uniform Commercial Code (the "Code" or the "UCC"). That Article primarily deals with secured transactions in most items of *personal property* (as distinguished from real property). With some individual state variations, Article 9 has been enacted in all the states, the District of Columbia, Guam, the North Mariana Islands, and the Virgin Islands. No part of the Code has been enacted in Puerto Rico.

The 1962 version of Article 9, once in force in most American jurisdictions, was superseded by the 1972 version in all jurisdictions.

The 1972 version of the Code was subsequently revised with technical changes to conform with later versions of other Articles of the Code. In 1994,

Article 9 also was revised to deal with security interests in investment securities under UCC Article 8 which also was revised in 1994.

This Nutshell discusses the 1972 version as revised prior to 1999. References to the 1972 Article 9 are to that version with subsequent revisions prior to 1999, as indicated above.

This Nutshell also discusses the 1999 version of Article 9. In 1998, the Code sponsoring bodies (the American Law Institute and the National Conference of Commissioners on Uniform State Laws) approved an entirely new version of Article 9. That new version is referred to here as the 1999 Article 9, when it was submitted to the states for enactment. The new 1999 Article 9 consists of a substantial reorganization of revised 1972 Article 9, a renumbering of most sections, and the inclusion of a number of new provisions.

b. The Comments to the Code

Reference also is made at various places in this Nutshell to Official Comments to sections of the Uniform Commercial Code. For example, a reference to Comment 3 to 1972 § 9-103 is to the Official Comment numbered 3 of the Uniform Commercial

Code drafters of the 1972 version. A reference to Comment 3 to 1999 § 9-103 is to the Official Comment number 3 of the drafters which follows and discusses some aspect of § 9-103 of the 1999 version. Although the Comments to the various Code sections do not themselves have the force of statutory law, they are valuable aids in the interpretation of such Code sections and have been extensively utilized by courts in Code cases.

c. Other Writings

Secured Transactions under Article 9 of the Uniform Commercial Code is the subject of discussion in a large number of law review articles and published books. A Hornbook that deals extensively with Article 9 is White and Summers, Uniform Commercial Code, 5th ed., Student Edition, West Publishing Co., 2000. Article 9 (as well as other Articles of the Code) also is discussed in Stone, Uniform Commercial Code in a Nutshell, 4th ed., West Publishing Co., 1995.

An exhaustive discussion of the background of secured transactions under the Code and under prior law is the early two-volume set, Gilmore, Security Interests in Personal Property, Little, Brown & Co., 1965. Another discussion of secured transactions under the Code is Clark, The Law of Secured Transactions Under the Uniform Commercial Code, Revised edition 1993 with Supplements, Warren, Gorham & Lamont.

d. Uniform Commercial Code Generally

The Uniform Commercial Code deals with secured transactions, the subject matter of this Nutshell, in Article 9. Other aspects of commercial transactions are covered in other Articles of the Code. Thus, Article 2 deals with Sales, Article 3 with Negotiable Instruments, Article 4 with Bank Deposits and Collections, Article 5 with Letters of Credit, Article 7 with Documents of Title and Article 8 (as revised in 1994) with Investment Securities. Article 6 deals with bulk transfers, but that Article was repealed in a number of states and revised in most remaining states.

Article 1 of the Code sets forth a number of General Provisions, including definitions of a number of terms and rules of construction, which affect all other Articles of the Code, including Article 9. There are also provisions at the end of the UCC that deal with the effective date of the various Articles of the Code in the enacting jurisdiction, continue the validity of commercial transactions entered into before the effective date of the various Articles and list statutes repealed by the Code.

While this Nutshell discusses secured transactions under Article 9, reference will be made where appropriate to provisions in other Articles of the Code, and particularly to various General Provisions and definitions in Article 1.

The Uniform Commercial Code was drafted during the period following World War II as a joint project of the American Law Institute and the National Conference of Commissioners on Uniform State Laws, referred to as the Code sponsors. The drafting represented the work of a large number of lawyers, judges, law professors and others. Later versions of the various Articles of the Code, including the 1999 version of Article 9, were drafted by other groups of lawyers, judges, law professors and others, again as a joint project of the American Law Institute and the National Conference of Commissioners on Uniform State Laws.

e. *Variations in Enactment of the Code*

The term, *Uniform Commercial Code*, is a misnomer at least to some degree. The various enacting jurisdictions have modified a number of individual

Code sections with non-uniform variations from the Official Text.

Although this Nutshell refers where appropriate to the revised 1972 and 1999 versions of the Code, it is impractical in a work of this nature to discuss individual state non-uniform modifications of particular Code sections of Article 9. The student of Article 9 who is concerned with the enactment in any particular jurisdiction should examine the specific enactment of that jurisdiction, to determine the existence of any non-uniform variations of individual sections from the Official Text of the Code sponsors.

f. Pre-Code Statutes Replaced by Code

The Uniform Commercial Code, in Articles other than Article 9 on Secured Transactions, replaces certain former uniform statutes. Article 9 itself also replaces some former statutes, including two former uniform statutes: the Uniform Trust Receipts Act and the Uniform Conditional Sales Act. The former uniform statute had rather widespread enactment; the latter uniform law on conditional sales had rather limited enactment.

A number of non-uniform state statutes covering

secured transactions are also superseded by Article 9. Those include chattel mortgage laws enacted in virtually all states, non-uniform statutes governing conditional sales and other non-uniform statutes governing assignments of accounts receivable and factor's liens. The replaced statutes covered parts of the secured transactions area now covered comprehensively in Article 9.

§ 2. Purpose and Policy of Article 9

§ 9-101 of the 1972 Article 9, as revised, and the 1999 version of Article 9 states that Article 9 may be cited as *Uniform Commercial Code–Secured Transactions*.

The aim of Article 9 is to provide a simple and unified structure within which the immense variety of present-day secured financing transactions can be carried out with less cost and more certainty than under pre-Code law. The general purpose of Article 9 is stated in the following material taken from the beginning of the Comment to 1972 § 9-101:

This Article sets out a comprehensive scheme for the regulation of security interests in personal property and fixtures. It supersedes prior legislation dealing with such security devices as chattel mortgages, conditional sales, trust receipts, factor's liens and assignments of accounts receivable.

Note that there is a similar statement in Comment 1 to 1999 § 9-101.

Consumer installment sales and consumer loans present special problems of a nature which makes special regulation of them inappropriate in a general commercial codification. Many states now regulate such loans and sales under small loan acts, retail installment selling acts and the like. Note, however, that the 1999 revision of Article 9 includes some special rules for "consumer goods," "consumer goods transactions," and "consumer transactions." See Comment 4 to 1999 § 9-101. Such special rules are discussed at various places in this Nutshell.

Under all versions of the Article, distinctions based on form or the label given a transaction are not controlling, unless the transaction takes the form of a "pledge" where the secured creditor is in possession of the collateral or produces a "purchase money security interest" (both of which are discussed and defined elsewhere in this Nutshell), in which case the Article in some instances treats the transaction differently from other secured transactions. For some purposes there are distinctions based on the type of property which constitutes the collateral–industrial and commercial equipment, business inventory, farm products, consumer goods, accounts receivable, documents of title and other intangibles. 1999 Article 9 also covers some additional kinds of property (such as computer software) not covered in the 1972 version. Where appropriate, the Article states special rules applicable to financing transactions involving a particular type of property. Despite the statutory simplification, a greater degree of flexibility in the financing transaction is allowed than was possible under pre-Code law.

In both the 1972 and 1999 versions of Article 9, a more rational filing system replaces the former system of different files for each security device which is subject to filing requirements. Thus, not only is the information contained in the files made more accessible but the cost of procuring credit information and, incidentally, of maintaining the files, is greatly reduced.

The rules set out in both the 1972 and 1999 versions of Article 9 are principally concerned with two relationships: the secured creditor-debtor relationship and the relationship of the secured party to purchasers from and creditors of the debtor.

§ 3. Secured Transactions Within Article 9

a. *Definition of Secured Transaction*

Article 9 of the Uniform Commercial Code under either the 1972 or 1999 versions primarily deals with *secured transactions in personal property*.

A *secured transaction* within the scope of Article 9 of the Code might be considered as any transaction which is *intended* to create in favor of one person a *security interest* in the *personal property* of someone else.

A secured transaction is one which produces for the benefit of the secured creditor a "lien" in the personal property of the debtor. The lien serves two functions for the creditor: (1) if the debtor defaults, *i.e.*, fails to pay the secured debt, the secured creditor may take possession of the personal property subject to the lien and use it to satisfy the debt; (2) if other creditors of or buyers from the debtor, or a bankruptcy trustee asserts a claim to the debtor's personal property, the creditor may be able to acquire a priority position through the lien. In these two regards, it may be said the personal property subject to the lien "secures" payment of the debt owed the secured creditor.

It must be kept in mind that Article 9 covers

secured transactions for the most part *only in personal property*. While personal property within the scope of Article 9 includes *fixtures* (goods related to real estate), Article 9 does not apply to any real estate security interest, such as a mortgage or deed of trust. See § 5 of this chapter which lists excluded transactions.

A secured transaction in personal property ordinarily arises in two basic kinds of transactions: (1) a loan made to the owner of personal property which is secured by that property; and (2) a purchase of personal property on credit wherein the buyer gives a security interest in the purchased property either to the seller or to the person who makes a loan to enable the buyer to buy the property. This latter type of transaction creates a *purchase money security interest*, similar to a conditional sale under pre-Code law. See discussion in § 9c(2) of this chapter.

Under the 1972 version of Article 9, in any secured transaction, the property subject to the security interest (including accounts and chattel paper which have been sold) is referred to as the *collateral*. See 1972 § 9-105(1)(c). The 1999 Article 9 in § 9-102(a)(12) defines *collateral* as the property subject to a security interest or agricultural lien. The term "collateral" includes proceeds of collateral, accounts, chattel paper, payment intangibles, and promissory notes that have been sold, and goods that are the subject of a consignment.

The term "secured transaction" is not expressly defined in the Code, although there is a definition of the term "security interest" in § 1-201(37), which basically defines that term as "an interest in personal property or fixtures which secures payment or performance of an obligation." The definition of "security interest" in § 1-201(37) continues by considering whether certain transactions (such as a sale of goods with reservation of title in the seller, a lease of goods, or a consignment) may create a security interest. That definition is expanded under the 1999 UCC. Further discussion of "leases" and "consignments" occurs later in this Nutshell. See Chapter 2, § 6d, e.

Although the term "secured transaction" is not defined, 1972 § 9-102(1) declares that Article 9 applies "(a) to any transaction (regardless of its form) which is intended to create a security interest in personal property or fixtures including goods, documents, instruments, general intangibles, chattel paper or accounts; and also (b) to any sale of accounts or chattel paper."

There is an expanded statement in 1999 § 9-109(a) which declares that except for certain excluded transactions (see § 5 of this chapter), Article 9 applies to:

(1)   a transaction, regardless of its form, that creates a security interest in personal property or fixtures by contract;

(2)   an agricultural lien;

(3)   a sale of accounts, chattel paper, payment intangibles, or promissory notes;

(4)   a consignment;

(5)   a security interest arising under certain provisions in the Articles on sales or leases of goods; and

(6)   a security interest arising under certain provisions on bank deposits and collections or letters of credit.

In summary, a secured transaction might be outlined as involving (1) a debt, (2) a debtor, (3) a creditor or secured party, (4) personal property or fixtures making up the security or collateral, (5) an agreement which may take the form of a pledge, or control of the collateral by the secured party, or a security interest where the debtor is in possession.

Ordinarily, the debtor is the borrower on the security of the personal property collateral or the credit purchaser of the personal property that serves as the collateral. In certain instances, a third person may put up the collateral as security for the loan and the debtor may also be a third person serving as surety or guarantor of the obligation.

b. *Intention of the Parties*

A secured transaction is *consensual* in nature and requires that there be an *agreement* between the parties, the debtor and the secured party. For example, under the 1972 version of Article 9, such an agreement must be in writing and meet certain requirements unless the secured party has possession or control of the collateral or the personal property which is security for the debt. For discussion of the requirements of agreements under both the 1972 and 1999 versions of the Article, see Chapter 2.

The basic test of the existence of a secured transaction in personal property usually is *whether the parties intended that a security interest exist.* Absent such an intention, Article 9 normally does not apply. However, without regard to intent to create a security interest, Article 9 applies to most sales of accounts and chattel paper. See § 4 of this chapter.

It follows that Article 9 does not apply to a non-consensual lien on personal property, such as a statutory lien, although the 1999 version of Article 9 includes coverage of agricultural liens for certain purposes.

Example 1. Dealer A had been financing the purchase of his inventory for resale with finance company B. B notified A that B intended to terminate the financing relationship and A then negotiated with a second finance company C for the latter to take over A's inventory financing. While the negotiations were under way, A received a shipment of new inventory from the manufacturer. The latter mistakenly billed the shipment to B and B mistakenly paid the manufacturer for the shipment. After the shipment arrived on A's premises, B discovered the mistake and took possession of the items shipped. There is no secured transaction between A and B covering that shipment and Article 9 does not apply.

Example 2. A entered into a contract for builder B to construct a building on A's premises. When B failed to complete construction, surety company C (which had issued a performance bond to B) took over and completed the work. After completion, A paid the amount due for the work to C which asserted its common-law right of subrogation to amounts that had been due from A to B under the contract. D, the trustee in bankruptcy of B, claimed the amount paid by A to C on the ground that C had not taken action under Article 9 to perfect its security interest in that amount. There is no secured transaction, since C's right to payment by A arose under common-law rights of subrogation. Thus, C is entitled to retain the payment even though C did not perfect a security interest under Article 9.

c. Additional Coverage in 1999 Article 9

The 1999 Article 9 expands the coverage of kinds of property subject to secured transactions in certain respects. Coverage in the 1999 version includes (as covered in Comment 4a to 1999 § 9-101): Deposit accounts, sales of payment intangibles and promissory notes, health-care-insurance receivables, nonpossessory statutory agricultural liens, consignments, supporting obligations and property securing rights to payment, commercial tort claims, transfers by States and governmental units of States, nonassignable general intangibles, promissory notes, health-care-insurance receivables, and letter-of-credit rights.

§ 4. Sales of Accounts, Chattel Paper, Payment Intangibles, or Promissory Notes

1972 Article 9 in § 9-102(1)(b) expressly applies, not only to transactions intended to create security interests in personal property, but also to any sale of accounts or chattel paper. The 1999 Article 9 in § 9-109(a)(3) similarly applies to a sale of accounts or chattel paper and additionally applies to a sale of payment intangibles or promissory notes. The reason for the rule subjecting such sales to Article 9 is that commercial financing on the basis of accounts and chattel paper "is often so conducted that the distinction between a security transfer and a sale is blurred," with the buyer treated as a secured party and the buyer's interest treated as a security interest. See Comment 2 to 1972 § 9-102. The definitions of the terms "account," "chattel paper," "payment intangibles," and "promissory note" are considered later in this chapter. See § 7b, c and e.

Comment 4 to 1999 § 9-109 states that the approach treating sales of accounts and chattel paper "generally has been successful in avoiding difficult problems of distinguishing between transactions in which a receivable secures an obligation and those in which the receivable has been sold outright. In many commercial financing transactions the distinction is blurred. Comment 4 continues by noting the expansion of 1999 § 9-109(a)(3) to include the sale of a "payment intangible" and the sale of a "promissory note."

Although, as stated above, 1999 Article 9 applies to sales of accounts, chattel paper, payment intangibles or promissory notes, certain sales or assignments are completely excluded from coverage under Article 9. See discussion in § 5g of this chapter.

§ 5. Excluded Transactions

There are a number of transactions that are excluded from Article 9 coverage. 1972 § 9-104 simply lists a number of transactions to which Article 9 does not apply. 1999 § 9-109(c) speaks of certain transactions that may not be within Article 9 and 1999 § 9-109(d) lists other transactions to which Article 9 does not apply. The exclusions in both the 1972 and 1999 versions of Article 9 have some similarities and some differences.

a. Both versions exclude certain transactions subject to federal law at least to some extent. 1972 § 9-104(a) excludes a security interest subject to any statute of the United States to the extent that such statute governs the rights of parties to and third parties affected by transactions in particular kinds of property. 1999 § 9-109(c)(1) declares that Article 9 does not apply to the extent that a statute, regulation, or treaty of the United States preempts Article 9. Both versions probably have the same meaning, but it is clear in the 1999 version that the exclusion applies only where there is federal preemption and not to areas where federal law merely deals with some subject matter also within Article 9. The important thing to remember is that certain matters must be researched on a federal as well as state level. For example, where ship mortgages, aircraft titles, patents and copyrights, railroad equipment and some interstate commercial vehicles are involved, federal law may be preemptive.

b. 1972 Article 9 does not apply to a transfer by a government or governmental subdivision or agency under § 9-104(e). Under 1999 § 9-109(c)(2) Article 9 does not apply where another statute of the enacting state governs the creation, perfection, priority, or enforcement of a security interest created by that state or a governmental unit of that state. 1999 § 9-109(c)(3) also states that Article 9 does not apply to the extent that a statute of another state or county or governmental unit of the same, other than a statute generally applicable to security interests (such as Article 9 of another state), expressly governs creation, perfection, priority or enforcement of a security interest created by the other state, county, or governmental unit. In other words, Article 9 of the enacting state defers to statutes of another state or foreign country only to the extent that the other statutes contain rules applicable specifically to security interests created by the particular governmental unit of the other jurisdiction.

c. 1972 § 9-104(m) excludes from Article 9 a transfer of an interest in a letter of credit other than the right to proceeds of a written letter of credit. 1999 § 9-109(c)(4) states somewhat similarly that Article 9 does not apply to the extent the rights of a transferee beneficiary or nominated person are independent and superior under the letter-of-credit Article (§ 5-114) dealing with assignment of proceeds of a letter of credit.

d. Article 9 does not apply to a landlord's lien under 1972 § 9-104(b). That exclusion is continued in 1999 § 9-109(d)(1) except for an agricultural lien. Agricultural liens are within 1999 Article 9 for certain purposes.

e. Article 9 does not apply to a lien given by statute or rule of law for services or materials under 1972 § 9-104(c). That exclusion is continued in 1999 § 9-109(d)(2) except for an agricultural lien. Those liens are often referred to as "artisan's liens." Other provisions (1972 § 9-310 and 1999 § 9-333) set forth rules of priority of any lien for services or materials as against an Article 9 security interest.

f. Transfer or assignment of a claim for wages, salary or other compensation of an employee is excluded from Article 9 under both 1972 § 9-104(d) and 1999 § 9-109(d)(3). Such assignments are regulated by other federal and state statutes and present important social issues that other law addresses.

g. Article 9 does not apply to certain sales or assignments of accounts or chattel paper that by their nature have nothing to do with commercial financing transactions. Thus, sales of accounts or chattel paper as part of the complete sale of a business are excluded. Assignments of accounts or chattel paper for the purpose of collection only are similarly excluded. A transfer or assignment of a right of payment under a contract to an assignee that is also obligated to perform under the contract is also excluded. Finally, a transfer or assignment of a single account to an assignee in full or partial satisfaction of a preexisting indebtedness is excluded. See 1972 § 9-104(f) and 1999 § 9-104(d)(4)-(7). The 1999 provisions also refer to sales or assignments of payment intangibles or promissory notes in § 9-109(d)(4), (5) and (7).

In short, if a business is sold to another person who takes over the seller's accounts, Article 9 does not apply. If a business turns over overdue accounts to a collection agency, Article 9 does not apply. If a contract is assigned to another person who is to take over the assignor's obligations and also to receive the assignor's rights to payment, Article 9 does not apply. If a business owes money to another and assigns to the other person the proceeds of a single account owed to the business by a third person, Article 9 does not apply.

h. Article 9 does not apply with respect to a transfer of an interest in or assignment of a claim under a policy of insurance. Such transactions are also special and do not fit easily into a general secured transactions statute. However, Article 9 provisions apply with respect to proceeds and priorities in proceeds of insurance policies. See 1972 § 9-104(g). For example, if an automobile that is collateral in a secured transaction is destroyed in an accident, the secured party has a security interest in the payment made to the policyholder by the insurance company under a "collision" insurance policy.

The same exclusion is in 1999 § 9-109(d)(8) but there is an exception for an assignment by or to a health-care provider of a health-care receivable and any subsequent assignment of a right to payment in the 1999 enactment. Certain 1999 provisions apply to health-care receivables.

i. Article 9 does not apply to a right represented by a judgment other than a judgment taken on a right to payment that was collateral under 1972 § 9-104(h) and 1999 § 9-109(d)(9).

j. Article 9 does not apply to a right of setoff under 1972 § 9-104(i). The same rule applies under 1999 § 9-109(d)(10) to a right of recoupment or setoff but two exceptions to the general exclusion are added. One of the exceptions applies to a setoff against a deposit account that is collateral. The second recognizes the right of an obligor on an account, chattel paper, or general intangible to raise claims and defenses against an assignee (secured party). See Comment 14 to 1999 § 9-109.

"Recoupment" is the legal ability to subtract from any payment due the amount the person trying to collect the debt (or that person's predecessor) happens to owe the debtor. "Setoff" is a common law right that allows parties to net out mutual debts. In essence, a setoff may occur where two parties are debtors to each other as to separate credit transactions and one party defaults. The other party may then reduce the defaulted obligation by reducing his debt to the defaulting party.

k. Article 9 does not apply to the creation or transfer of an interest in or lien on real estate, including a lease or rents thereunder. However, a security interest in fixtures is within the scope of Article 9. See 1972 § 9-104(j). 1999 § 9-109(d)(11) is similar. The provision refers not only to fixtures but also to fixture filings. The 1999 provision also permits a security agreement covering both real and personal property and permits certain liens (in 1999 § 9-203 and 9-308) on real property.

Issues have arisen as to whether a mortgagee's

interest (the note payable to the mortgagee and real estate mortgage which secures it) when used as collateral falls within the scope of Article 9. It appears when the note and mortgage are used as collateral to secure payment of an extension of credit to the mortgagee, the transaction falls within the scope of Article 9. However, should the mortgagor use its interest in the real estate as collateral for an extension of credit, the transaction does not fall within the scope of Article 9. Similar issues have arisen regarding land sale contracts. There is a split of authority regarding whether a vendor's interest when used as collateral is within the scope of Article 9. Most probably, the vendee's interest when used as collateral in a transaction would involve a transaction outside the scope of Article 9.

l. A transfer of a tort claim is excluded in 1972 § 9-104(k). That exclusion is narrowed in 1999 § 9-109(d)(12) to exclude only tort claims that are other than "commercial tort" claims. 1999 Article 9 applies to commercial tort claims as well as assignments of tort claims that constitute proceeds of other collateral (such as a right to payment for destruction of inventory serving as collateral).

m. Deposit accounts are excluded in 1972 § 9-104(l) except with respect to proceeds and priorities in proceeds. That exclusion is narrowed in 1999 § 9-109(d)(13) to exclude only an assignment of a deposit account in a consumer transaction. In short, non-consumer deposit accounts when used as collateral fall within 1999 Article 9's scope. Proceeds and priorities in proceeds of both consumer and non-consumer accounts are within 1999 Article 9's scope.

§ 6. Parties to Secured Transaction

a. Debtor

The principal parties to a secured transaction are the *debtor* and the *secured party*, terms which are defined in the Code.

"Debtor" under the 1972 UCC means "the person who owes payment or other performance of the obligation secured, whether or not he owns or has rights in the collateral, and includes the seller of accounts or chattel paper. Where the debtor and the owner of the collateral are not the same person, the term 'debtor' means the owner of the collateral in any provision of the Article dealing with the collateral, the obligor in any provision dealing with the obligation, and may include both where the context so requires." See 1972 § 9-104(1)(d).

The 1999 UCC in § 9-102(a)(28) redefines "debtor" as (A) a person having an interest, other than a security interest or other lien in the collateral, whether or not that person is an obligor; (B) a seller of accounts, chattel paper, payment intangibles, or promissory notes; or (C) a consignee.

Comment 2 to 1999 § 9-102 explains the changed definition, which also introduces the terms "obligor" and "secondary obligor" absent from the 1972 Article 9. In most instances, the "debtor" is one who has a stake in the proper enforcement of the security interest by virtue of a non-lien interest in the property, usually an ownership interest. In most instances, the "debtor" is also an "obligor." That term is defined in 1999 § 9-102(a)(59) and usually is the person who owes the debt. A "secondary obligor" is defined in 1999 § 9-102(a)(71) and usually indicates a person who is a surety or guarantor of the debt.

The 1999 definition of "debtor" also continues the 1972 definition of "debtor" as a seller of accounts and chattel paper and also includes a seller of payment intangibles or promissory notes. The 1999 definition further defines a "debtor" as including a consignee of goods. 1999 Article 9 removes from the Sales Article 2 most aspects of consignment sales and transfers such consignment transactions to 1999 Article 9.

Other terms that may be synonymous with the term "debtor" would include "borrower" or "buyer." A "buyer" might include a person who purchases goods on credit and gives a "purchase-money security interest" in the goods for the unpaid price.

b. *Secured Party*

Under 1972 § 9-105(m) the term "secured party" means "a lender, seller or other person in whose favor there is a security interest, including a person to whom accounts or chattel paper have been sold. When the holders of obligations issued under an indenture of trust, equipment trust agreement or the like are represented by a trustee or other person, the representative is the secured party."

The term "secured party" is redefined in 1999 § 9-102(a)(72) as a person in whose favor a security interest is created or provided for under a security agreement, whether or not any obligation to be secured is outstanding; a person that holds an agricultural lien; a consignor; a person to which accounts, chattel paper, payment intangibles, or promissory notes have been sold; a trustee, indenture trustee, agent, collateral agent, or other representative in whose favor a security interest or agricultural lien is created or provided for; or a person that holds a security interest arising under certain provisions of Articles 2, 2A, 4 and 5.

The references to a person holding an agricultural lien and to a consignor are new (the latter reference again recognizing the transfer of much of the law of consignment transactions from Article 2 to 1999 Article 9). The references to certain provisions of Articles 2, 2A, 4 and 5 recognize certain security interests given in sections of those Articles that apply also under 1972 Article 9 but do not require a security agreement or filing. The reference to payment intangibles or promissory notes is added to the reference to the purchaser of accounts and chattel paper.

Other terms which might apply to a "secured party" include "lender," "obligee," "financer" or "seller." The latter term would include a person who sells goods on credit and takes a purchase-money security interest for the unpaid price.

c. Account Debtor

Still another term used in Article 9 is "account debtor," defined as "the person who is obligated on an account, chattel paper or general intangible." See 1972 § 9-105(1)(a). 1999 § 9-102(a)(3) is almost identical in defining "account debtor" but adds a statement: "[t]he term does not include persons obligated to pay a negotiable instrument, even if the instrument constitutes part of chattel paper."

Example 1. A buys widgets from B on credit and gives B a security interest in the widgets for the unpaid price by means of a signed security agreement and a promissory note. B assigns the security agreement and indorses the note to C, as security for a debt owed by B to C. C is the assignee and secured party, B is the assignor and debtor and A is the account debtor. The note and security agreement together are chattel paper.

Example 2. B sells widgets to A on open account and B assigns the account due from A to C as security for a debt owed by B to C. C is the assignee and secured party, B is the assignor and debtor and A is the account debtor.

Comment 5b to 1999 § 9-102 states that the rules in various provisions of 1999 Article 9 dealing with an "account debtor" do not apply where an assignment of chattel paper is evidenced by a negotiable instrument. Rather, the assignee's rights are governed by UCC Article 3.

§ 7. Collateral: Definition and Classes

The term *collateral* is defined in 1972 § 9-105(1)(c) as the property subject to a security interest. The term includes accounts and chattel paper which have been sold.

Collateral is defined in 1999 § 9-102(a)(12) as the property subject to a security interest or agricultural lien. The term includes: proceeds to which a security interest attaches; accounts, chattel paper, payment intangibles, and promissory notes that have been sold; and goods that are the subject of a consignment.

The 1999 definition adds proceeds, sales of payment intangibles and promissory notes and also adds goods that are the subject of a consignment. The definition also includes property subject to an agricultural lien.

There are different classes of collateral under both the 1972 and 1999 versions of Article 9. The Article frequently treats secured transactions differently depending upon the class of collateral involved. Thus, it is important to understand which class of collateral is involved in a particular secured transaction.

Goods are defined in 1972 § 9-105(1)(h) as including "all things which are movable at the time the security interest attaches or which are fixtures, but does not include money, documents, instruments, investment property, accounts, chattel paper, general intangibles, or minerals or the like (including oil and gas) before extraction. 'Goods' also includes standing timber which is to be cut and removed under a conveyance or contract for sale, the unborn young of animals, and growing crops."

The definition of "goods" in 1999 § 9-102(a)(44) is rather lengthy. It basically covers the first clause of the 1972 definition (all things that are movable when a security interest attaches). The definition includes fixtures, standing timber to be cut and removed under a conveyance or contract for sale, the unborn young of animals, and crops. Crops include those produced on trees, vines, or bushes (something not specified in the 1972 definition). The 1999 definition also adds as goods manufactured homes. "Goods" in the 1999 definition also includes a computer program embedded in goods and any supporting information provided in connection with a transaction relating to the program if (i) the program is associated with the goods in such a manner that it customarily is considered part of the goods, or (ii) by becoming the owner of the goods, a person acquires a right to use the program in connection with the goods. The term does not include a computer program embedded in goods that consist solely of the medium in which the program is embedded. Similar to the 1972 definition of "goods," the term "also does not include accounts, chattel paper, commercial tort claims, deposit accounts, documents, general intangibles, instruments, investment property, letter-of-credit rights, letters of credit, money, or oil, gas, or other minerals before extraction."

a. Goods. Goods are classified as follows:

(1) *Consumer goods* are goods used or bought for use primarily for personal, family or household purposes. See 1972 § 9-109(1) and 1999 § 9-102(a)-(24).

Example. Homeowner gives a security interest in his household furniture to Secured Party.

(2) *Farm products* under 1972 § 9-109(3) are "crops or livestock or supplies used or produced in farming operation or products of crops or livestock

in their unmanufactured states (such as ginned cotton, wool-clip, maple syrup, milk and eggs), and if they are in the possession of a debtor engaged in raising, fattening, grazing or other farming operations. If goods are farm products they are neither equipment nor inventory."

Farm products under 1999 § 9-102(a)(34) are "goods, other than standing timber, with respect to which the debtor is engaged in a farming operation and which are crops grown, growing, or to be grown, including crops produced on trees, vines, and bushes, and aquatic goods produced in aquacultural operations. Farm products would also include livestock, born or unborn, including aquatic goods produced in aquacultural operations and supplies used or produced in a farming operation or products of crops or livestock in their unmanufactured states."

The 1999 definition expands the 1972 definition to cover crops growing on trees, vines and bushes and "aquatic goods," such as fish on a fish farm or hatchery or cultivated oysters. It is stated that standing timber is not a "farm product." Presumably, standing timber to be cut is "inventory."

(3) *Inventory* are goods under 1972 § 9-109(4) held by a person who holds them for sale or lease or to be furnished under contracts of service or if he

has so furnished them, or if they are raw materials, work in process or materials used or consumed in a business. Inventory of a person is not to be classified as equipment.

In 1999 § 9-102(a)(48), *inventory* is similarly defined as goods, other than farm products, which are leased by a person as lessor; are held by a person for sale or lease or to be furnished under a contract of service; are furnished by a person under a contract of service; or consist of raw materials, work in process, or materials used or consumed in a business.

(4) *Equipment* consists of goods used or bought for use primarily in business (including farming or a profession) or by a nonprofit organization or governmental subdivision or agency. Equipment is not included in the definitions of inventory, farm products or consumer goods. See 1972 § 9-109(2). In 1999 § 9-102(a)(33), *equipment* is merely defined as goods other than inventory, farm products, or consumer goods.

Example. Manufacturer gives a security interest in the machinery used in the factory to Secured Party.

Comment 4a to 1999 § 9-102 notes:

"The classes of goods are mutually exclusive. For example, the same property cannot simultaneously be both equipment and inventory. In borderline cases—a physician's car or a farmer's truck that might be either consumer goods or equipment—the principal use to which the property is put is determinative. Goods can fall into different classes at different times. For example, a radio may be inventory in the hands of a dealer and consumer goods in the hands of a consumer."

It is stated that goods are "equipment" if they do not fall into another category. That is also true under 1972 § 9-109. See Comment 3 to that provision.

(5) *Fixtures* are goods that have become so related to particular real estate or real property that an interest in them arises under real estate law. See 1972 § 9-313(1)(a) and 1999 § 9-102(a)(41). However, no security interest arises under Article 9 in ordinary building materials incorporated into an improvement on land. See 1972 § 9-313(2) and 1999 § 9-334(a).

In short, real estate law governs whether goods are fixtures; but when they are fixtures, property rights are governed both by real estate law and the law of personal property.

Examples of fixtures. A furnace affixed to a

house or other building; counters permanently affixed to the floor of a store; a sprinkler system installed in a building.

Note as to fixtures that as personal property under the Code, fixtures are also either consumer goods or equipment. It is difficult to conceive of goods being both inventory and fixtures, since they are not normally affixed to real estate while being held for sale in the ordinary course of business. Crops are farm products but are not fixtures, even though they have a relation to real estate. Personal property that is attached to realty but is easily removable (such as carpeting tacked to a floor) is not a fixture.

(6) *Accessions* are goods installed in or firmly affixed to other goods (such as a new motor installed in an automobile). See 1972 § 9-314(1) and 1999 § 9-102(a)(1) for a similar definition. But easily removable goods installed on other goods (such as tires mounted on the wheels of an automobile) are not accessions.

b. Indispensable Paper. This expression does not appear in the Code as such, though the Comment to 1972 § 9-106 refers to an "indispensable writing." Indispensable paper covers various categories of paper which are negotiable or which are to some extent dealt with as if negotiable. This category has also been referred to as *semi-intangibles* or *commercial specialties*.

(1) *Document* means document of title, such as a bill of lading or warehouse receipt. See 1972 § 9-105(1)(f) and 1999 § 9-102(a)(30). See also the Article 1 definitions of *bill of lading* in § 1-201(6), *document of title* in § 1-201(15) and *warehouse receipt* in § 1-201(45). As to the 1999 Code, see also § 7-201(2).

(2) *Instrument* means most commonly a negotiable instrument (draft, check, certificate of deposit or note). See 1972 § 9-105(1)(i) and 1999 § 9-102(a)(47). Note that "instrument" does not include "investment property."

(3) *Investment property* most importantly means an investment security such as stocks, bonds or the like but also includes commodity accounts and contracts. See 1972 § 9-115 and 1999 § 9-102(a)(49). An investment security can be certificated or uncertificated. See § 9a(3) of this chapter for discussion.

(4) *Chattel paper* means a writing or writings which evidence both a monetary obligation and a security interest in or lease of specific goods. When a transaction is evidenced both by such a security

agreement or a lease and by an instrument or series of instruments, the group of writings taken together constitutes chattel paper. See 1972 § 9-105(1)(b). 1999 § 9-102(a)(11) similarly defines *chattel paper*.

Example. A dealer sells a tractor to a farmer on conditional sales contract or purchase money security interest. The conditional sales contract is a *security agreement*, the farmer is the *debtor*, the dealer is the *secured party* and the tractor is the type of *collateral* defined as *equipment*. The dealer then transfers the contract to his bank either by outright sale or to secure a loan. Since the conditional sales contract is a security agreement relating to specific equipment, the conditional sales contract is now the type of collateral called *chattel paper*. In this transaction between the dealer and his bank, the bank is the *secured party*, the dealer is the *debtor*, and the farmer is the *account debtor*. *If a promissory note is included with the conditional sales contract or security agreement, the writings taken together are chattel paper.*

c. Intangibles. This type of collateral is purely intangible, that is, intangibles not evidenced by an indispensable writing but which may be the subject of a commercial financing transaction.

(1) *Account* under the 1972 Code means any right to payment for goods sold or leased or for services rendered which is not evidenced by an instrument or chattel paper, whether or not it has been earned by performance. This covers the ordinary account receivable. Rights arising under a ship charter are also accounts. See 1972 § 9-106 and Comment. The 1999 Code similarly defines "account." See 1999 § 9-102(a)(2).

Example. Dealer sells goods to users on open account (on an unsecured basis) wherein the users have 60 days in which to pay. Dealer assigns the accounts to Bank either by outright sale or to secure a loan. In this transaction between Dealer and Bank, Bank is the *secured party*, Dealer is the *debtor* and the several users are the *account debtors*.

(2) *General intangibles* means any personal property (including things in action) other than goods, accounts, chattel paper, documents, instruments and money, i.e., purely intangible collateral which is not an account.

Examples. Goodwill, literary rights, rights to performance, and also copyrights, trademarks and patents if not excluded from the applicability of Article 9 as security interests subject to any statute of the United States. See 1972 § 9-106 and Comment and 1999 § 9-109(a)(42).

d. Proceeds includes "whatever is received upon the sale, exchange, collection or other disposition of collateral or proceeds * * *. Money, checks, deposit accounts, and the like are 'cash proceeds.' All other proceeds are 'non-cash proceeds.'" See 1972 § 9-306(1). Similarly, see 1999 § 9-102(a)(64).

Example. Dealer gives a security interest in his inventory to User-Buyer. User-Buyer pays a cash down payment and trades in his old car. He pays the balance by check. The cash, trade-in car and check are all proceeds of the inventory collateral. Note that when the used car traded in is itself sold again by Dealer, other proceeds arise from that sale and might be considered as *proceeds of proceeds* in connection with the original sale of the new car.

e. Other kinds of collateral also referred to in both the 1972 and 1999 versions of Article 9 include:

(1) *Timber to be cut.* 1972 §§ 9-105(1)(h) and 9-402 and 1999 §§ 9-102(a)(44)(ii) and 9-502.

(2) *Minerals (including oil and gas).* 1972 §§ 9-

103, 9-105(1)(h) and 9-402, which cover minerals upon extraction; and 1999 §§ 9-502, 9-301(4), 9-102(a)(6) and 9-102(a)(44).

(3) *Motor vehicles.* 1972 § 9-302 and 1999 § 9-311.

(4) *Mobile goods* (goods used in more than one jurisdiction). 1972 § 9-103. There is no reference to "mobile goods" in the 1999 Article 9.

(5) *Money.* 1972 §§ 9-304(1) and 9-305; and 1999 §§ 9-312, 9-313.

New kinds or classes of collateral are created in the 1999 version of Article 9. These include:

(1) *Deposit accounts* (including non-consumer bank accounts). 1999 § 9-102(a)(29).

(2) *Payment intangibles* (a general intangible under which the account debtor's principal obligation is a monetary obligation). 1999 § 9-102(a)(61).

(3) *Health-care insurance receivable* (essentially an interest or claim under a health insurance policy). 1999 § 9-102(a)(46).

(4) *Supporting obligations* (essentially a letter-of-credit right or secondary obligation that supports payment of an account, chattel paper and document, a general intangible, an instrument, or investment

property). 1999 § 9-102(a)(77).

(5) *Commercial tort claims* (essentially where the claimant is an organization or the claim is business related). 1999 § 9-102(a)(13).

(6) *Letter-of-credit right* (essentially a right to payment under a letter of credit). 1999 § 9-102(a)(51).

§ 8. Attachment and Perfection of Security Interest

Article 9 of the Uniform Commercial Code speaks in terms of two different concepts in connection with a security interest in personal property collateral: *attachment of a security interest* and *perfection of a security interest.*

Attachment of a security interest might be considered as equivalent to creation of a security interest; in other words, unless there is attachment of a security interest, there is no security interest whatever. However, once a security interest has attached, the secured party can enforce the interest and realize on the collateral, at least as against the debtor himself.

The additional step of *perfection of a security*

interest is necessary when the secured party seeks to enforce the interest against third persons who assert interests in the collateral, such as other creditors of the debtor, a bankruptcy trustee should the debtor file bankruptcy, or persons to whom the collateral is transferred. Where perfection takes place, the security interest is enforceable, not only against the debtor, but also against most (though not all) third persons with claims against the collateral.

For discussion of attachment of a security interest, see Chapters 2 and 3.

For discussion of perfection of a security interest, see Chapters 4, 5 and 6.

§ 9. Particular Security Devices

Neither the 1972 nor the 1999 versions of Article 9 place great emphasis on the form a secured transaction takes, with the exception of a "pledge" (when the secured party has possession of the collateral) and a transaction that produces by its form a "purchase money security interest." However, it is helpful from a practical standpoint to have some understanding of how secured transactions have been and still are structured.

a. *Pledge or Possessory Security Interest.*

(1)   *General Characteristics.*   A *pledge*, considered as a transaction, is a bailment or delivery of goods or property by way of security for a debt or engagement, or as security for the performance of an act. Another definition is that a *pledge* is a security interest in a chattel or in an intangible represented by an indispensable instrument (such as formal, written evidence of an interest in an intangible so representing the intangible that the enjoyment, transfer, or enforcement of the intangible depends upon possession of the instrument), the interest being created by a bailment for the purpose of securing the payment of a debt or the performance of some other duty. See Restatement, Security, § 1.

It is necessary not only that there be an agreement to pledge, *but also that there be delivery of possession* to the pledgee or secured party (or in some instances to a third person acting for the secured party). *There is no pledge where the debtor remains in possession*, even where he purportedly acts as agent for the secured party.

The earliest form of secured transaction in personal property was the pledge and it is still used to secure loans in situations where the item pledged does not have to be retained by the borrower.

Pledges may be used to secure loans on such valuables as jewelry (the pawnbroker business). Pledges are often used where the collateral consists of *instruments*, such as stock certificates, bonds, promissory notes and the like, or *negotiable documents,* such as bills of lading or warehouse receipts.

On the other hand, a pledge is impossible with respect to complete intangibles which do not consist of documents or instruments that confer property rights on one in possession. This is made clear in 1972 § 9-305, which provides that a security interest may be perfected by possession (without filing) with respect to letters of credit, advises of credit, goods, instruments, money, negotiable documents or chattel paper. (Money was added in the 1972 version of § 9-305 as a possible subject to a possessory security interest.) 1999 § 9-313 permits a security interest to be perfected by taking of possession only when the collateral is goods, instruments, negotiable documents, money or tangible chattel paper. Accounts, commercial tort claims, deposit accounts, investment property, letter-of-credit rights, letters of credit, money, oil, gas or other minerals before extraction are excluded. See Comment 1 to 1999 § 9-313. Under the 1999 Code, a secured party may perfect a security interest in certificated securities by taking delivery of the certificated security. See 1999

§ 9-313(a) and Comment 6; see also § 8-301. Thus, a pledge is meaningless with respect to accounts or general intangibles, although such items of personal property may be assigned.

Under the 1972 Code, no written security agreement is necessary when the collateral is pledged or in the possession of the secured party. 1972 § 9-203(1)(a). Also, under the 1972 Code, a security interest is perfected without filing when the collateral is in the possession of the secured party. 1972 §§ 9-302(1)(a) and 9-305. Similarly, as to the 1999 Code, see §§ 9-203 and 9-313.

If a secured party has an unperfected security interest in collateral in the debtor's possession (as where the secured party failed to file a financing statement), the secured party nonetheless obtains a perfected security interest if he repossesses the collateral after the debtor's default. Such a secured party who has repossessed has all the rights and duties of a pledgee or secured party in possession. See 1972 § 9-501(1) and Comment 2. See also 1999 § 9-601(b) and Comment 4.

(2) *Field Warehousing*. A security interest may be perfected under the Code without filing where the collateral is in the possession of the secured party. See 1972 §§ 9-302(1)(a) and 9-305. See also 1999

§ 9-203 and 9-313. However, *either the secured party or a third person acting for the secured party must be in possession.* If the debtor is in possession or has ready access to the pledged property, the security interest remains unperfected; there is no pledge.

There is a special form of pledge transaction known as field warehousing. This is an arrangement whereby a pledgor may have necessary access to the pledged goods, while the goods are actually in the custody and control of a third person, *acting as a warehouseman on the pledgor's premises.*

Field warehousing is often employed as a security device in inventory financing where the financer or secured party desires to maintain close control over the borrower's inventory and have the advantages of being a pledgee of the property. The device is employed in financing manufacturers or wholesalers in seasonal industries (for example, a manufacturer of Christmas tree ornaments). The device is also useful where the manufactured products must be aged or cured or where they are accumulated over a period of time and then disposed of all at once.

The field warehousing operation is carried out through employment by the financer of a warehouseman who leases space on the borrower's premises at a nominal rate and sets up a warehouse in that space where the borrower's unsold inventory is stored. Warehouse receipts are usually issued by the warehouseman covering the goods in storage and those documents are delivered to the financer. Thus, the goods in the field warehouse are in effect pledged to the financer.

The major difficulty under pre-Code law with field warehousing was that such a transaction was often not regarded as a proper pledge where the borrower was permitted too easy access to the goods. For effective field warehousing, it is necessary that the space for the field warehouse be effectively segregated from the remainder of the borrower's premises. This may be done by taking a room that can be locked or other space that can be partitioned off, with access denied any unauthorized person. The field warehouse company usually employs a custodian, and the custodian is often a former employee of the borrower (such as a shipping clerk) who is placed on the warehouseman's payroll.

Many of the problems as to the effectiveness of the field warehousing operation arise from the fact that the custodian (as a former and possible future employee of the borrower) is likely to allow the borrower too ready access to the goods, thus destroying the effectiveness of the transaction as a pledge.

A secured party under the Code who desires to conduct a field warehouse on the borrower's premises may avoid the risk inherent in too loose supervision of the warehouse operations by filing a financing statement under Article 9. In this manner, the secured party retains a perfected security interest in the warehoused goods, even if the field warehouse operation is not properly conducted. In other words, the secured party can maintain as much control as is desired through the field warehouse; yet the secured party need not risk the consequences of a lapse of control. He can file under Article 9 and have a perfected security interest, regardless of whether he maintains tight or loose control over the borrower's inventory.

In fact, it would seem advisable to file under Article 9, even where the field warehousing operation is properly conducted. In particular, filing is advisable if it is contemplated that periodic release to the borrower of the warehoused goods is necessary. Moreover, filing may be helpful where any question of the propriety of the disposition of the goods by the secured party after the borrower's default is at issue.

(3) *Investment Property.* The 1972 version of

Article 9 was significantly amended regarding security interests in investment securities and the like in 1994. These amendments change the method by which secured transactions in such collateral are structured. The 1994 amendments, which involve changes both to Article 8 and to the 1972 Article 9, deal not only with stocks and bonds represented by physical pieces of paper, known as *certificated securities* [see § 8-102(a)(4)], but also with similar rights against an issuing corporation that are evidenced by a registration in a computer at the corporation, known as *uncertificated securities* [see § 8-102(a)(18)]. The amendments also recognize the current method of holding securities in an account with a stockbroker in which the stockholder's ownership is reflected merely by a bookkeeping entry in the stockbroker's records, known as a *securities entitlement* [see § 8-102(a) (17)]. The 1994 amendments to Article 9 combine these methods of owning securities with similar ownership rights in commodity contracts and accounts. The 1994 Code refers to all such property as *investment property*. See § 9-115 (1972 version as amended in 1994).

There are essentially two methods of structuring a secured transaction in investment property. One method does not involve taking possession or control of the investment property by the secured party; rather the secured party, after attaching the security interest, will file a financing statement. See § 9-115(4)(b) (1972 version as amended in 1994). Under the second method, the secured party takes "control" of the investment property. See § 9-115(4)(a) (1972 version as amended in 1994). There are different ways to take control of the investment property. For example, a secured party has control over a certificated security by taking possession of it, along with any necessary indorsements. See §§ 8-106(a), (b) and 8-301(a). The 1999 version of Article 9 does not substantially change how a secured transaction should be structured to obtain perfection of a security interest in investment property. See Comment 4(d) to 1999 § 9-101. As to perfection of security interests in investment property, see discussion at Chapter 4, § 4b.

b. *Chattel Mortgage*

At common law, the only known security devices were the mortgage of real estate and the pledge of chattels. Obviously, a pledge was of little value, where, by the nature of the transaction, it was necessary that the debtor have possession of the collateral. It necessarily followed that the device of recording a mortgage could be utilized for tangible personal property, as well as real estate.

In the 19th century, a number of statutes were enacted validating chattel mortgages upon the filing or recording of such instruments at a local public office. The style of such a transaction itself was apparently borrowed from the concept of recording a mortgage on real estate. Such chattel mortgage filing or recording statutes persisted, often in rather fragmentary form, until replaced by Article 9 of the Code.

The usual characteristics of a chattel mortgage were a debt owed the mortgagee by the mortgagor and an agreement subjecting specified personal property as security for the debt. By statute, such chattel mortgages were generally declared void against such persons as other secured or lien creditors of the borrower or purchasers of the collateral, unless the mortgage was filed or recorded as prescribed by statute or unless the mortgagee took possession of the collateral.

In general, the chattel mortgage instrument itself had to be filed or recorded and had to describe the property covered and the obligation or debt secured by the mortgage. Some pre-Code statutes required that the chattel mortgage be signed by the mortgagor and be witnessed or acknowledged before a notary. Some other statutes required inclusion of a sworn affidavit that the mortgage had been given in good faith or that it had been given for good consideration.

A chattel mortgage may still be used under the Uniform Commercial Code if it complies with the relatively simple Code requirements necessary in connection with any security agreement, and a chattel mortgage may be filed under the Code if it complies with the relatively simple requirements as to form for a filed financing statement.

c. Conditional Sale

(1) *General Characteristics.* Another form of security device which developed during the 19th century was the so-called *conditional sale* or sale with reservation of title in the seller. Such a sale might be made conditional on the occurrence or non-occurrence of some event, and thus not final until the described event had taken place or had not. But the term *conditional sale* (also sometimes called a "retain title" sale) came to mean a sale in which title was reserved in the seller until the purchase price had been paid in full. Thus, a seller might sell goods on installment credit and, by agreement, retain title

to the goods until all installments were paid by the buyer. The agreement might permit the seller to repossess the goods upon any default on the part of the buyer, such as delay in paying a due installment of the price.

In most states under pre-Code law, conditional sales were distinguished from chattel mortgages. The conditional sale device could be used only by a seller of the goods and could not be used by one lending on the security of goods. (A chattel mortgage could be used for either an installment sale of goods or a loan secured by goods.) However, conditional sales were considered desirable because at common law such a sale was effective to retain title in the seller without the necessity of filing or recording, even when the buyer had possession. Some states permitted conditional sales without filing or recording even up to the time of enactment of the Code. However, other states enacted the Uniform Conditional Sales Act or a non-uniform statute which required the filing or recording of conditional sales transactions in order to permit the unpaid seller to retain rights to the goods as against the buyer's creditors.

Transactions under the Uniform Commercial Code may be cast in the form of conditional sales, and a conditional sales agreement may serve as a security agreement if it meets the rather simple Code requirements for such an agreement. A transaction in the form of a conditional sale under the Code gives rise to a purchase money security interest, which is discussed below.

(2) Purchase Money Security Interest

To some extent, some of the pre-Code functional concepts of conditional sales have been retained in the Article 9 provisions dealing with purchase money security interests. Section 9-107 of the 1972 Code declares that a security interest is a *purchase money security interest* to the extent that it is...

(a) taken or retained by the seller of the collateral to secure all or part of its price; or

(b) taken by a person who by making advances or incurring an obligation gives value to enable the debtor to acquire rights in or the use of collateral if such value is in fact so used.

The 1999 Article 9 similarly defines purchase money security interest although 1999 § 9-103 takes a slightly different approach. 1999 § 9-103 first indicates that "purchase money collateral" means goods or software that secures a purchase money obligation and then provides that a purchase money obligation is one that an obligor incurs as all or part of the price of the collateral or for value given to enable the debtor to acquire rights in or use of the collateral if the value is in fact so used. See 1999 § 9-103(a). That section then applies these definitions to purchase money security interests in goods [1999 § 9-103(b)], software [1999 § 9-103(c)], and to consignors [1999 § 9-103(d)].

A secured transaction that produces a purchase money security interest is probably the most important and most common of secured transactions under Article 9. It gives the secured party certain advantages not given with respect to a non-purchase money security interest. For one thing, a secured party with a purchase money security interest has ten days under the 1972 Code and twenty days under the 1999 Code after the debtor obtains the collateral to file, and such filing relates back to the time the debtor obtained possession for most purposes. See 1972 §§ 9-301(2) and 9-312(4) and 1999 §§ 9-317(e) and 9-324(a). However, the ten-day or twenty-day period does not apply to inventory under 1972 § 9-312(3) and 1999 § 9-324. Such a purchase money secured party also has, if his interest is timely perfected, priority over other perfected non-purchase money security interests. See 1972 § 9-313(3) and (4) and 1999 § 9-324(a) and (b).

The Code follows pre-Code law of many states

which permitted conditional sales without filing by permitting perfection of a purchase-money security interest in consumer goods without filing. Thus, many secured transactions of relatively large total volume but of relatively small individual dollar amounts are perfected without filing under 1972 § 9-302(1)(d) and 1999 § 9-309(1).

However, filing or compliance with certificate of title laws is necessary with respect to motor vehicles. 1972 § 9-302(1)(d) also requires a fixture filing to secure priority over certain conflicting real estate interests in some cases where consumer goods are fixtures. The 1999 version would also require a fixture filing. See 1999 §§ 9-309, Comment 3, and 9-334.

Example 1. A desires to buy widgets from B and enters into an agreement with B whereby A pays $100 cash as a down payment and agrees to pay $100 a month for 12 months. B retains a security interest in the widgets which are collateral for A's obligation to make the monthly payments. B has taken a purchase money security interest in the widgets. If B assigns the interest to C, C also acquires a purchase money security interest in the widgets.

Example 2. A desires to buy widgets from B for

a price of $1,200. A borrows $1,100 from C and, with the borrowed sum and $100 of his own, purchases the widgets from B. A agrees to pay $100 a month for 12 months for the loan and also gives C a security interest in the widgets as collateral for A's obligation to make the monthly payments. C has taken a purchase money security interest in the widgets, even though C did not sell the widgets to A. C has a purchase money security interest whether he makes the loan by directly paying $1,100 to the seller B or whether C advances the $1,100 to A and A applies that sum, plus $100 of his own, to purchase the widgets from B.

Example 3. A borrows money from B and gives B a security interest in widgets already owned by A as collateral for A's obligation to repay the loan. B does not have a purchase money security interest in the widgets.

d. *Other Security Devices*

(1) *Trust Receipts.* A form of financing was developed to finance importers of goods and automobile and appliance dealers by the use of "trust receipts." Under this form of financing, an importer or dealer might finance his inventory by delivering to the lender a paper called a "trust receipt," which

recognized that title to the goods received by the borrower was in the lender, while the borrower was in possession. This form of financing was often legally unsatisfactory under pre-Code chattel mortgage and conditional sales statutes; but its effectiveness was made clear under the Uniform Trust Receipts Act. Under that Act, a lender could obtain a security interest in inventory items in the borrower's possession by obtaining signed trust receipts for such items from the borrower and by filing a rather simple form of statement (similar to an Article 9 financing statement) in a central state office. Financing using the trust receipt device may also be carried on under Article 9 of the Code.

(2) *Factor's Liens.* Another method of inventory financing, used to finance shifting stocks of small items of inventory, was by use of a device whereby a factor (lender) had by agreement a lien on inventory in the borrower's possession. Some states had non-uniform statutes permitting the factor to perfect a lien by filing a notice of lien in a public office.

(3) *Assignments of Accounts Receivable.* When inventory is sold by a manufacturer, wholesaler or other seller, it is often sold on open account, thereby creating an "account receivable." In many instances, such accounts may be assigned to a lender as secu-

rity for advances made to the borrower (the manufacturer or seller of inventory). In some instances, such accounts were sold outright to a factor. Because of difficulty in effectively financing such accounts under pre-Code law, so-called non-uniform "assignment of accounts receivable" statutes were enacted in some but not all states. Some of the statutes provided for the filing of a notice of assignment in a public office. The Code clearly permits the financing of accounts and sets forth the effect of assignment of accounts in 1972 § 9-318 and 1999 §§ 9-404 through 9-406. Perfection of assignments of accounts may be accomplished by filing under Article 9.

(4) *Miscellaneous Security Devices. Leases* of goods and *consignments* of goods are also sometimes in such form as to be secured transactions. In particular, the so-called *bailment lease* (often used in Pennsylvania) has been used as a security device closely resembling a conditional sale. Such security devices or others, not referred to here, may also be secured transactions under Article 9. Another kind of security device is an *equipment trust* taken on such items as railway equipment, buses, airplanes and like items.

CHAPTER 2

THE SECURITY AGREEMENT

§ 1. Necessity of Agreement

A security interest cannot attach, and thus cannot be enforceable against the debtor with respect to the collateral, unless there is an agreement. Such an agreement is referred to as a *security agreement*. See 1972 § 9-203(1) and 1999 §§ 9-203, 9-102(a) (73). The term "security agreement" is defined as "an agreement which creates or provides for a security interest." 1972 § 9-105(1)(l) and 1999 § 9-102(a)(73).

Agreement is defined in § 1-201(3) as "the bargain of the parties in fact as found in their language or by implication from other circumstances including course of dealing or usage of trade or course of performance * * *. Whether an agreement has legal consequences is determined by the provisions of [the Uniform Commercial Code], if applicable; otherwise by the law of contracts * * *."

The agreement in a secured transaction is also a *contract*. The latter term is defined as "the total legal obligation which results from the parties' agreement as affected by [the Uniform Commercial Code] and any other applicable rules of law."

Even where the secured party is in possession of the collateral, it must be kept in mind that an agreement is necessary, although it need not be in writing. Thus, a judgment creditor who seizes a debtor's property pursuant to attachment, garnishment or execution has no security interest under Article 9 of the Code. The rights of such a creditor are governed by law outside the Code.

The requirements regarding the security agreement are different to some extent in the Revised 1972 Article 9 and the 1999 Article 9. Therefore, discussion will begin with the requirements of the Revised 1972 Article and then will separately turn to the 1999 requirements.

§ 2. Revised 1972 Article 9 Security Agreement Requirements

a. Requirement of Writing

Under 1972 § 9-203(1), it is necessary that the secured party be in *possession* of the collateral (that there be a pledge transaction), or that the collateral is investment property and the secured party has control, or that there be a *written security agreement* meeting certain requirements. The formal requisites under the 1972 Article 9 of such a written agreement are discussed in § 2c of this chapter.

The requirement of a writing (in the absence of possession or control as to investment property) is not only a condition to the enforceability of a security interest against third parties, but is in the nature of a *statute of frauds*. Unless the secured party is in possession of the collateral or the collateral is investment property that the secured party controls, his security interest absent a sufficient writing *is not enforceable even against the debtor*, and cannot be made so on any theory of equitable mortgage or the like. If a person has advanced money, he is of course a creditor and, like any creditor, is entitled after judgment to appropriate process to enforce his claim against the debtor's assets. However, such a creditor does not have the rights given a secured party upon default under 1972 § 9-501 et seq. See Comment 5 to 1972 § 9-203.

A "writing" is defined at § 1-201(46) as including printing, typewriting or any other intentional reduction to tangible form. Thus, the definition of "writing" precludes an "electronic" security agreement or any other intangible medium as satisfying the security agreement requirement for attachment of the security interest.

It should be noted that a second writing is associated with an Article 9 secured transaction. It is termed the "financing" or "finance" statement. The financing statement is filed in a public office to perfect the security interest thereby making the security interest to the extent possible effective against third-party claimants. Occasionally, parties to a secured transaction mistakenly use only a financing statement. Some courts have held that the financing statement alone will not suffice as a security agreement even though the financing statement contains a signature of the debtor and a description of the collateral. Other courts have held that the financing statement coupled with other written evidence of the intention to create a security interest, i.e., a promissory note, correspondence between the parties, will suffice as a security agreement. Still other courts have found that the financing statement alone will serve as a security agreement. Remember that without a security agreement the security interest will not attach, and in effect does not exist. For further discussion of attachment of a security interest, see Chapter 3, § 1. Financing statements and their relation to perfection are discussed in Chapter 5.

b. *When Writing Is Not Legally Necessary*

A written security agreement is not legally necessary when the secured party is in possession of the collateral, commonly called a "pledge." Where there is no written security agreement, the security interest attaches when the secured party takes possession. 1972 § 9-203(1). Perfection also takes place when the secured party is in possession. 1972 §§ 9-302(1)(a) and 9-305.

Although a written agreement is not legally necessary when the secured party is in possession, a writing may nonetheless be desirable in order to set forth the various rights of the parties, the debt secured and like matters.

The requirement of a written security agreement is also dispensed with under the 1972 Article 9 in a few special situations which, though technically within Article 9, are not the ordinary type of secured transactions. See 1972 § 9-203(1).

First, no written security agreement is necessary to create a security interest of a collecting bank under § 4-208. A collecting bank has a security interest in items and proceeds thereof held for collection under that Article 4 provision when it permits the withdrawal or application of credit given for an item, i.e., a deposited check, when it gives credit available for withdrawal as a matter of right, or when it makes an advance on or against an item.

Example. Bank B takes a check on deposit from its customer A, drawn by D on Bank C. B permits A to withdraw the amount of the check before collection is made (B permits A to draw against uncollected funds). B has a security interest in the check which may be enforced against the drawer D if the check is not paid by Bank C. No security agreement is necessary. Likewise, no filing is necessary.

Second, no written security agreement is necessary when a security interest arises under UCC Article 2 on Sales, or UCC Article 2A on Leases. Under 1972 § 9-113, a security interest arising solely under the Article on Sales or the Article on Leases is also subject to Article 9 on Secured Transactions, except that to the extent that and so long as *the debtor does not have or does not lawfully obtain possession of the goods*: (a) no security agreement is necessary; (b) no filing is required to perfect the security interest; and (c) the rights of the parties on default are governed by Articles 2 and 2A. The above rules apply only when the buyer has not received possession of the goods in a sales transaction; if the buyer receives possession of the goods, with the seller reserving title or a security interest for the price, Article 9 fully applies and a written security agreement is necessary.

Third, no written security agreement is necessary to create a security interest in investment property over which the secured party has acquired control. Most importantly, investment property includes securities such as stocks, whether certificated or uncertificated. See 1972 § 9-115(1)(f), as revised. A secured party has control in essence when the secured party becomes the owner of the investment property or when a third party has control but agrees it will comply with orders given by the secured party.   See 1972 § 9-115(1)(e) and § 9-106. Generally, as to investment property, see Chapter 1, § 9a(3) and Chapter 4, § 4b.

c. *Formal Requisites of Written Security Agreement Under Revised 1972 Article 9*

(1) *Debtor's Signature*

The security agreement must be signed by the debtor. See 1972 § 9-203(1). The Code at § 1-201(39) defines "signed" as including any symbol executed or adopted by a party with present intention to authenticate a writing.

There is no requirement in the Code that the

security agreement also be signed by the secured party but general principles of law outside the Code determine the extent to which a non-signing secured party is bound. Obviously, if the secured party is not bound, there is no secured transaction, i.e., no contract.

It might be noted that no "formal" or "complete" signature of the debtor is necessary, and the principles set forth in § 1-201(39) and Comment 39 to § 1-201 may be utilized in determining whether a signature exists. It is also not necessary that the signature be acknowledged, nor is any sworn affidavit of consideration or the like necessary. The signature also need not be witnessed.

There is no requirement that the signature be under seal. However, a signature under seal in a jurisdiction which still gives special effect to a contract under seal may be given such special effect, as by subjecting the transaction to a longer statute of limitations than exists with respect to an unsealed contractual obligation. This special effect may not exist where the security agreement under seal is also a contract of sale of goods on credit. See § 2-203.

If the signature of the debtor is made by an agent, the general common-law concepts of the law of agency determine whether the signature is effective.

See § 1-103 which preserves supplementary general principles of law and equity, including the law of principal and agent.

For other discussion of the effectiveness of a signature, see the discussion in connection with the signing of a financing statement in Chapter 5, § 4c.

(2) *Description of Collateral*

A written security agreement must contain a description of the collateral.   1972 § 9-203(1). However, there is no requirement (as sometimes existed under pre-Code law) that the description be specific or detailed (as where the collateral be described by kind or type, model number, serial number or the like). In many instances, blanket descriptions are all that is necessary.

In this connection, 1972 § 9-110 states that "any description of personal property * * * is sufficient whether or not it is specific if it reasonably identifies what is described."

It should be noted that a description of collateral is also necessary in a filed financing statement. Thus, nearly the same principles applicable to description in a financing statement apply to description in a security agreement. See Chapter 5,

§ 4f.

(3) *Description of Real Estate*

In certain instances, the security agreement must describe real estate. Under 1972 § 9-203(1)(a) of the Code, a description of land is necessary when the security interest covers *crops* growing or to be grown or *timber* to be cut.

Where a description of land is necessary in a security agreement, such description need not be the formal or technical style used generally when land is described in a real estate deed or mortgage. In this connection, "any description of * * * real estate is sufficient whether or not it is specific if it reasonably identifies what is described." 1972 § 9-110.

Thus, a description of land by street number or location is often sufficient, although a very loose or indefinite description may be insufficient. For discussion of description of land in a financing statement under certain circumstances, see Chapter 5, § 3g.

§ 3.   1999   Article   9   Security Agreement Requirements

a. *Requirement of a Record*

Although there are exceptions discussed below, 1999 Article 9 requires a *record* of the security agreement in order that the security interest attach, that is, be enforceable against the debtor with respect to the collateral. *Specifically*, the debtor must have authenticated a security agreement. See 1999 § 9-203(b)(3)(A). A *security agreement* means an agreement that creates or provides for a security interest. See 1999 § 9-102(a)(73).

A debtor can authenticate a security agreement in two ways. The debtor might *sign* a written security agreement. See 1999 § 9-102(a)(7)(a). *Signed* includes any symbol executed or adopted by a party with the present intention to authenticate a writing. See § 1-201(39). As indicated previously, a *writing* includes printing, typewriting or any other intentional reduction to tangible form. See § 1-201(46).

The 1999 Article 9 also recognizes intangible security agreements providing that a debtor *authenticates* a security agreement by executing or otherwise adopting a symbol, or by encrypting or similarly processing a *record* in whole or in part, with the present intention of adopting a record. See 1999

§ 9-102(a)(7)(b). A *record* means information that is inscribed on a tangible medium or which is stored in an electronic or other medium and is retrievable in perceivable form.   See 1999 § 9-102(a)(69). Thus, the 1999 Code adjusts Article 9 to reflect current commercial practice that may include electronic security agreements. See Comment 9, 1999 § 9-102.

b. *When Record Is Not Legally Necessary*

As discussed previously with respect to the 1972 Article 9 (see § 2b of this chapter), there are situations in which a writing is not necessary. Similarly, under the 1999 Article 9 it remains the case that under some circumstances a *record* of a security agreement is not necessary. Where there is no such record, if the collateral is not a certificated security and is in the possession of a secured party pursuant to the debtor's security agreement, the security interest will still attach.   See 1999 §§ 9-203(b) (3)(B), 9-313. When the secured party takes possession of the collateral, the secured transaction is commonly called a *pledge*.

Although a record of the security agreement is not legally necessary when the secured party is in possession, a record may nonetheless be desirable in order to set forth the various rights of the parties, the debt secured and like matters.

The requirement of a record of the security agreement is also dispensed with under the 1999 Article 9 in a few special situations which, though technically within Article 9, are not the ordinary type of secured transaction.

First, it continues to be the case that no record of a security agreement is necessary to create a security interest of a collecting bank under § 4-208. Second, no record of a security agreement is necessary when a security agreement arises under UCC Article 2 on Sales or under UCC Article 2A on Leases. See 1999 § 9-110. As to these matters, see discussion at § 2b of this chapter.

Third, the 1999 Code does not require a record of the security agreement if the collateral is a certificated security in registered form and the security certificate has been delivered to the secured party pursuant to the debtor's security agreement. See 1999 §§ 9-203(b)(3)(C), 8-301. Generally, as to investment securities collateral, see Chapter 1, § 9a(3) and Chapter 4, § 4b.

Fourth, the 1999 Code does not require a record of the security agreement if the collateral is a deposit account, electronic chattel paper, investment property, or letter-of-credit rights, and the secured party has *control* of such property. See 1999 §§ 9-203(b)(3)(D), 9-104 through 9-107. *Control* under these 1999 Code sections essentially requires the secured party to have the collateral transferred to it or that the secured party otherwise have control over the collateral pursuant to an instruction contained in an authenticated record.

c. *Formal Requirements of Record of Security Agreement Under 1999 Article 9.*

(1) *Debtor's Authentication*

The 1999 Code requires the debtor to *authenticate* the security agreement. 1999 § 9-203(b)(3)(A). Recall from prior discussion that a security agreement is an agreement that creates or provides for a security interest. See 1999 § 9-102(a)(73). Authentication can occur in two ways. One method of authentication occurs when the debtor signs a written security agreement. See 1999 § 9-102(a)(7)(a). *Signed* includes any symbol executed or adopted by the party with the present intention to authenticate a writing. See § 1-201(39). A second method of authentication occurs when the debtor executes or otherwise adopts a symbol, or encrypts or similarly processes a *record* in whole or in part, with the present intention of adopting the record. See 1999 § 9-102(a)(7)(b). A *record* is information that is inscribed on a tangible medium or which is stored in an electronic or other medium and is retrievable in perceivable form. See 1999 § 9-102 (a)(69).

Other matters related to the requirement of a signature under the 1972 Code carry over to the 1999 Code. Thus, there remains no requirement of a *formal* or *complete* signature of the debtor, a signature need not be under seal, and agency concepts from the common law remain applicable where an agent signs or otherwise authenticates a security agreement on behalf of a principal. See UCC § 1-201(39), Comment 39 to § 1-201, § 2-203, and § 1-103. See for other discussion of signatures, Chapters 3 and 5.

(2) *Description of Collateral*

The record of the security agreement must contain a description of the collateral. See 1999 § 9-203 (b)(3)(A). As is the case under the 1972 Code, there is no requirement that the description be specific or detailed. In this connection, 1999 § 9-108(a) states that "a description of personal...property is sufficient, whether or not it is specific, if it reasonably identifies what is described."

The 1999 Code provides examples of reasonable identification. See 1999 § 9-108(b). A description of collateral reasonably identifies the collateral if it identifies the collateral by specific listing, category, a type of collateral defined in the Code, quality, computational or allocational formula or procedure or any other method, if the identity of the collateral is objectively determinable. On the other hand, the 1999 Code as to the security agreement does not permit supergeneric descriptions such as "all the debtor's assets" or "all the debtor's personal property." See 1999 § 9-108(c).

Investment property is treated somewhat differently. Subject to one caveat, such collateral must be described as "investment property" or by the terms "security entitlement," "securities account," or "commodity account," where appropriate. The description also is sufficient if it describes the underlying financial asset or commodity account. See 1999 § 9-108(d).

The above-mentioned caveat is provided in 1999 § 9-108(e). As to collateral in the form of a security entitlement, a securities account or commodity account, and commercial tort claim, or in a consumer transaction, or as to consumer goods, a description only by the type of collateral defined in the UCC is insufficient. For example, "all existing and after-acquired investment property" without more would be an insufficient description. See 1999 § 9-108, Comment 5.

(3) *Description of Real Estate*

The 1999 Article 9 requires in certain instances that the record of the security agreement describe real estate. Under 1999 § 9-203(b)(3)(A), description of the land concerned is necessary if the security interest is in timber to be cut. As is the case under the 1972 Code, the description need not be the formal or technical style used generally when land is described in a real estate deed or mortgage. A description of real property is sufficient, whether or not it is specific, if it reasonably identifies what is described. See 1999 § 9-108(a). The only significant change is that when the collateral is crops, unlike the 1972 Code [see discussion at § 2c(3) of this chapter], under the 1999 Article 9 a description of the real estate is not required in the record of the security agreement.

§ 4. Grant of Security Interest

The security agreement must create or provide for a security interest. This accords with the definition of *security agreement* set forth in § 1 of this chapter. In other words, if the security agreement does not contain some language indicating that a security interest in described collateral is granted, the agreement is not a security agreement. However, neither the 1972 nor the 1999 version of Article 9 require particular language to evidence the grant of a security interest, both versions of the Article being silent on the matter.

Example 1. Debtor signed a promissory note for $10,000 payable to Creditor and also signed a standard-form financing statement which listed the collateral as "all widgets in Debtor's possession." No separate security agreement was signed. Some courts have held that there is no security interest, since there is no language in either the note or the filed financing statement *granting a security interest,* even though the financing statement signed by the debtor properly described the collateral. A few decisions treat the financing statement also as satisfying the requirement of a security agreement, particularly where other writings exist which reflect the intention of the parties to create a security interest when coupled with the financing statement.

Example 2. Debtor signed a promissory note payable to Creditor for $150,000 which stated that it is secured by a security agreement between Debtor and T (a prior lender) and by a financing statement filed by T. The note further stated that it is secured by security interests in a security agreement to be delivered by debtor to creditor (a subsequent lender who paid off the $65,000 former loan to T and advanced an additional $85,000) which security agreement covers the collateral also covered in the prior security agreement. No new security agreement was entered into between Debtor and Creditor, but a financing statement in proper form and describing the same collateral covered in the earlier security agreement with T was properly filed. There was also "a group of letters" between Debtor and Creditor "constituting the course of dealing between the parties." The note, financing statement and correspondence, together, are sufficient to establish that the parties intended a security agreement to be created and are sufficient to create a security interest.

It might be noted that the cases in accord with Example 1 above take a strict view and require a more or less formal security agreement. Those cases that hold a financing statement suffices as a security agreement, notwithstanding the lack of explicit granting language, take the most liberal view in not requiring a formal security agreement. The cases in accord with Example 2 fall between the two views and recognize that a security agreement may exist from a combination of writings.

While it is necessary under the 1972 and 1999 Codes that a written security agreement be signed by the debtor or a record of security agreement be authenticated by the debtor, describe the collateral (and in some instances describe real estate) and perhaps have language that can be taken as evidencing an intent to grant a security interest, writings and other records purporting to evidence other kinds of transactions may nonetheless be considered as evidencing secured transactions. Such "disguised" secured transactions are discussed in § 6a of this chapter.

§ 5. Necessity of Reference to Proceeds

Under the 1972 Article 9, *proceeds* includes whatever is received by the debtor upon the sale, exchange, collection or other disposition of collateral or proceeds. 1972 § 9-306(1). A similar definition is given *proceeds* under the 1999 Article 9. See 1999 § 9-102(a)(64). The secured party would like to have a security interest in such proceeds. The

Code permits attachment of a security interest to traceable, that is identifiable, proceeds. See 1972 § 9-306(2) and 1999 § 9-315(a)(2).

The 1972 and 1999 Codes take the position that *no reference to proceeds is necessary in the security agreement.* See 1972 § 9-203(3) which states that "unless otherwise agreed, a security agreement gives the secured party the right to proceeds ...." 1999 § 9-203(f) states that "[t]he attachment of the security interest in collateral gives the secured party the right to proceeds ...."

These Code provisions are based on the assumption that parties to a secured transaction intend to cover proceeds, unless otherwise agreed. There appears to be no purpose in requiring a specific reference to proceeds in a security agreement, and such a requirement would likely be a trap for a secured party who was careless in drafting a security agreement.

§ 6. Agreement in Other Form as Security Agreement

a. *"Disguised" Security Agreements*

Although a security agreement must meet the basic requirements described in §§ 2 and 3 of this chapter, certain kinds of transactions covered by written agreements and purportedly not labeled as secured transactions may nonetheless be so regarded. In other words, some transactions may be cast in other forms in writings but still fall within the category of secured transactions and thus within the scope of UCC Article 9. This has been the case under the 1972 Code and will continue to be so under the 1999 Code, although the 1999 Code has made some significant changes, particularly regarding consignments.

The transactions purportedly agreed upon may so closely resemble secured transactions as to be considered secured transactions, no matter how "disguised" in terminology. Examples such as sales reserving title in the seller, bills of sale, leases and consignments are discussed below.

b. *Reservation of Title in Seller*

It is declared in Article 2 of the Code governing Sales that any retention or reservation by the seller of title (property) in goods shipped or delivered to the buyer is limited in effect to a reservation of a security interest. See §§ 2-401(1) and 2-505. Similarly, as to leases see § 2A-508(5). In other words, a sale of goods in a transaction whereby title is expressly retained by the seller until the buyer pays the price is a secured transaction within the scope of Article 9, and the seller has a security interest in the goods for the payment of the price. Such a transaction under pre-Code law was often considered a conditional sale.

While the rule of § 2-402(1) described above applies when the buyer obtains delivery of the goods without paying the price, UCC Article 9 sets forth a different rule to govern instances where the buyer has not received possession of the goods. Under 1972 § 9-113 and 1999 § 9-110, no security agreement is necessary nor is any filing required to perfect the security interest. Moreover, the rights of the parties on default are governed by Article 2 on Sales. In any other respect, Article 9 governs the transaction.

c. Bill of Sale

Article 2 of the Uniform Commercial Code on Sales applies to transactions in goods, but does not apply to any transaction which, although in the form of an unconditional contract to sell or present sale, is intended to operate only as a security transaction. See § 2-102. While under the 1972 Article 9 a written security agreement is required when the secured party is not in possession of the security or collateral, and under the 1999 Article 9 an authenticated record is usually required, and although a security agreement is defined in 1972 § 9-105(1) and 1999 § 9-102(a)(73) as an agreement which creates or provides for a security interest, this does not reject the deeply rooted doctrine that a bill of sale, although absolute in form, may be shown to have been in fact given as security. Under Article 9, as under prior law, a debtor may show by parol evidence that a transfer purporting to be absolute was in fact one for security and may then, on payment of the debt, assert his fundamental right to return of the collateral and execution of an acknowledgment of satisfaction.

d. *Lease of Personal Property*

A secured transaction may arise under either the 1972 or 1999 versions of Article 9 where personal property is leased and the lease is intended as security. See 1972 §§ 9-102(1)(a) and (2) and 1999 § 9-109(a). Some difficulty has arisen in cases where a lease is regarded as a secured transaction and where the lessor (secured party) failed to file under Article 9 and thus had an unperfected security interest. Leases of personal property often closely resemble installment purchases of goods with retention of title in the seller until payment is made in full.

In this connection, the definition of security interest in § 1-201(37) states in part:

"... Whether a transaction creates a lease or security interest is determined by the facts of each case; however, a transaction creates a security interest if the consideration the lessee is to pay the lessor for the right to possession and use of the goods is an *obligation for the term of the lease not subject to termination by the lessee....*" [Emphasis added.]

In addition to an obligation for the term of the lease, one of four other criterion must be satisfied for the "lease" to be considered a security agreement:

(1) The original term of the lease must be equal to or greater than the remaining economic life of the goods; or

(2) The lessee is bound to renew the lease for the remaining economic life of the goods or is bound to become the owner of the goods; or

(3) The lessee must have an option to renew the lease for the remaining economic life of the

goods for no additional consideration upon compliance with the lease agreement; or

(4) The lessee must have an option to become the owner of the goods for no additional consideration or nominal consideration upon compliance with the lease agreement.

The Code also sets forth factors of a lease agreement that do not indicate the agreement creates a security interest. See, in that regard, § 1-201(37).

Example 1. Equipment was leased by B to A at a monthly rate with A having an option at the end of the lease period to purchase the equipment and have 85 percent of the rental payments applied toward such purchase. Such a lease is a secured transaction where the lessee is obligated to pay the lessor for the term of the lease and has no right of termination. See § 1-201(37).

Example 2. Equipment was leased from B to A at a monthly rate with A having an option at the end of the lease period to purchase the equipment and have 75 percent of the rental payments applied toward such purchase up to but not exceeding 75 percent of the price. Such a lease is *not* a secured transaction even if the lessee could not terminate the lease, because the lessee still must pay more than a *nominal amount* to purchase the equipment at the end of the lease period. See § 1-201(37).

e. *Consignment of Personal Property*

(1) *Treatment of Consignments Under 1972 Article 9*

A consignment might be described as an entrustment or bailment of goods by one person (consignor) to another person (consignee) under an arrangement whereby the consignee is to sell the goods for the consignor and remit the sales proceeds to him. If the consignee is unable to sell the goods, he may return them to the consignor. In the Sales Article of the Code, such a consignment is considered a *sale or return*. See § 2-326(1)(b).

Under the 1972 Code, unless a consignment is intended as security, reservation of title thereunder by the consignor is not a security interest, but a consignment sale is in any event subject to the provisions on consignment sales in § 2-326. See § 1-201(37). This means that, in most instances, even if a consignment is not intended as security, compliance with the filing provisions of Article 9 is necessary under § 2-326(3)(c) in order to protect the interest of the consignor in the consigned goods from claims of the consignee's creditors. See §§ 2-

326(2) and (3)(c). For discussion of consignment filing, see Chapter 5, § 12.

Most consignments are not intended as security, and are thus under the 1972 Code not subject to the provisions of Article 9 except the filing requirements (in most instances) and the "priority" provision of the 1972 § 9-114. However, under the 1972 Code some consignments are intended as security and are thus subject to Article 9 in its entirety.

Example 1. A consigned machines to B under an arrangement whereby A retained title to the machines. B was permitted to sell the machines but only at a fixed minimum price. The consignment is not a secured transaction, although A must file a UCC Article 9 financing statement in order to protect his right to the unsold machines against B's creditors.

Example 2. A sold widgets to B. When B was unable to pay for the widgets, the parties entered into a transaction whereby B resold the widgets back to A but B remained in possession. A then entered into an agreement consigning the widgets to B with a term of the consignment agreement stating that the consignor had a security interest in the widgets. B at all times remained in possession of the widgets. Not only must A file a UCC Article 9 financing statement in order to protect his interest in the widgets against creditors of B, but the consignment is an intended secured transaction within Article 9 of the Code.

(2) *Treatment of Consignments Under 1999 Article 9*

A significant change regarding consignment transactions has been made under the 1999 version of Article 9. The 1999 Article flatly states that the Article applies to consignments. See 1999 § 9-109(a)(4). The 1999 Article § 9-102(a)(20) defines "consignment" as a transaction, regardless of its form, in which a person delivers goods to a merchant for the purpose of sale. The merchant must deal in goods of this kind under a name other than the name of the person making delivery and must not be an auctioneer and the merchant must not generally be known by its creditors to be substantially engaged in selling goods of others. See 1999 § 9-102(a)(20)(A). The aggregate value of the goods must be $1,000 or more at the time of delivery. See 1999 § 9-102(a) (20)(B). The goods must not be consumer goods immediately before delivery [1999 § 9-102(a)(20) (C)] and the transaction must not create a security interest that secures an obligation [1999 § 9-102(a) (20)(D)].

The gist of the 1999 changes is that some "true" consignments as described above, that is a bailment of goods for the purpose of sale by the bailee, are within the scope of UCC Article 9. In most consignment transactions, the consignor will file a financing statement in order to protect its interest against creditors of the consignee, much as occurs under the 1972 Article 9 and § 2-326(3)(c). Additionally, a true consignment under the 1999 Article 9 is subject to all of Article 9, except where otherwise stated, because the true consignment is within the scope of the 1990 Article 9. Thus, the rules pertaining to lien creditors, buyers, attachment and perfection, and the priority of competing security interests apply to consigned goods. The 1999 Article does provide that the relationship of the consignor and consignee is left to other law and that the consignor has no duties under Part 6 of the 1999 Article 9 that pertains to default and enforcement of security interests. See 1999 § 9-109, Comment 6.

§ 7. Other Terms in Security Agreement

a. *Freedom of Contract*

A security agreement or record may, and usually does, contain a number of "optional" provisions in addition to those required under 1972 § 9-203(1) and

1999 § 9-203(b)(3)(A).

The Uniform Commercial Code permits broad freedom of contract with respect to provisions which may be incorporated in a security agreement. Under the 1972 Article 9, § 9-201 declares that, except as otherwise provided by the Code, "a security agreement is effective according to its terms between the parties, against purchasers of the collateral and against creditors." Note also that the last paragraph of the Comment to 1972 § 9-101 states that the rules set out in Article 9 are principally concerned with the limits of the secured party's protection against purchasers from and creditors of the debtor. It then states: "Except for the procedure on default, freedom of contract prevails between the immediate parties to the secured transaction." The 1999 Article 9 similarly honors this freedom of contract approach. See 1999 § 9-201.

A consonant provision applicable to the Code generally, § 1-102(3), permits variation of Code provisions by agreement, except as otherwise provided in the Code, and then states that "the obligations of good faith, diligence, reasonableness and care" prescribed by the Code may not be disclaimed by agreement. However, the parties "may by agreement determine the standards by which the performance of such obligations is to be measured if such standards are not manifestly unreasonable."

In addition to the general requirements of good faith, diligence, reasonableness and care, referred to above, some other Article 9 provisions as they may affect third persons may not be varied by agreement between the debtor and the secured party. These include provisions as to priorities between the secured party and a third person, such as purchasers of the collateral, other creditors of the debtor and other secured parties (1972 §§ 9-301, 9-306 through 9-310, 9-312 through 9-315 and 1999 §§ 9-315, 9-317, 9-320, 9-322 through 9-324, 9-330 through 9-331, 9-333 through 9-336).

Moreover, the freedom of contract permitted under Article 9 may be limited by regulatory statutes outside the Code governing such matters as usury, small loans, retail installment sales or the like. Other consumer-protection statutes such as the Uniform Consumer Credit Code also fall within that category. See 1972 §§ 9-201 and 9-203(4) and 1999 § 9-201.

Some other provisions which are ineffective if included in a security agreement include:

(1) A term prohibiting transfer of the debtor's equity in the collateral, 1972 § 9-311 and 1999 § 9-401(b). See Chapter 3, § 9.

(2) A term waiving priority rules of Article 9, unless assented to by affected third persons, Comment to 1972 and 1999 § 9-201.

(3) A term waiving or varying certain rights and duties upon default, 1972 § 9-501(3) and 1999 § 9-602.

(4) An "unconscionable" term in a contract for the sale of goods, § 2-302. This latter restriction applies in a sale of goods on credit creating a security interest in the goods, but it is not so clear as to the extent that "unconscionability" affects a secured transaction arising under other circumstances.

Some other limitations on freedom of contract are discussed in this chapter in connection with after-acquired property provisions in security agreements and provisions permitting the secured party to accelerate payment or to require additional collateral.

b. *After-Acquired Property as Collateral*

(1) *Generally May be Covered*

With exceptions discussed below relating to consumer goods, "a security agreement may provide that any or all obligations covered by the security agreement are to be secured by after-acquired collateral." 1972 § 9-204(1) and 1999 § 9-204(a).

Examples of after-acquired property clauses which are effective include clauses such as "all inventory now or hereafter acquired by Debtor"; "all accounts due or to become due to Debtor"; or "all contents of Debtor's restaurant together with all property and articles now, and which may hereafter be used or mixed with, added to or attached to or substituted for, any of the foregoing property."

Still another example is the following: The security interest of the secured party under this agreement extends to all collateral of the kind which is the subject of this agreement which the debtor may acquire at any time during the continuation of this agreement in connection with the operation of the business of the debtor.

The coverage of after-acquired property permitted under the Code accepts the principle of a "continuing general lien" and rejects the judicial attitude of former law against after-acquired property clauses. The widespread nineteenth century prejudice against the "floating charge" was based on a feeling, often inarticulate in the opinions, that a commercial borrower should not be allowed to encumber all his assets present and future, and that for the protection not only of the borrower but of his other creditors a cushion of free assets should be preserved. Article 9 rejects that view on the ground that it was not effective under pre-Code law. A number of pre-Code devices such as field warehousing, trust receipts and factor's liens could be used to avoid the former rule against encumbrance of all of the debtor's assets. See Comment 2 to 1972 and 1999 § 9-204.

After-acquired property that may be embraced in a security agreement may include the *increase* of existing collateral.

Example. A security agreement covering all cattle of the debtor also covers the increase where one of the group of cattle covered gives birth to a calf.

Moreover, after-acquired property may include the *products* of collateral.

Example. Raw materials which are covered in a security agreement are converted into a finished product, which is also covered.

Notwithstanding that a security interest may be taken in after-acquired property, this does not mean that the interest is proof against subordination or defeat. In this connection, 1972 § 9-108 should be consulted on when a security interest in after-acquired collateral is not security for an antecedent debt (and thus subject to possible attack if the debtor becomes bankrupt), and 1972 §§ 9-312(3) and (4) and 1999 § 9-324 should be consulted on when such a security interest may be subordinated to a conflicting purchase money security interest of another person in the same collateral.

(2) *Limitations as to Consumer Goods and Crops*

"No security interest attaches under an after-acquired property clause to consumer goods other than accessions . . . when given as additional security unless the debtor acquires rights in them within ten days after the secured party gives value." 1972 § 9-204(2). Similarly, see 1999 § 9-204(b). The 1999 Code also does not permit attachment of a security interest by way of an after-acquired property clause to a commercial tort claim. See 1999 § 9-204(b)(2).

This limitation departs from the general policy of permitting security interests to cover after-acquired property in order to protect a necessitous consumer from encumbering all his present and future assets. However, consumer goods acquired within 10 days after the secured party gives value may be covered.

Accessions may also be covered. For example, if a security interest is taken in an automobile and a new engine is installed, the security interest may cover the engine.

c. *Future Advances*

"Obligations covered by a security agreement may include future advances or other value whether or not the advances or value are given pursuant to commitment." 1972 § 9-204(3). Similarly, see 1999 § 9-204(c). An advance is made pursuant to commitment "if the secured party has bound himself to make it, whether or not a subsequent event of default or other event not within his control has relieved or may relive him from his obligation." 1972 § 9-104(1)(k) and 1999 § 9-102(a)(68).

Example of "future advance" clause: The security interest herein created shall also secure all other indebtedness, obligations and liabilities of the debtor to the secured party, now existing and hereafter arising, including future advances, howsoever evidenced or created, actual, direct, contingent or otherwise.

At common law and under chattel mortgage statutes there was a vaguely articulated prejudice against future advance agreements comparable to the prejudice against after-acquired property interests. In line with the policy of Article 9 permitting after-acquired property interests, future advances are also validated, provided only that the obligation be covered in the security agreement. See Comment 5 to both 1972 and 1999 § 9-204. However, if the security agreement fails to provide for future advances, the security interest taken in the collateral arguably will cover only the original debt and not future advances made.

Example. Debtor borrowed $25,000 on a promissory note. A security agreement was also signed describing the collateral as "all widgets in Debtor's possession." The security agreement also stated that the collateral "secures payment of the debt evidenced by the note of the same date and also any and all liabilities of Debtor to Creditor under this agreement or said note or any renewal or extension thereof." Debtor later borrowed an additional $25,000 and gave another note for that sum. The collateral covered in the security agreement does not secure the additional borrowing, since the security agreement provided only for renewals or extensions of the original debt and not for additional indebtedness.

On the other hand, where a priority dispute arises

involving UCC Article 9 claimants, some courts have held that even though a security agreement does not expressly include a future advance clause, a later advance will be secured by the security interest created by the security agreement. Other courts, in the case of a priority dispute involving UCC Article 9 claimants have held to the contrary and required an express future advance clause to be included in the security agreement for a later advance to be effectively secured by the security interest created in that security agreement.

Recognition of the validity of the security interest on after-acquired property and the security interest for future advances facilitates the financing of *inventory* and *accounts* (accounts receivable) where the collateral turns over, e.g., a mortgage on a shifting stock of goods. The secured party thus may make present and future advances to the debtor (often referred to as revolving credits) secured by both present and after-acquired inventory or accounts or both. This results in what is often called a *floating lien*. See Comment 2 to both 1972 and 1999 § 9-204.

d. Option to Accelerate Payment or Require Additional Collateral

Frequently, a security agreement calling for payments at fixed times will have a provision for acceleration of payment. Acceleration may be specified at the secured party's option upon the happening of certain events, such as nonpayment of principal or interest on the debt, nonperformance by the debtor of duties required of him in the security agreement, bankruptcy or insolvency on the part of the debtor, or even events beyond the debtor's control, such as the debtor's death (or the death of the key individual in the debtor's organization). Such provisions are generally given effect.

Another type of acceleration provision permits the secured party to accelerate payment "at will" or "when he deems himself insecure" or in words of similar import. The right of the secured party to accelerate at his option under such a provision is limited in § 1-208; the secured party may act only "if he in good faith believes that the prospect of payment or performance is impaired." However, the burden of establishing lack of good faith is on the party against whom the power has been exercised.

In other words, under such a provision, the secured party may not accelerate payment at whim or for some reason not related to the prospect of payment by the debtor, but the debtor must prove that any acceleration made was capricious and not related to the prospect of payment.

Another kind of provision sometimes found in security agreements permits the secured party to require the debtor to put up additional collateral upon the happening of certain events, such as impairment of the market value of the existing collateral. Sometimes, a provision as to additional collateral merely permits the secured party to require such "at will" or "when he deems himself insecure" or in words of similar import. Section 1-208 restricts this right to require additional collateral at will only if the secured party "in good faith believes that the prospect of payment or performance is impaired." However, the burden of establishing lack of good faith is on the party against whom the power has been exercised.

§ 8. Additional "Optional" Terms

Some additional provisions (discussed elsewhere in this chapter and in Chapter 3, § 3) which may be included in a security agreement include: (1) giving the debtor liberty to use or dispose of the collateral or to make his own collections of accounts of chattel paper; (2) waiver by the debtor of defenses when the security interest is assigned; (3) subordination of the security interest in favor of the interest of a third person; (4) permitting future advances or covering after-acquired property; (5) permitting acceleration or requiring additional collateral; or (6) giving or limiting sales warranties.

Some other optional terms may also be included which are not specifically dealt with in Article 9. Such terms may include the following:

a. *The amount of debt and the terms of payment.*

Unlike some pre-Code chattel mortgage statutes, the security agreement does not have to set forth the debt or related matters. However, it is obvious that there must be a debt or obligation, and the security agreement or some other writing (such as a promissory note) generally sets forth provisions respecting the debt. This may include principal, interest or finance charges (subject to limitations in usury or consumer credit statutes outside the Code), other charges permitted by law, provision for attorneys' fees and costs of collection where permitted by law, provision for confession of judgment where permitted by law, and some statement of the terms of repayment, maturity and like matters.

b. Duties of the debtor respecting the collateral.

These may include duties relating to care or maintenance of the collateral, keeping it at a designated place, using it only in a certain manner, or payment of taxes, insurance premiums and other expenses connected with the collateral.

c. Other duties or restrictions on the debtor.

These may include the furnishing of financial statements or reports to the secured party, restrictions on the payment of dividends or other distribution of profits, restrictions on the incurring of other indebtedness or the subjecting of the collateral to other liens or security interests.

d. Duties as to proceeds.

The security agreement may require the debtor to turn over proceeds from the sale of collateral periodically to the secured party, to execute written assignments of accounts and similar matters.

e. Events of default.

A security agreement generally sets forth various

acts or occurrences that may constitute events of default. The most common event of default is nonpayment of principal or interest or nonpayment of an installment when due. Other events may consist of failure on the part of the debtor to comply with other duties or requirements set forth in the security agreement, unauthorized sale or removal of the collateral, bankruptcy or insolvency of the debtor, failure of the debtor to pay debts to third persons when due and many other possible acts or occurrences. Upon the happening of one or more events of default, the secured party is generally given the option of accelerating payment and may resort to the "default" provisions of Article 9 (1972 §§ 9-501 through 9-507 and 1999 §§ 9-601 through 9-628). However, the secured party may not take "default" action in the absence of an event of default set forth in the security agreement. See Chapter 9, § 1.

§ 9. Subordination Agreements

Sometimes a security interest may be subordinated by agreement to another security interest or to a claim of some other person. Nothing in Article 9 prevents subordination by agreement by an person entitled to priority. 1972 § 9-316; 1999 § 9-339.

However, the agreement must be made by the person willing to subordinate his interest; his rights cannot be adversely affected by an agreement to which he is not a party. See Comment to 1972 and 1999 § 9-316.

A related provision of Article 1, drafted as an "optional provision" and not enacted in all Code jurisdictions, permits subordination of one obligation to payment of another obligation by agreement of the subordinating person with either the obligor or the beneficiary of the other obligation. However, such a subordination does not itself create a security interest as against either the common debtor or a subordinated creditor, and the provision is declared as stating the existing law (common law) and not changing it. Section 1-209.

There is nothing in the above provision to prevent an agreement in which a creditor subordinates his interest to another creditor and also gives a security interest in his right to payment from the debtor to such other creditor.

CHAPTER 3

RELATIONSHIP OF THE PARTIES PRIOR TO DEFAULT

§ 1. Attachment of Security Interest

Attachment of a security interest might be considered as equivalent to creation of a security interest. In other words, unless there is attachment of a security interest, there is no security interest whatever. But once a security interest has attached, the secured party has the right to enforce the security and realize on the collateral, at least against the debtor himself.

Additionally, attachment of a security interest is necessary in order that the security interest can be perfected, thereby making it to the extent possible effective against third parties, including a bankruptcy trustee. Perfection of security interests is discussed in Chapters 4, 5 and 6.

There are some differences between the 1972 and 1999 Codes regarding attachment. Accordingly, the discussion of attachment that follows is separated.

a. Attachment Under the 1972 Code

For a security interest to attach to collateral, three requirements must be met under 1972 § 9-203(1):

First, *there must be an agreement*. This agreement must be in writing and meet certain requirements unless the secured party is in possession of the collateral. For discussion of the requisites of a security agreement, see Chapter 2.

Second, *value must be given*. This requirement is discussed in § 1a(1) of this chapter which follows.

Third, *the debtor must have rights in the collateral*. This requirement is discussed in § 1a(2) of this chapter which also follows.

A security interest is said to *attach* when it becomes enforceable against the debtor with respect to the collateral Attachment occurs as soon as all of the events described above have taken place, unless an explicit agreement postpones the time of attaching. 1972 § 9-203(2).

(1) Requirement of Value

A security interest cannot attach unless *value* is given. 1972 § 9-203(1)(b). The term "value" is defined in § 1-201(44), which states that a "person gives 'value' for rights if he acquires them:

(a) in return for a binding commitment to extend credit or for the extension of immediately available credit whether or not drawn upon and whether or not a charge-back is provided for in the event of difficulties in collection; or

(b) as security for or in total or partial satisfaction of a pre-existing claim; or

(c) by accepting delivery pursuant to a pre-existing contract for purchase; or

(d) generally, in return for any consideration sufficient to support a simple contract."

From the above definition, it can be seen that *value* is not only *consideration* in the ordinary sense under the law of contracts, but is also the taking of security for an *antecedent debt*. In this regard, the concept of value goes beyond the ordinary rules of the law of contracts which generally reject the enforceability of a promise based on past consideration.

Example 1.   Debtor purchased goods from Creditor on open account. When Debtor is unable to pay, he enters into a security agreement granting Creditor a security interest in the goods. Value is given, even though the security interest is for an antecedent debt. The same is true if Debtor gives Creditor a security interest in goods other than those sold by Creditor.

Consideration in the ordinary sense used in the law of contracts is also value.

Example 2. Pursuant to a security agreement or conditional sales agreement, Seller sells or agrees to sell goods to Buyer on credit and reserves a security interest in the goods to secure the balance of the price. Value is given when Seller sells or agrees to sell the goods.

Example 3. Debtor bought goods from Seller on open account. When Debtor is unable to pay, he enters into a security agreement with Lender granting Lender a security interest in the goods. Lender assumes Debtor's debt to Seller. Value is given.

In connection with the definition of value as including a binding commitment to extend credit or the extension of credit, difficulty has sometimes arisen in determining in particular fact situations whether value was given at the time the secured party indicated its willingness to extend credit or at the later time that credit was extended.

Example 4. Debtor, desiring to purchase widgets from Seller, requested a loan of the purchase price from Lender, and Debtor signed a security agreement granting Lender a security interest in the widgets for any loan that Lender might make for the purchase price. Seller delivered the widgets to Debtor and billed Debtor for the price. Debtor forwarded the bill to Lender and the latter paid Seller. Value was not given until Lender paid the bill, since there was no earlier commitment to extend credit.

Example 5. The same facts exist as in Example 4 above, except that the security agreement provided that Lender promised to make the loan if Debtor purchased the widgets. Value was given at the time the security agreement was entered into, since there was a commitment to extend credit at that time.

(2) Requirement That Debtor Have Rights in the Collateral

A security interest cannot attach unless the debtor has rights in the collateral. 1972 § 9-203(1)(c). The term "rights" is not defined [except that § 1-201(36) declares that "rights" includes remedies]. Undoubtedly, a debtor who owns the collateral has *rights* in it. Presumably, a debtor also has rights in the collateral when it is delivered to him or when he is in possession, whether or not he has legal title or ownership, at least in most instances. In certain other instances, a debtor not in possession may also have rights in the collateral.

Example 1. Buyer enters into an agreement with Lender to finance purchase of an automobile and gives Lender a security interest in the automobile. Buyer then goes to Dealer and enters into a binding written contract for sale of a specific automobile then in Dealer's showroom. Buyer has rights in the automobile at the time he enters into the contract for sale even though he has not obtained delivery. The reason is that Buyer has a special property and insurable interest in the automobile under § 2-501(1) in the Article on Sales. If Buyer had merely entered into a contract with Dealer to buy a particular kind and model of automobile at a stated price, but no specific car had been identified in the contract, Buyer would have no rights in any particular car meeting the description of the contract for sale.

Example 2. Financer repossessed an automobile and delivered it to Dealer for repairs. Dealer had entered into a security agreement with Second Financer covering all of Dealer's inventory. Second Financer has no security interest in the automobile since Dealer has no rights in that particular car.

b. Attachment Under the 1999 Code

Much like the 1972 Code, the 1999 Code provides that for a security interest to attach to collateral three requirements must be met. See 1999 § 9-203(b). The three requirements are as follows:

First, *value* must be given. This requirement is discussed in § 1b(1) of this chapter which follows.

Second, the debtor must have *rights* in the collateral. This requirement is discussed in § 1b(2) of this chapter which also follows.

Third, there must be an *agreement*. The debtor usually must have authenticated a security agreement. 1999 § 9-203(b)(3)(A). This requirement of an authenticated security agreement is discussed at Chapter 2, § 3a. There are situations in which an authenticated security agreement is not necessary. 1999 § 9-203(b)(3)(B), (C) and (D). All of these situations are discussed at Chapter 2, § 3b.

The 1999 Code provides that a security interest attaches to collateral when it becomes enforceable against the debtor with respect to the collateral. This is the case unless an agreement expressly postpones the time of attachment. 1999 § 9-203(a).

(1) Requirement of Value

A security interest cannot attach under the 1999 Code unless value is given. 1999 § 9-203(b)(1). The term "value" is defined in § 1-201(44) and has not been redefined by the 1999 Code within Article 9. The § 1-201(44) definition of value was previously discussed at § 1a(1) of this chapter. That same discussion is applicable to the 1999 Code.

(2) Requirement That Debtor Have Rights in the Collateral

A security interest cannot attach under the 1999 Code unless the debtor has rights in the collateral. Specifically, the 1999 Code provides that the debtor must have rights in the collateral or the power to transfer rights in the collateral to a secured party. 1999 § 9-203(b)(2). The discussion of the 1972 Code requirement that the debtor have rights in the collateral is applicable to the 1999 Code. See § 1a(2) of this chapter.

Official Comment 6 to 1999 § 9-203 elaborates on this "rights" requirement beyond the Official Comments to 1972 § 9-203. The 1999 Official Comment indicates that a debtor's limited rights in collateral, short of full ownership, are sufficient for a security interest to attach. However, the Comment mentions a "baseline" rule that a security interest attaches only to whatever rights a debtor may have. The Comment notes that there are exceptions to the baseline rule that enable a debtor to transfer, and a security interest to attach to, greater rights than the debtor has. Thus, 1999 § 9-203(b)(2) adds the phrase "or the power to transfer rights in the collateral to a secured party." These exceptions to the baseline rule are embodied in the priority rules of 1999 Code found in §§ 9-317—9-339 (1999).

Example. The owner of some pottery gives possession of the pottery to an art gallery and authorizes the gallery to sell the pottery for the owner, the gallery to receive a commission upon making a sale. If the art gallery cannot sell the pottery within six months, the pottery must be returned to the owner. This transaction is a "consignment." Assume that Big Bank has previously made a loan to the gallery and the gallery granted Big Bank a security interest in all of its inventory of art presently owned and after acquired. Under the Code, the consigned pottery is subject to the claims of the gallery's creditors. In other words, Big Bank's security interest will attach to the consigned pottery because the debtor-gallery has the power to transfer rights to the secured party. If the security interest has priority over the owner-consignor's interest under an applicable priority rule, Big Bank will be able to enforce the security interest in the consigned pottery even though the gallery held only a consignee's interest in the pottery. For example, if the owner of the pottery does not file a financing statement and does not give notice to Big Bank, Big Bank has priority over the owner-consignor's interest. See 1999 §§ 9-316, 9-324(b) and § 2-236(3)(c). For other discussions of consignments, see Chapter 2, § 6e.

§ 2. Title to the Collateral

Article 9 of the Code does not determine whether *title* to the collateral is in the debtor or in the secured party and adopts neither a "title theory" nor a "lien theory" of security interests. Pre-Code chattel mortgage laws of some states adopted a "title theory" whereby title was in the mortgagor while the mortgagee had a lien on the property.

Instead, Article 9 declares in 1972 and 1999 § 9-202 that rights, obligations and remedies under Article 9 do not depend on the location of title in the debtor or in the secured party. In other words, *title is largely irrelevant in a secured transaction under Article 9*.

The location of title may be relevant under other law for certain other purposes outside the scope of Article 9, as for example determining the owner of goods under a tax law. However, the location of title is not relevant under the Code in any instance where a secured party petitions for reclamation of the collateral in a bankruptcy proceeding.   See Comments to 1972 §§ 9-101 and 9-102.

Where title is relevant, the use of a form traditionally regarded as determinative of title might be considered as evidencing the intention of the parties. Moreover, where a secured transaction arises in connection with a sale of goods, the location of title to the extent that it is relevant may be determined by resorting to § 2-401.

§ 3. Right of Debtor to Use or Dispose of Collateral

It is a matter for agreement between the debtor and secured party whether the debtor is to have possession of the collateral. It is also a matter for agreement whether the debtor has the right to sell the collateral, to receive and handle the proceeds of sale or to collect accounts of those to whom the debtor makes sales.

"A security interest is not invalid or fraudulent against creditors by reason of liberty in the debtor to use, commingle or dispose of all or part of the collateral (including returned or repossessed goods) or to collect or compromise accounts or chattel paper, or to accept the return of goods or make repossessions, or to use, commingle or dispose of proceeds, or by reason of the failure of the secured party to require the debtor to account for proceeds or replace collateral." But this "does not relax the requirement of possession where perfection of a security interest depends upon possession of the collateral by the secured party or by a bailee." 1972 § 9-205. Similarly, see 1999 § 9-205.

In other words, pre-Code holdings of a number of jurisdictions which invalidated security interests where the debtor was permitted freely to sell the collateral, collect the proceeds of sale and collect assigned accounts receivable are overturned by the Code. Comment 1 to 1972 § 9-205 and Comment 2 to 1999 § 9-205 expressly declare that the Code repeals the rule of Benedict v. Ratner, 268 U.S. 353 (1925) and similar cases which held such arrangements void because the debtor was given unfettered dominion or control over the collateral. The Benedict v. Ratner rule was sometimes thought to require lenders to observe a number of needless and costly formalities. For example, the debtor had to make daily remittances to the lender of all collections received, even though the account remitted was immediately returned to the debtor in order to keep the loan at an agreed level. See Comment 2 to 1972 and 1999 § 9-205.

1972 and 1999 §§ 9-204 and 9-205 thus have the effect of validating a floating charge or lien on shifting stock. It is a matter of agreement between the debtor and secured party as to the amount of policing or control the latter may exercise over the debtor's business operations or the control of the debtor's collateral. The Code provisions also permit both "notification" and "non-notification" financing secured by accounts. In other words, the agreement may permit the debtor to collect his own accounts from account debtors without the necessity of giving notice to the account debtors that the accounts have been assigned. The agreement may also permit the secured party to notify the account debtors of the assignment and directly collect the accounts from such account debtors. See Comments 3 and 5 to 1972 § 9-205 and Comment 2 to 1999 § 9-205.

§ 4. Rights and Duties When Secured Party Has Possession

Some common-law principles of law as to rights and duties of the respective parties when there is a pledge are codified in 1972 and 1999 § 9-207, which applies to a pledge. Such principles are summarized as follows:

a. The pledgee (secured party in possession) *must use reasonable care in the custody and preservation of the collateral.* Where the collateral is an instrument or chattel paper, reasonable care includes taking necessary steps to preserve rights against prior parties unless otherwise agreed.

Example 1. Debtor A pledged some stock of X Corporation owned by A with B to secure a loan from B to A. While B was in possession, X issued some rights to existing stockholders to purchase additional shares of X stock, which rights would expire if not exercised by a stated date. B, knowing of the existence of such rights, failed to notify A of their existence before the expiration date. B is liable to A for any loss sustained by A caused by B's failure, and B would be considered to have failed to exercise due care under § 9-207.

Example 2. Debtor F placed some stock of Y Corporation owned by F with G to secure a loan from G to F. While G was in possession, the stock declined greatly in value but G failed to sell. G as pledgee is not responsible for the decline in market value, particularly since F had equal opportunity with G to stay apprized of the declining value of the stock.

b. Expenses incurred in connection with the collateral are chargeable to the debtor and are also secured by the collateral.

c. The risk of accidental loss or damage is on the debtor to the extent of any deficiency in insurance coverage.

d. Any increase of the collateral, such as a stock dividend paid on pledged stock, becomes additional security for the debt. Any money received from the collateral, such as a cash dividend on pledged stock, may be remitted to the debtor but if not must be applied to the debt.

e. The collateral must be kept identifiable, but fungible collateral may be commingled. In other words, if collateral such as stock is pledged, it must be kept identifiable as the property of the particular debtor. But fungible collateral [see definition of *fungible* in § 1-201(17)] such as pledged grain may be commingled with other similar collateral, such as a quantity of grain in a warehouse.

f. The pledgee may repledge the collateral upon terms which do not impair the debtor's right to redeem it. In other words, a pledgee or secured party may himself use the pledged collateral as security for his own debt and repledge it to a second pledgee. But under 1972 § 9-207 the original debtor's right of redemption must not be impaired. In other words, the repledge may not be for a debt in excess of that owed by the original pledgor. 1999 § 9-207 is silent regarding the debtor's right of redemption. See Comment 5 to 1999 § 9-207. Also, the first pledgee faces possible liability if he repledges to a second pledgee who is known to be irresponsible.

g. A pledgee is liable for any loss caused by failure to exercise due care or any other failure described above, but does not lose his security interest. That rule is specified in 1972 § 9-207(3). The rule is implied in 1999 § 9-207(a) on the pledgee's general duty of care. See also 1999 § 9-625(b).

h. Under limited circumstances, the pledgee may use or operate the collateral. This may be done to preserve it, or pursuant to court order, or (except with respect to consumer goods) as permitted in the security agreement.

§ 5. Rights When Secured Party Knows That Third Person Owns the Collateral

It is clear under the Code that a third person may sometimes put up for the debtor the collateral which is security for the debt, and such a third person falls within the definition of "debtor" in 1972 § 9-105(1) (d) and 1999 § 9-102(a)(28), even though not personally liable for the debt.

Certain rights are given a third person who puts up the collateral *when the secured party knows that the collateral is owned by the third person*, under 1972 § 9-112. The 1999 Code has no equivalent provision to that of 1972 § 9-112 because the 1999 definition of "debtor" makes it clear that provisions of Article 9 apply to one who has an interest in the collateral even though not personally liable for the debt. See Comment 2(a), 1999 § 9-102. In short, under the 1999 Code such third persons enjoy the same rights automatically that had to be separately set forth under the 1972 Code at § 9-112.

Those rights of the third person include the right to receive from the secured party any surplus arising from collections made from account debtors or obligors and any surplus resulting from sale of the collateral. In addition, the third person *is not liable for any deficiency* following sale of the collateral, unless otherwise agreed.

Additional rights of such a third person include the following:

(a) to receive from the secured party statements of account of the indebtedness and of the collateral; and to recover any losses for failure of the secured party to furnish such;

(b) to receive notice of and to object to a secured party's proposal to retain the collateral in satisfaction of the indebtedness;

(c) to redeem the collateral;

(d) to obtain injunctive or other relief if the secured party is not proceeding in accordance with the provisions of the Code governing rights after default.

It should be repeated that the above rules apply only if the secured party knows that the collateral belongs to a third person. Short of such knowledge, the secured party may deal exclusively with the debtor who owes the obligation. Nor is the secured party under any duty of inquiry, and the Code does not deal with the matter of the authority of a debtor to put up property owned by someone else. See Comment to 1972 § 9-112 and 1999 § 9-605.

§ 6. Right of Debtor to Statement of Account or List of Collateral

A procedure is set forth in both 1972 § 9-208 and 1999 § 9-210 whereby a debtor may obtain from a secured party a statement of the amount due on the obligation and a statement of the collateral. Under 1972 § 9-208(1) the debtor may sign a statement of his belief of the amount of unpaid indebtedness as of a certain date and send it to the secured party with a request that it be approved or corrected and returned to the debtor. The debtor has a similar right to request approval or correction of a list of collateral.

Under 1972 § 9-208(2) the secured party must comply with the debtor's request within two weeks after receipt. If the secured party claims a security interest in all of a particular type of collateral owned by the debtor, he may indicate such and need not approve or correct an itemized list of collateral. If the secured party without reasonable cause fails to comply, he is liable for any loss caused to the debtor thereby, and under certain circumstances may not claim a security interest in collateral not shown in the debtor's request. If the secured party has assigned his security interest, he must disclose the name and address of his successor in interest.

The debtor is entitled to such a statement once

every six months without charge, but the secured party may charge not over $10 for each additional statement furnished. 1972 § 9-208(3).

A third person who has put up the collateral (where this is known to the secured party) has the same rights and a secured party failing to comply is liable for any resulting loss. See 1972 § 9-112(a) and (e).

The purpose of the Code section is to provide a procedure whereby a debtor may obtain from the secured party a statement of the amount due on the obligation and in some cases a statement of the collateral. Comment 1 to 1972 § 9-208.

The financing statement filed may disclose only that a secured party may have a security interest in specified types of collateral. Third parties are normally told neither the amount of the obligation secured nor which particular assets are covered. Since subsequent creditors and purchasers may legitimately need more detailed information, it is necessary to provide a procedure under which the secured party will be required to make disclosure. On the other hand, the secured party should not be required to disclose details to any casual inquirer or competitor who asks for them. Thus, the right to demand disclosure is given only to the debtor, who will typically request a statement in connection with negotiations with subsequent creditors and purchasers, or for the purpose of establishing his credit standing and proving which of his assets are free of the security interest. See Comment 2 to 1972 § 9-208.

The 1999 Code also provides that a debtor may request information from the secured party. See 1999 § 9-210. The debtor can submit an authenticated record and request thereby a list of the collateral, a statement of account, or an accounting. The secured party has 14 days after receipt in which to respond. Under the 1999 Code, if the secured party fails to comply with the request for information, the secured party is liable to the debtor for $500 and for any damages caused by its failure. 1999 § 9-625(f). Additionally, to the extent a party is mislead by the secured party's failure to respond to a request for a list of collateral, the secured party may claim an interest only as shown on the debtor's list. 1999 § 9-625(g).

§ 7. Modification or Exclusion of Sales Warranties

Under the 1972 Code, when a seller retains a purchase money security interest in goods, Article 2 on Sales governs the sale and any disclaimer, limitation or modification of the seller's warranties. 1972 § 9-206(2). Although the 1999 Code has no provision on point, the comments make it clear that Article 2 of the Code governs any disclaimer, limitation, or modification of the seller's warranties. See Comment 4 to 1999 § 9-403.

In other words, if a seller of goods on credit takes a purchase money security interest in the goods, the Sales Article of the Code governs the existence of warranties concerning the quality of the goods and also governs the effectiveness of any attempt in the security agreement to exclude or limit such sales warranties. Warranties arising in connection with sales of goods may be express (§ 2-313) or implied (§§ 2-314 and 2-315), and a warranty of title is also generally given (§ 2-312). The effectiveness of language in a written sales agreement to exclude express or implied warranties is limited; such exclusions must meet certain standards (§ 2-316).

By making the Sales Article applicable, either the 1972 or 1999 Codes have the effect of preventing a buyer from inadvertently abandoning his warranties by a "no warranties" term in the security agreement, when warranties have already been created under the sales agreement. Where the sales transaction and the purchase money security transaction are evidenced by only one writing, that writing may disclaim, limit or modify warranties but only to the extent permitted by Article 2. See Comment 3 to 1972 § 9-206 and Comment 4 to 1999 § 9-403.

Example.   In connection with the sale of a quantity of widgets, a written sales contract expressly warranted the "marketability" of the goods. A separate written security agreement granting a purchase money security interest in the widgets to the seller for the price contained a statement whereby the buyer acknowledged delivery of the goods purchased "without warranty, guarantee or representation of any kind or nature." The attempted exclusion in the security agreement is ineffective, since Article 2 governs the sales warranties and attempts to disclaim them. Thus, in an action by the seller to enforce payment under the security agreement, the buyer may defend on the basis that the widgets were not marketable and the sales warranty was breached.

§ 8. Secured Party Not Obligated on Debtor's Contract

The mere existence of a security interest or authority given to the debtor to dispose of or use collateral does not impose contract or tort liability upon the secured party for the debtor's acts or omissions. 1972 § 9-317 and 1999 § 9-402.

The Comments to 1972 § 9-317 and 1999 § 9-402 state that there were a few common-law decisions which suggested, if they did not hold, that a secured party who gave his debtor liberty of sale might be liable, as for example for breach of warranty, on the debtor's contracts of sale. This theory was grounded on the law of agency, the debtor being regarded as selling agent for the secured party as principal. 1972 § 9-317 and 1999 § 9-402 reject that theory.

The rights of a secured party as assignee may be subject to setoff for claims of an account debtor against the assignor under 1972 § 9-318.   In addition,1999 § 9-404(b) and Comment 3 make it clear that the account debtor may not go further and assert affirmative rights of recovery from the assignee over and above any amounts assigned, for a default on the part of the assignor.

Example. Buyer bought a machine from Seller on credit. Seller assigned his right to the unpaid price to Financer. Because of a defect in the machine, Buyer sustained personal injuries. While Buyer (unless he has validly waived his defenses against an assignee) may set off his claim against the assigned payments due on the machine, Buyer may not recover damages, over and above the payments due, from Financer on a theory of breach of warranty or other "products liability" theory of recovery.

§ 9. Transferability of Debtor's Rights in the Collateral

The debtor's rights in collateral may be *voluntarily* or *involuntarily* transferred (by way of sale, creation of a security interest, attachment, levy, garnishment or other judicial process) notwithstanding a provision in the security agreement prohibiting any transfer or making the transfer constitute an event of default. 1972 § 9-311 and 1999 § 9-401.

In other words, the debtor can always voluntarily transfer his equity in the collateral subject to the security interest. His equity may also be reached by third persons, such as other creditors, but subject to the security interest if perfected. The security agreement may not prohibit such a transfer, but it can make the transfer an event of default. However, even in the latter case, the transferee takes subject to the security interest.

Where a security interest is in inventory, difficult

problems arise with reference to attachment and
levy. If a debt of $100,000 is secured by inventory
worth $200,000, the debtor's equity may be reached.
But if by attachment and levy certain units of the
inventory are seized, the determination of the
debtor's equity in the units seized is not a simple
matter. The solution to this problem is left to the
courts, but procedures such as marshaling of assets
may be appropriate. See Comment 3 to 1972 § 9-
311 and Comment 6 to 1999 § 9-401.

§ 10. Rights Between Parties Where Security Interest Is Assigned

a. *Right to Assign; Prohibition of Assignment Ineffective*

Sometimes a security interest (and the right to
payment of the debt secured by the security interest)
is assigned or transferred to a third person who as
assignee becomes the secured party. Such an
assignment is frequently contemplated in cases
where a seller of goods on credit takes a purchase
money security interest and then assigns that interest
to a bank or finance company. Such a purchase
money security interest normally gives rise to
chattel paper (conditional sales agreement) wherein
the buyer gives the seller a security interest in the

goods sold. The chattel paper is then assigned by the seller to the bank or finance company.

Assignments are also often made of *accounts* or *general intangibles* which are rights to payment of money. In short, accounts, general intangibles and chattel paper may be the subject of assignment under Article 9. The person who is obligated on such an assigned account, chattel paper or general intangible is the *account debtor*, under the definition in 1972 § 9-105(1)(a) and 1999 § 9-102(a)(3). Where there is a sale (including an assignment without recourse) of an account or chattel paper, the transaction is within the scope of Article 9. 1972 § 9-102(1)(b) and 1999 § 9-109(a)(3). See Chapter 1, § 4.

The rights between the various parties, the account debtor, the assignor and the assignee, are dealt with in 1972 § 9-318 and 1999 §§ 9-404 – 406 which cover such matters as the availability of defenses of the account debtor against the assignee, the right of the account debtor and the assignor to modify their contract and the right of the account debtor to pay the assignor. These are dealt with in subsequent discussion in this section.

Discussed elsewhere are the effect of perfection of a security interest taken by an assignor on the rights of an assignee (see Chapter 4, § 9) and the indication of an assignment on a filed financing statement or a separate statement of assignment (see Chapter 5, § 9).

It should be noted here, however, that an attempt in a contract between an account debtor and an assignor to prohibit assignment or to require the consent of the account debtor to assignment is *ineffective with respect to an account or a general intangible*, under 1972 § 9-318(4). Similarly, under 1999 § 9-406(d)(1), an attempt to prohibit, restrict or require the consent of the account debtor or person obligated on a promissory note to the assignment or transfer or, or the creation, attachment, perfection, or enforcement of a security interest in, is ineffective with respect to an account. chattel paper, payment intangible, or promissory note.

Comment 4 to 1972 § 9-318 points out that, in theory, such a prohibition was given effect under prior law, but that in practice most courts construed purported prohibitions of assignments in such manner as to be ineffective. See also Comment 5 to 1999 § 9-406.

b. *Right of Account Debtor to Assert Defense Against Assignee*

Under the 1972 Code, where there has been an assignment, the account debtor may assert a right to set off against the amount due under the account, chattel paper or general intangible assigned, some defense or claim which the account debtor may have against the assignor.   Under pre-Code law, an assignee was traditionally subject to defenses or setoffs existing before an account debtor had been notified of the assignment. See Comment 1 to 1972 § 9-318.

The 1972 Code not only continues, but expands and clarifies the traditional rule permitting such a setoff.   Under 1972 § 9-318(1)(a), the account debtor may at any time assert against the assignee any defense which may arise from the contract between the account debtor and the assignor.   *It makes no difference whether the breach giving rise to the defense occurs before or after the account debtor is notified of the assignment.*   See 1972 § 9-318(1)(a) and Comment 1.   In other words, an assignee of rights under a contract stands in the shoes of the assignor and has no greater rights against the account debtor than did the assignor.

Example 1. A entered into a contract with B for

B to construct a building on A's land. B assigned his right to payment from A to C for a loan made by C to B. C notified A to make all payments due under the contract to C. When B failed to complete the construction, A withheld the final payment under the contract. C has no claim against A. Moreover, if A had made the final payment to C before learning that B had abandoned the job, A could recover the payment from C as having been made by mistake, where C had not changed his position after receiving payment (as by making an additional loan to B).

Under the 1972 Code, where an account, chattel paper or general intangible has been assigned, the account debtor may also have claims against the assignor which arise independently of the contract giving rise to the subject matter of the assignment. The assignee is subject to all such independent claims which accrue before the account debtor is notified of the assignment, *but is not subject to such independent claims which accrue after the account debtor is notified.* See 1972 § 9-318(1)(b) and Comment 1.

Example 2. On April 1, Buyer entered into a contract with Seller for delivery by Seller of a quantity of widgets on June 1. On May 1, Buyer entered into a second contract with Seller for delivery by Seller immediately of another quantity of widgets. Seller assigned the amount due under the latter contract to Bank on May 2 and delivered the widgets to Buyer that same day. Bank notified Buyer of assignment of the amount under the second contract. Seller failed to make delivery on June 1 under the first contract. Buyer asserted a setoff against the payment due Bank under the assignment of the second contract for damages arising from Seller's breach of the first contract. The setoff may not be made, since the claim accrued on June 1 after Buyer had been notified of the assignment, and arose under a contract independent of the one assigned.

In summary, 1972 § 9-318(1) permits an account debtor to set off against an assignee a defense or claim arising under the contract which has been assigned, and also any defense or claim independent of the contract assigned, but such independent defense or claim must have accrued before the account debtor is notified of the assignment. Any such rights of setoff may be waived by a term in the contract between the assignor and the account debtor. For discussion of agreements to waive defenses or claims against an assignee, see § 10c of this chapter.

The 1999 Code is substantially similar. Unless an account debtor has made an enforceable agreement not to assert defenses or claims against an assignee, the account debtor may assert such defenses or claims under circumstances similar to those of 1972 § 9-318(1). Under 1999 § 9-404(a) (1), the rights of the assignee are subject to all terms of the agreement between the account debtor and the assignor and any defense or claim in recoupment arising from the transaction that gave rise to the contract. "Recoupment" is the legal ability to subtract from any payment due the amount the person trying to collect the debt (or that person's predecessor) happens to owe the debtor. See Comment 3 to 1990 § 3-305. Under 1999 § 9-404(a) (2), the rights of an assignee also are subject to any other defenses or claims of the account debtor against the assignor which accrues before the account debtor receives a notification of the assignment authenticated by the assignor or the assignee.

The 1999 Code does provide some qualifications to the general rule discussed above that an assignee is subject to the claims and defenses of the account debtor. In general, the claim of an account debtor against an assignor may be asserted against an assignee only to reduce the amount the account debtor owes. 1999 § 9-404(b). However, a separate consumer protection law that provides otherwise will preempt. 1999 § 9-404(c). Also as to consumer

account debtors, 1999 § 9-404(d) preserved the
effectiveness of the notice required by the Federal
Trade Commission to the effect that defenses and
claims of the consumer are preserved and are
assertable against an assignee, including a claim that
would lead to affirmative recovery. See Comment
4 to 1999 § 9-404(d). Finally, 1999 § 9-404 does
not apply to an assignment of health-care insurance
receivables. 1999 § 9-404(e).

c. *Waiver of Defenses Against Assignee*

The 1972 Code validates an agreement by a
buyer or lessee that he will not assert against an
assignee any claim or defense which he may have
against the seller or lessor. 1972 § 9-206(1). This is
an exception to the general rule set forth in 1972
§ 9-318(1) that the rights of an assignee are subject
to defenses or claims arising between the account
debtor and the assignor.

The rules of 1972 § 9-206(1) permitting an
agreement not to assert a defense may be summarized as follows:

(1) Such an agreement is enforceable by an
assignee who takes the assignment for value, in
good faith and without notice of a claim or defense.

(2) A buyer who as part of one transaction signs both a negotiable instrument and a security agreement makes such an agreement not to assert a claim or defense, whether or not such an agreement is specified in either writing.

(3) Such an agreement is not enforceable by an assignee with respect to so-called "real defenses" which may be asserted against a holder in due course of a negotiable instrument under 1990 § 3-305(a)(1), (b).   Real defenses include infancy; duress, lack of legal capacity, or illegality which under applicable law nullifies an obligation; fraud that induced the obligor to sign the instrument with neither knowledge nor reasonable opportunity to learn of its character or its essential terms; or discharge of the obligor in an insolvency proceeding. See 1990 § 3-305(a)(1).

(4) The validity of an agreement not to assert a defense against an assignee is declared to be subject to any statute or decision which establishes a different rule for buyers or lessees of *consumer goods*. In other words, it is left to statutes outside the Code or decisional law whether defenses can be cut off against an assignee where secured transactions involving consumer goods are involved.

Example 1. Debtor purchased equipment from

Seller and signed a conditional sales contract for the unpaid price. The contract contained no "waiver of defense" clause and was not accompanied by a negotiable note. Seller assigned the conditional sales contract to Financer. The equipment did not operate properly and was worthless to Debtor. Debtor may refuse to pay Financer the amount due under the assigned contract. On the other hand, if the assigned contract had contained a "waiver of defense" clause in favor of any assignee or had been accompanied by a negotiable promissory note or other instrument, Debtor would be barred from asserting the defense against Financer if the latter had taken for value, in good faith and without notice of a claim or defense.

Example 2. Debtor-farmer purchased a tractor from Seller and signed a conditional sales contract which contained a waiver of defense clause in favor of any assignee. The clause is effective to bar a setoff asserted because the tractor is defective. The tractor is not consumer goods.

Example 3. Debtor purchased consumer goods from Seller on a conditional sales contract which contained a clause stating: "Debtor agrees to settle all claims against Seller directly with Seller and will not set up any such claims against Seller as defense, counterclaim, set off, cross complaint or otherwise in any action for the purchase price or possession of the collateral brought by any assignee of this contract." Seller assigned the contract to Financer. There is no statute or prior decision in the state barring such a waiver of defense clause with respect to consumer goods. The agreement is given effect.

Example 4. Under the facts of Example 3, there is prior decisional law protecting buyers of consumer goods notwithstanding use of a "waiver of defense" clause in a conditional sales agreement. Buyer may assert a defense of nondelivery of the consumer goods.

CAVEAT.   While 1972 § 9-206(1) takes a "neutral" position as to the effectiveness of an agreement waiving defenses against an assignee with respect to buyers and lessees of *consumer goods*, the trend of legislation outside the Uniform Commercial Code is clearly to prohibit or sharply limit such agreements or the use of negotiable notes cutting off defenses.   Such agreements are now ineffective in a number of states and may be ineffective anywhere under Federal consumer protection statutes and regulations thereunder.

The 1999 Code is substantially similar. It validates an agreement between an account debtor and an assignor not to assert against an assignee any claim or defense that the account debtor may have against the assignor if the assignee takes the assignment for value, in good faith, without notice of a claim of a property or possessory right to the property assigned, and without notice of a defense or claim in recoupment of the type that may be asserted against a person entitled to enforce a negotiable instrument under 1990 § 3-305(a). See 1999 § 9-403(b). This is an exception to the general rule set forth in 1999 § 9-404(a) that the rights of an assignee are subject to a defense or claim arising between the account debtor and the assignor. The 1999 Code also makes it clear that in any event the assignee is subject to the so-called real defenses that are assertable against a holder in due course or a negotiable instrument under 1990 § 3-305(a)(1), (b). Additionally, separate consumer protection law is given preemptive effect. See 1999 § 9-403(d), (e) and Comments 5 and 6 to 1999 § 9-403.

d. *Right of Account Debtor and Assignor to Modify Contract*

Prior law was in confusion as to whether modification of an executory contract by an account debtor and an assignor without the assignee's consent was possible after notification of an assignment. The

1972 Code in § 9-318(2) takes the position that modification of, or substitution for, a contract which is agreed upon by the account debtor and the assignor is effective without the assignee's consent, even after notification of the assignment given the account debtor. However, the modification or substitution must be in good faith and in accordance with reasonable commercial standards.

The assignee acquires corresponding rights under the modified or substituted contract, and no modification or substitution may affect a right to payment which has been fully earned by performance. The agreement between the assignor and assignee (secured party) may not effectively prohibit modification or substitution of the underlying contract by agreement between the assignor and the account debtor, but it may make such a modification or substitution a breach by the assignor. See § 9-318(2) of the 1972 Code.

Comment 2 to 1972 § 9-318 states that the above rule is sound and necessary in view of the realities of large scale procurement, as for example in the area of government contracts.

Example. A has a prime contract with the government for A to manufacture gadgets. A enters into a subcontract with B for the latter to manufacture widgets, which are parts used in the manufacture of gadgets. B assigns payments due from A under the subcontract to financer C. The government subsequently exercises its right to modify the prime contract by reducing the quantity of gadgets ordered from A. A enters into a corresponding modification with B under the subcontract reducing the quantity of widgets to be delivered by B. The modification is binding on C. However, the modification only affects executory rights and cannot cut off a right of C to collect assigned amounts due from A to B for widgets already delivered by B to A. See Comment 2 to 1972 § 9-318 for discussion of problems arising in connection with government contracts upon which this Example is based.

The 1999 Code is substantially similar. A modification or a substitution for an assigned contract under the 1999 Code is effective against an assignee if made in good faith. 1999 § 9-405(a). This is the case to the extent that the right to payment or a part thereof under an assigned contract has not been fully earned by performance or the right to payment or a part thereof has been fully earned by performance and the account debtor has not received notice of the assignment. 1999 § 9-405(b); see also 1999 § 9-406(a). However, the 1999 Code gives preemptive effect to consumer protection law outside the Code and also makes 1999 § 9-405 inapplicable to an assignment of a health-care-insurance receivable. 1999 § 9-405(c), (d).

e. *Right of Account Debtor to Pay Assignor*

Under the 1972 Code, the account debtor is entitled to pay the assignor until the account debtor receives notification that the amount due or to become due has been assigned and that payment is to be made to the assignee. 1972 § 9-318(3).

So long as the assignee permits the assignor to collect claims or leaves him in possession of chattel paper which does not indicate that payment is to be made at some place other than the assignor's place of business, the account debtor may pay the assignor even though he may know of the assignment. In such a situation an assignee who wants to take over collections must notify the account debtor to make further payments to him. See Comment 3 to 1972 § 9-318.

It should be kept in mind that the account debtor is protected in paying the assignor until he *receives notification* otherwise. In this connection, § 1-201(26) states that a person receives a notice or notification when it comes to his attention or when it is duly delivered at the place of business through which the contract was made or at any other place held out as the place for receipt of such communications. Thus, notice is not received by the account debtor merely because there is a filing with respect to an assignment. Moreover, notice is not received merely because the account debtor might have reason to believe that an assignment has been made.

The Code also has a provision protecting the right of an account debtor who is notified of an assignment and who is directed to pay the assignee to have the authenticity of the assignment verified. In this respect, 1972 § 9-318(3) states that a notification which does not reasonably identify the rights assigned is ineffective. The provision also states that, if requested by the account debtor, the assignee must seasonably furnish reasonable proof that the assignment has been made and unless he does so the account debtor may pay the assignor. See also Comment 5 to 1972 § 9-318.

Example 1. Buyer contracted to purchase machines from Seller. Seller assigned its accounts (including that of Buyer) to Financer. Financer sent written notice of assignment to Buyer by certified mail stating that Buyer was to pay Financer the amounts due for the machines. Buyer's personnel handling incoming mail failed to deliver the notice to Buyer's accounting department and Buyer continued to pay Seller for the machines. Financer has a claim against Buyer for the payments made to Seller.

Example 2. A agreed to sell machines for B and received from B a letter authorizing A to sell the machines and then stating: "You are authorized to pay the sum of $10,000 from the proceeds of the sale to C," followed by C's address. A did not pay $10,000 from sales proceeds to C. In an action by C against A for $10,000, it was held that there was nothing in the letter to indicate an intention on the part of B to transfer the sales proceeds or any part of them to C, or to give notice of an assignment to C.

The 1999 Code is substantially similar, tracking with 1972 § 9-318(3). Thus, an account debtor on an account, chattel paper, or a payment intangible may discharge its obligation by paying the assignor until the account debtor receives an authenticated notice of the assignment. 1999 § 9-406(a). The 1999 Code specifies when the notice is effective [1999 § 9-406(b)] and that the account debtor can require proof of the assignment [1999 § 9-406(c)]. Separate consumer protection law is given preemptive effect [1999 § 9-406(h)] and § 9-406 indicates that it is inapplicable to assignment of health-care-insurance receivables [1999 § 9-406(i)].

CHAPTER 4

PERFECTION OF SECURITY INTEREST

§ 1. Perfection Generally

"A security interest is perfected when it has attached and when all of the applicable steps required for perfection have been taken." 1972 § 9-303(1). Similarly, see 1999 § 9-308(a).

Although *attachment* of a security interest with or without perfection is necessary to give a secured party rights in the collateral against the debtor, a secured party may maximize his rights against third persons having claims to the collateral by taking whatever action is necessary to *perfect* his interest. A secured party with an attached but unperfected security interest has but limited rights against third persons.

"A perfected security interest may still be or become subordinate to other interests * * * but in general after perfection the secured party is protected against creditors and transferees of the debtor and in particular against any representative of creditors in insolvency proceedings instituted by or against the debtor." 1972 § 9-303, Comment 1. Similarly, see 1999 § 9-308, Comment 2.

In other words, the holder of a perfected security interest is able in most circumstances to realize on the collateral against the claim of a subsequent lien creditor or a representative of creditors such as a receiver or an assignee for the benefit of creditors. As to the rights of the secured party when the debtor is bankrupt, see Chapter 8. Moreover, such a perfected security interest is superior to the security interest of a third person in the same collateral which is not perfected or which is subsequently perfected, although there are certain exceptions to this rule. In addition, a perfected security interest has priority over buyers of the collateral, although some classes of buyers prevail over even a perfected security interest.

Various methods exist for the perfection of a security interest. In all cases, perfection cannot take place before the security interest has attached under 1972 § 9-303(1) and 1999 § 9-308(a), and additional steps often must be taken to perfect before or after the security interest has attached. The particular method which is effective to perfect a security interest depends on the kind of personal property serving as collateral in the secured transaction, and sometimes on the nature of the transaction itself. The various methods of perfection common to both the 1972 and 1999 versions of Article 9 (which are discussed in detail in this chapter) are as follows:

(1) automatic perfection when the security interest attaches;

(2) temporary perfection;

(3) perfection through a pledge or the secured party taking possession of the collateral;

(4) the filing of a financing statement in one or more public filing offices (Note that this is the most common method of perfection. Filing is discussed at § 5 of this chapter and is considered in detail in Chapter 5.);

(5) filing or registration or compliance with a certificate of title requirement pursuant to federal law or a treaty;

(6) compliance with a state certificate of title law or central filing under a state statute other than the Uniform Commercial Code;

(7) taking the necessary steps to perfect with respect to investment property.

This chapter first discusses the above methods of

perfection found only in the 1972 Code or that are common to both the 1972 and 1999 versions of Article 9. It then turns to discussion of methods of perfection of security interests that are provided for only in the 1999 version of Article 9. See § 12.

§ 2. Perfection Upon Attachment Alone

a. *Purchase Money Security Interest in Consumer Goods*

In certain instances, it is not necessary that any steps be taken to perfect a security interest other than attachment of that interest. In other words, with respect to certain kinds of collateral, a security interest is automatically perfected when it attaches. No action such as filing or the taking of possession of the collateral is necessary.

The most significant type of security interest which is automatically perfected upon attachment alone is a *purchase money security interest in consumer goods* (with certain exceptions if the consumer goods are fixtures or motor vehicles). See 1972 § 9-302(1)(d) and 1999 §§ 9-310(b)(2) and 9-309(1). (Note that the definition of *purchase money security interest* is considered in Chapter 1, § 9c(2). The definition of *consumer goods* is considered in

Chapter 1, § 7a.) This follows the rule of many jurisdictions under pre-Code law which did not make security interests in consumer goods arising from conditional sales or bailment leases subject to filing requirements. See 1972 § 9-302 Comment 4.

The policy behind this rule is that it is sometimes unwise to require filing where the benefits of public filing are outweighed by the disadvantages of filing with respect to a large number of transactions involving rather small amounts of credit and collateral of relatively low value. Filing for such transactions merely clutters the files, inconveniences those involved in the filing process and may result in expenses for filing fees disproportionate to amounts of credit given.

Although purchase money security interests in consumer goods are perfected without filing, it should be noted that filing with respect to such collateral is permitted on an optional basis. Under 1972 § 9-307(2) and 1999 § 9-320(b), unless a financing statement is filed a third person who buys consumer goods from the consumer-debtor may take free of the security interest even though perfected, if the third person also uses the goods for consumer purposes. See 1972 § 9-302 Comment 4 and 1999 § 9-320 Comment 5.

It should be kept in mind that 1972 § 9-302(1)(d) and 1999 §§ 9-309(1), 9-311(a) and (b) require filing if the consumer goods are a motor vehicle required to be registered, and a fixture filing is required for priority over conflicting interests in fixtures to the extent provided in 1972 § 9-313 and 1999 § 9-334. In other words, if the collateral is a motor vehicle purchased for personal or family use, a security interest may be perfected only by filing or by complying with a state certificate of title law. The same may be true under 1972 § 9-302(3)(b) and 1999 § 9-311(a)(2) with respect to such consumer goods as boats, trailers or mobile homes subject to a state certificate of title law. If the consumer goods collateral is a fixture (such as a furnace affixed in a dwelling house), a security interest may be perfected by attachment but fixture filing is necessary in order to obtain priority over certain real estate interests.

Example 1. Buyer purchases a combination stereo-television set from Seller on installment credit for personal, family or household purposes. The purchase is made under a written security agreement. The set is delivered to Buyer's home. Upon delivery, the security interest attaches and is perfected upon attachment. If Seller assigns the security interest to Financer, the security interest continues perfected. See 1972 §§ 9-302(1)(d) and

(2) and 1999 §§ 9-310(b)(2), 9-309(1), and 9-310(c).

Example 2. Under the facts of Example 1, seller sells the set for cash, but Buyer borrows from Financer and uses the money to pay Seller. The security interest is perfected in favor of Financer upon attachment, since Financer has a purchase money security interest. See 1972 §§ 9-107(b), 9-302(1)(d) and 1999 §§ 9-103, 9-310(b)(2), 9-309(1).

Example 3. Buyer purchases an automobile from Dealer on installment credit for personal, family or household purposes. The purchase is made under a written security agreement. The car is delivered to Buyer. Upon delivery, the security interest attaches but is not perfected unless a financing statement is filed or there is compliance with an applicable state certificate of title law. See 1972 §§ 9-302(1)(d), (3)(b) and (c), and 1999 §§ 9-309(1), 9-311(b)(2).

Example 4. Buyer purchases a furnace from Seller on installment credit for personal, family or household purposes. The purchase is made under a written security agreement. The furnace is installed as a fixture in Buyer's home. Under 1972 § 9-302(1)(d) and 1999 § 9-309(1), the security interest is perfected upon attachment, but a fixture filing is necessary for priority over certain real estate interests under 1972 § 9-313 and 1999 § 9-334.

b. *Isolated Assignments of Accounts*

1972 § 9-302(1)(e) provides that filing is not necessary to perfect a security interest in an assignment of accounts which does not alone or in conjunction with other assignments to the same assignee transfer a significant part of the outstanding accounts of the assignor. Similarly, see 1999 §§ 9-309(2) and 9-310(b)(2).

The effect of 1972 § 9-302(1)(e) and 1999 § 9-309(2) is to permit perfection upon attachment alone with respect to isolated assignments of accounts. This rule is justified on the ground that casual or isolated assignments which no one would think of filing should not be subject to invalidation by reason of failure to file. On the other hand, any person who regularly takes assignments of a particular debtor's accounts should file. See Comment 5 to 1972 § 9-302 and Comment 4 to 1999 § 9-309.

Example. Assignor assigned accounts totaling $6,000 to Assignee for a cash consideration of $4,000. At that time, Assignor was doing about $10,000 worth of business every month. The assignment gave Assignee a perfected security interest in the accounts without the necessity of filing.

It should also be noted that 1972 § 9-104(f) and 1999 § 9-109(d)(4)-(7) completely exclude certain transfers of accounts from Article 9. See discussion of exclusions in Chapter 1, § 5.

c. *Other Instances*

In certain other instances, a security interest may be perfected without filing. Such perfection takes place with respect to the following kinds of collateral:

(1) Temporary perfection as to instruments, certificated securities, negotiable documents, or goods in possession of a bailee other than one who has issued a negotiable document of title, for not over 21 days or in proceeds for not over 10 days. 1972 §§ 9-302(1)(b), 9-304(4), (5), and 9-306(3). Similar provisions are included in the 1999 Code but the time limit is 20 days and not 21 days. See 1999 §§ 9-312(e)-(h) and 9-315(d). See discussion of temporary perfection in the next section of this chapter.

(2) A security interest created by an assignment

of a beneficial interest in a trust or a decedent's estate. 1972 § 9-302(1)(c). Similarly, under the 1999 Code, a security interest created by an assignment of a beneficial interest in a decedent's estate. 1999 § 9-309(13).

(3) A security interest of a collecting bank in an item taken for collection (such as a check taken on deposit when the bank permits the depositor to withdraw the proceeds before the check is collected). 1972 § 9-302(1)(f) and 1999 § 9-309(7).

(4) A security interest arising under Article 2 of the Code on Sales or Article 2A of the Code on Leases where the debtor-buyer/lessee does not have possession of the goods. 1972 §§ 9-302(1)(f) and § 9-113. As to the 1999 Code, see 1999 § 9-309(6).

(5) A security interest in investment property under 1972 (as revised in 1994) § 9-302(1)(h). See also 1972 (as revised in 1994) §§ 9-115 and 9-116. As to the 1999 Code, see 1999 § 9-309(10).

(6) An assignment for the benefit of all the creditors of the transferor, and subsequent transfers by the assignee thereunder. 1972 § 9-302(1)(g) and 1999 § 9-309(12).

§ 3. Temporary Perfection in Certain Collateral

a. *The 1972 Code Temporary Perfection Provision*

Automatic perfection of a security interest in certain collateral without the necessity of filing or possession by the secured party is permitted for a temporary period of 21 days under 1972 § 9-304(4) and (5). The 1999 Code has some similar but yet slightly changed provisions that are discussed at § 3b of this chapter. After the expiration of the 21-day period, the security interest becomes unperfected unless other proper steps (such as filing or the taking of possession) are taken before the end of 21 days. See 1972 § 9-304(6).

Under 1972 § 9-304(4), a security interest "in instruments, certificated securities, or negotiable documents is perfected without filing or the taking of possession for a period of 21 days from the time it attaches to the extent that it arises for new value given under a written security agreement."

Comment 4 to 1972 § 9-304 points out that the 21-day period runs from the date of attachment of the security interest, and further declares that there is no limitation on the purpose for which the debtor is in possession but that the secured party must have given new value under a written security agreement. For example, this provision permits lenders who make loans secured by negotiable documents of title to one who is purchasing the goods represented by the documents for early resale, to do so without the necessity of the lender filing or taking possession of the documents.

A different kind of 21-day temporary perfection is covered in 1972 § 9-304(5). Under that provision, a secured party who already has a perfected security interest in a negotiable document or goods in the possession of a bailee who has not issued a negotiable document on the goods, may release the document to the debtor or make the goods available to him for one of the purposes specified in 1972 § 9-304(5)(a), without losing perfection, for 21 days.

Example 1. A bank which has acquired a bill of lading by honoring drafts under a letter of credit subsequently turns over the bill of lading to its importer-customer. The customer then uses the bill of lading to obtain the goods for the purpose of resale or one of the other purposes specified in the Code provision. See Comment 2 to 1972 § 9-303 and Comment 4 to 1972 § 9-304.

In addition, a secured party who has a perfected security interest in an instrument or a certificated security may retain that interest for 21 days after delivering the instrument to the debtor "for the purpose of ultimate sale or exchange or of presentation, collection, renewal or registration of transfer." 1972 § 9-304(5)(b).

Example 2. A bank has possession of a stock certificate owned by a borrower. The issuer offers an exchange of stock in connection with a corporate merger, and the bank releases the certificate to the borrower so that the exchange may be effected.

The evident reason for permitting such temporary perfection is to avoid cluttering the files with records of exceedingly short-term transactions and also to allow the debtor freedom in handling the collateral in such short-term transactions. However, it should be kept in mind that, even though a security interest is temporarily perfected in such transactions, the debtor is in a position to give a superior title or interest to a third person by making an unauthorized transfer to the latter under 1972 §§ 9-308 and 9-309.

There is a cross reference to 1972 § 9-304(5)(a) to clarify the position of a purchase money secured party who releases inventory to the debtor for a 21-day temporary period, as against another person who also has a security interest in inventory. See 1972 § 9-312(3) and Comment 3 to that provision.

Note: The temporary 21-day rule applied to "certificated securities" delivered to the debtor for certain purposes under 1972 § 9-304(5)(b). Generally, as to investment property and security interests in such property, see § 4b of this chapter and Chapter 1, § 9a(3).

b. *The 1999 Code Temporary Perfection Provisions*

The 1999 Code provisions regarding temporary perfection merit separate consideration. The 1999 Code indicates that a security interest in certificated securities, negotiable documents, or instruments is perfected without filing or the taking of possession for a period of 20 days from the time it attaches. However, the temporary perfection applies only to the extent the security interest arises for new value given under an authenticated security agreement. 1999 § 9-312(e).

The 1999 Code also provides for temporary perfection in goods or documents made available to the debtor under some circumstances. 1999 §9-312(f). Specifically, the provision applies to a perfected security interest in a negotiable document or goods in possession of a bailee, other than one who has issued a negotiable document for the goods. The security interest remains perfected for 20 days without filing if the secured party makes available to the debtor the goods or documents representing the goods for either of two purposes. One purpose is to facilitate the sale or exchange of the goods or documents. The second purpose is to facilitate loading, unloading, storing, shipping, trans-shipping, manufacturing, processing or otherwise dealing with them in a manner preliminary to their sale or exchange. Similarly, a perfected security interest in a certificated security or instrument remains perfected for 20 days without filing if the secured party delivers the certificate or instrument to the debtor for the purpose of ultimate sale or exchange or presentment, collection, enforcement, renewal, or registration of transfer. 1999 § 9-312(g).

Finally, after the 20-day periods described above expire, the secured party must take steps to otherwise perfect the security interest to maintain perfection 1999 § 9-312(h).

§ 4. Perfection by Pledge or Possessory Security Interest

a. *Generally*

The kinds of personal property which may be the subject of a pledge or possessory security interest are listed in Chapter 1, § 9a. Such items include goods and collateral represented by a writing that may transfer a claim through delivery or through delivery plus indorsement. A writing capable of transferring the claim may be an instrument, a document or chattel paper. On the other hand, purely intangible collateral such as accounts and chattel paper cannot be pledged. Perfection as to such collateral is only by filing, although in certain instances there may be automatic perfection as to isolated accounts or perfection as proceeds. See 1972 §§ 9-302(1)(e), 9-306(2) and (3) and 1999 §§ 9-309(2) and 9-315(a), (c)-(e). Note that investment property, including a certificated security, is not included within the definition of "instrument." As to security interests in investment property, see § 4b of this chapter and Chapter 1, § 9a(3).

With respect to collateral that may be pledged, a security interest is perfected without filing if the collateral is in the possession of the secured party. See 1972 §§ 9-302(1)(a) and 9-305; 1999 §§ 9-310(b)(6) and 9-313. In fact, under the 1972 Code a security interest in instruments (other than instruments which constitute part of chattel paper) can be perfected *only* by the secured party taking possession, except in certain instances where there may be temporary perfection under 1972 § 9-304(4) and (5) or where proceeds are involved under 1972 § 9-306(2) and (3). For discussion of perfection of

security interests in instruments under the 1999
Code, see § 12h of this chapter. In addition, under
the 1972 and 1999 Codes, a security interest in
money may be perfected only by possession except
where the money is proceeds. See 1972 § 9-304(1)
and 1999 § 9-312(b)(3).

The common law rules on the degree and extent
of possession which are necessary to perfect a
pledge interest are not relaxed by any provision of
Article 9. See Comment 6 to 1972 § 9-205 and
Comment 3 to 1999 § 9-205. Possession may be by
the secured party himself or by an agent on his
behalf, but it is clear that *the debtor or a person
controlled by him cannot qualify as such an agent
for the secured party.* See Comment 2 to 1972 § 9-
305 and also the final sentence of 1972 § 9-205. As
to the 1999 Code, see Comment 3 to 1999 § 9-313
and also 1999 § 9-205(b).

b. *Investment Property*

The 1972 version of Article 9 was significantly
amended regarding security interests in investment
securities and the like in both 1972 and again in
1994. These amendments change the method by
which secured transactions in such collateral are
structured. The 1994 amendments, which involve

changes both to Article 8 and to the 1972 Article 9, deal not only with stocks and bonds represented by physical pieces of paper, known as *certificated securities* [see § 8-102(a)(4)], but also with similar rights against an issuing corporation that are evidenced by a registration in a computer at the corporation, known as *uncertificated securities* [see § 8-102(a) (18)]. The amendments also recognize the current method of holding securities in an account with a stockbroker in which the stockholder's ownership is reflected merely by a bookkeeping entry in the stockbroker's records, known as a *securities entitlement* [see § 8-102(a)(17)]. The 1994 amendments to Article 9 combine these methods of owning securities with similar ownership rights in commodity contracts and accounts. The 1994 Code refers to all such property as *investment property*. See § 9-115 (1972 version as amended in 1994).

There are essentially two methods of structuring a secured transaction in investment property. One method does not involve taking possession or control of the investment property by the secured party; rather the secured party, after attaching the security interest, will file a financing statement. See 1972 § 9-115(4)(b) (as amended in 1994). Under the second method, the secured party takes "control" of the investment property. See 1972 § 9-115(4)(a) (as amended in 1994). There are different ways to take control of the investment property. For example, a secured party has control over a certificated security by taking possession of it, along with any necessary indorsements. See §§ 8-106(a), (b) and 8-301(a). As to uncertificated securities, the secured party takes control by being registered as the owner of the stock in the records of the issuing corporation or takes other steps to make certain that it can reach the rights of the debtor in the event it needs to enforce the security interest. The other steps include, for example, having a stock-brokerage account of the debtor changed such that the secured party is the owner or entering an agreement with the stockbroker and the debtor whereby they agree to honor the order of the secured party regarding disposition of the investment property should the debtor default. See §§ 8-106(c) and (d). To insure priority of investment property generally as against other claimants, it is best to acquire control of the investment property as opposed to filing a financing statement. The Code gives to a controlling secured party priority over another secured party who has only filed a financing statement. See 1972 § 9-115 (5)(a).

The 1999 version of Article 9 does not substantially change how a secured transaction should be structured to obtain perfection of a security interest in investment property. See Comment 4(d) to 1999 § 9-101. Perfection by filing or control remains possible, with control having priority over filing as is the case under the 1972 version of the Article as amended in 1994. See 1999 §§ 9-102(a)(49), 9-106, 9-328 and § 8-106.

c. Where Collateral Is Held by Bailee

If collateral other than goods covered by a negotiable document is held by a third person as bailee, the secured party is deemed to have possession from the time the bailee receives notification of the secured party's interest. See 1972 § 9-305. Similarly, as to the 1999 Code, see 1999 § 9-313(c). Under the 1999 Code, with respect to collateral other than certificated securities and goods covered by a document of title, the secured party takes possession only when the third-person bailee has authenticated a record that acknowledges it holds the collateral for the secured party's benefit. See 1999 § 9-313(c) and Comment 4. This rule rejects the common-law doctrine that it is necessary for the bailee to attorn to the secured party or acknowledge that the property is held on the secured party's behalf. See Comment 2 to 1972 § 9-305. Similarly, under the 1999 Code, see Comment 3 to 1999 § 9-

313. The rationale behind this rule is explained as follows:

> "While ordinarily an agency cannot be created without consent of the agent * * * it is not considered desirable to require the consent of the third person [bailee] as a condition precedent to the creation of the pledge. The third person's duties are not altered in any material respect by the pledge. To make the third person's consent a test of the creation of the pledge would vest him with an arbitrary power of affecting the interests of the other parties. The third person of course may surrender the possession if he does not wish to be under any duty to the pledgee." Restatement, Security § 8 Comment a. Cf. UCC Sections 2-503(4), 2-509(2), 2-705(2)(b) and (c), 7-504(2) and (3).

Consonant with the above rule is 1972 § 9-304(3) which states: "A security interest in goods in the possession of a bailee [such as a warehouseman] other than one who has issued a negotiable document therefor is perfected by issuance of a document in the name of the secured party or by the bailee's receipt of notification of the secured party's interest or by filing as to the goods. Similarly, as to the 1999 Code, see 1999 § 9-312(c) and (d).

It should also be noted that 1972 § 9-304(2) states: "During the period that goods are in the possession of the issuer of a negotiable document therefore [such as a warehouseman who has issued a negotiable warehouse receipt or a carrier that has issued a negotiable bill of lading], a security interest in the goods is perfected by perfecting a security interest in the document, and any security interest in the goods otherwise perfected during such period is subject thereto." Similarly, as to the 1999 Code, see 1999 § 9-312(c) and (d). This provision takes the position that so long as a negotiable document covering goods is outstanding, title to the goods is locked up in the document and the proper way of dealing with the goods is through the document. Moreover, a security interest taken on the goods themselves while a negotiable document is outstanding is subordinate to a security interest taken in the document.

Under 1972 § 9-304(2), a debtor may pledge a negotiable document to a secured party and thus give the latter a perfected security interest in the goods, as well as in the document. Again, as to the 1999 Code, see 1999 § 9-312(c) and (d). See also, generally Article 7 of the Code and particularly §§ 7-403 and 7-502.

Similarly, the Code provides that a secured party

may perfect a security interest in investment property, i.e. stocks, by the giving of notice (through an agreement) to a third person (such as a bank, broker, or other person) who is in possession or control of the stock and is in an analogous position to that of a bailee. Generally, as to security interests in investment property, see § 4b of this chapter and Chapter 1, § 9a(3).

§ 5. Perfection by Filing

Generally, perfection as to most kinds of collateral is accomplished by filing a financing statement in a public office. See 1972 § 9-302(1) and 1999 § 9-310(a) which state that a financing statement must be filed to perfect all security interests, with certain exceptions discussed in the preceding sections of this chapter. As to the details of filing, including where to file and what to file, see Chapter 5.

In many instances, a security interest may be perfected either by filing or by possession. This applies to goods, chattel paper or negotiable documents. See 1972 §§ 9-302(1)(a), 9-304(1) and 9-305. See also 1999 §§ 9-310(b)(6) and 9-313. On the other hand, *filing is not effective to perfect a security interest in instruments* (other than instruments which constitute part of chattel paper) and also, under the 1972 Code, *in money*, except where instruments or money are proceeds. See 1972 § 304(1). Under the 1999 Code, filing is effective to perfect a security interest in instruments, but the creditor must take possession of money to perfect a security interest therein. See 1999 §§ 9-312(a) and 9-312(b)(3). Conversely, filing is the only general means of perfecting a security interest in accounts and general intangibles, although there are exceptions as to isolated accounts under 1972 § 9-302(1)(e) and 1999 § 9-309(2), as to assignment of an interest in a trust or estate under 1972 § 9-302(1)(c) and 1999 § 9-309(13) (estates only), and as to an assignment for the benefit of creditors under 1972 § 9-302(1)(g) and 1999 § 9-309(12).

As indicated above, filing under the 1972 Code is not effective to perfect a security interest in instruments. As to investment property, i.e. stocks, filing is a permissible means of perfection, although taking "control" of the investment property is a better method of perfection because it gives the secured party a better priority position in the collateral. See 1972 § 9-115(5)(a) (as revised in 1994) and 1999 § 9-328(1). For discussion of perfection of security interests in investment property, see § 4b of this chapter and Chapter 1, § 9a(3).

In certain instances, the filing requirements may

be complied with by registration or filing pursuant to a statute or treaty of the United States, by central filing under a state statute or by compliance with an applicable certificate of title law. See 1972 § 9-302(3) and (4) and 1999 § 9-311. See also discussion in the next two sections of this chapter.

§ 6. Perfection Where Filing is Required Under Federal Law

The filing provisions of Article 9 do not apply where the collateral is subject to a requirement of federal law under which there is a national registration or filing or a national certificate of title. Compliance with such federal requirement is equivalent to filing under Article 9. See 1972 § 9-302(3)(a) and (4), 1999 § 9-311(a)(1), (b). The 1972 and 1999 Codes make it clear that compliance with a treaty providing for international registration or an international certificate of title has the effect of filing under Article 9.

Filing or registration under a federal statute may be made with respect to such property as copyrights, trademarks, patents, aircraft, and rolling stock of a railroad. Where such filing requirements exist, they must be complied with for perfection, and filing under Article 9 is ineffective. On the other hand, where the security interest consists of the assignment of a claim against the United States, it is necessary both to file under Article 9 and to comply with the federal Assignment of Claims Act, which requires the giving of notice to contracting and disbursing officers and to sureties on bonds, but does not establish a national filing system. See Comment 8 to 1972 § 9-302 and Comment 2 to 1999 § 9-311.

§ 7.　Compliance With State Certificate of Title Law or Other Filing Requirement

The filing provisions of Article 9 do not apply where the collateral is subject to a state certificate of title law under which it is required that a security interest be indicated on a certificate of title or under which central filing is required under a state statute other than the Uniform Commercial Code. Compliance with such a certificate of title law or other state statute is equivalent to filing under Article 9. See 1972 § 9-302(3)(b),(4), and1999 §§ 9-310(b)(3), 9-311(a)(2), (3). Filing is not required to perfect a security interest in property subject to enumerated certificate of title statutes, except during the time when the goods are inventory held by a dealer for sale. 1972 § 9-302(3)(b), 1999 § 9-311(d).

The major items of collateral subject to certificate

of title laws which provide for indication of a security interest are motor vehicles, in probably the majority of states. However, filing is necessary with respect to motor vehicles in "nontitle" states (or states which do not have certificate of title laws providing for indication of a security interest on such a certificate as the means of perfecting a security interest). The certificate of title laws do not apply where motor vehicles are inventory held by a dealer for sale.

In some states, other items of collateral are also subject to certificate of title laws, such as boats.

Under 1972 § 9-302(3)(c) and 1999 § 9-311(a)(3), filing is not necessary where there is compliance with a certificate of title law of another state under the law of which indication of a security interest on the certificate is required as a condition of perfection.

The Code provides in 1972 § 9-302(3)(b), (4) and 1999 § 9-311(a)(2), (b) that filing under the Code is not necessary where the property is subject to a statute (separate from the UCC) of the state which provides for central filing. This has the effect of permitting filing where the debtor is a transmitting utility under a central filing statute, and such is clear under the Code which has provisions for central filing where the debtor is a transmitting utility.

§ 8.   Perfection as to Proceeds

"Proceeds" includes whatever is received upon the sale, exchange, collection or other disposition of collateral or proceeds. 1972 § 9-306(1), 1999 § 9-102(a)(64). See discussion of proceeds as collateral in Chapter 1, § 7d. Under 1972 § 9-306(2), a security interest in collateral which is sold, exchanged or otherwise disposed of "continues in any identifiable proceeds including collections received by the debtor." Similarly, see 1999 § 9-315(a)(2).

Under the 1972 Code it is not necessary to specifically file as to proceeds or make a specific reference to proceeds in a financing statement. In most instances, a filing as to collateral automatically covers proceeds and no action is necessary to perfect as to proceeds. See 1972 § 9-306(3), which provides that a security interest in proceeds is a continuously perfected security interest if the interest in the original collateral is perfected. The 1972 Code does provide that a perfected security interest ceases to be perfected ten days after receipt of the proceeds by the debtor unless one of four conditions are satisfied.

First, under the 1972 Code the security interest in

proceeds continues to be perfected beyond ten days of receipt by the debtor of the proceeds if a filed financing statement covers the original collateral and the proceeds are collateral in which a security interest may be perfected by filing in the office(s) where the financing statement has been filed. However, the continued perfection provision does not apply if the proceeds are acquired with cash proceeds and the financing statement fails to describe the collateral in a manner that includes the types of property constituting the proceeds. 1972 § 9-306(3)(a).

Second, under the 1972 Code the security interest in proceeds continues to be perfected beyond ten days of receipt by the debtor of the proceeds if the filed financing statement covers the original collateral and the proceeds are identifiable cash proceeds. 1972 § 9-306(3)(b).

Third, under the 1972 Code the security interest in proceeds continues to be perfected beyond ten days of receipt by the debtor of the proceeds if the original collateral was investment property and the proceeds are identifiable cash proceeds. 1972 § 9-306(3)(c).

Finally, under the 1972 Code the security interest in proceeds continues to be perfected beyond ten days of receipt by the debtor of the proceeds if the security interest in the proceeds is perfected before the expiration of the ten-day period. 1972 § 9-306(3)(d). In other words, the secured party is required to take action in order to perfect a security interest (i.e., take possession of a negotiable instrument or file a financing statement as to other collateral) when such perfection does not occur under of the above-discussed provisions.

Example 1. Lender filed a financing statement covering inventory of Borrower in State A where the inventory is kept. Borrower sold inventory on open account. Since Borrower's chief executive office is in State B, perfection as to accounts must be made by filing in State B under 1972 § 9-103(3). The security interest in the accounts continues perfected for ten days after they come into existence, but perfection is lost after that time unless Lender files as to accounts in State B before the end of that time. If Lender files in State B as to accounts at the time he files in State A as to inventory, the security interest in accounts is perfected without any ten-day limitation. See 1972 § 9-306(3). See also discussion as to the state in which to file in multistate transaction in Chapter 6.

Example 2. Lender filed a financing statement covering inventory of Borrower in State A where the inventory is kept and where Borrower has its only location. Borrower sold some inventory and took a check in payment. The check is cash proceeds, and the security interest in the check is perfected without the necessity of Lender taking possession. But if Borrower then used the check to pay for a machine to be used in Borrower's business, the machine is proceeds acquired with cash proceeds. Since the machine is equipment, it is not within the description of collateral in the financing statement which covered only inventory. The security interest in the machine continues for ten days after acquisition by Borrower. Perfection is lost at the end of that time if Lender does not file a financing statement covering the machine within that time. See 1972 § 9-306(3).

Example 3. Lender filed a financing statement covering inventory of Borrower in State A where the inventory is kept and where Borrower has its only location. Borrower sold some inventory and took a promissory note for the price from the buyer of the inventory. The security interest in the note is perfected for ten days after receipt of the note by Borrower. After that time, perfection is continued only if Lender has taken possession of the note during the ten-day period. The filing is ineffective, since the note is an "instrument" and is also "non-cash proceeds."

The perfection of security interests in proceeds under the 1999 Code is quite similar to the above-discussed provisions of the 1972 Code. Under the 1999 Code, it is not necessary to specifically file as to proceeds or make a specific reference to proceeds in a financing statement. In most instances, a filing as to collateral automatically covers proceeds and no action is necessary to perfect as to proceeds. See 1999 § 9-315(c), which provides that a security interest in proceeds is a perfected security interest if the security interest in the original collateral was perfected. The 1999 Code does provide that a perfected security interest in proceeds becomes unperfected on the 21st day after the security interest attaches to the proceeds unless one of three conditions are satisfied. See 1999 § 9-315(d).

First, under the 1999 Code the security interest in proceeds continues to be perfected beyond 20 days of attachment if a filed financing statement covers the original collateral, the proceeds are collateral in which a security interest may be perfected by filing in the office(s) in which the financing statement has been filed, and the proceeds are not acquired with cash proceeds. 1999 § 9-315(d)(1). This 1999 provision is derived from 1972 § 9-306(3)(a).

Second, under the 1999 Code the security

interest in proceeds continues to be perfected beyond 20 days of attachment if the proceeds are identifiable cash proceeds. 1999 § 9-315(d)(2). This 1999 provision is derived from 1972 § 9-306(3)(b).

Finally, under the 1999 Code the security interest in proceeds continues to be perfected beyond 20 days of attachment if the security interest in the proceeds is perfected other than under 1999 § 9-315(c) when the security interest attaches to the proceeds or within 20 days thereafter. 1999 § 9-315(d)(3). This 1999 provision is derived from 1972 § 9-306(3)(d) and requires the secured party to take action in order to perfect the security interest when such perfection does not occur because the security interest in the original collateral was not perfected.

§ 9. Perfection When Security Interest is Assigned.

"If a secured party assigns a perfected security interest, no filing * * * is required in order to continue the perfected status of the security interest against creditors of and transferees from the original debtor." 1972 § 9-302(2). Similarly, see 1999 § 9-310(c).

Example Buyer buys goods from Seller who

retains a security interest in them which he perfects (as by filing or even without filing if it is a purchase money security interest in consumer goods). Seller assigns the perfected security interest to X. The security interest, in X's hands and without further steps on his part, continues perfected against *Buyer's* transferees and creditors. If, however, the assignment from Seller to X was itself intended for security (or was a sale of accounts or chattel paper), X must take whatever steps may be required in order to be protected against *Seller's* creditors. See Comment 7 to 1972 § 9-302 and Comment 4 to 1999 § 9-310.

Although a secured transaction perfected against the original debtor by filing need not be further filed by an assignee of the security interest, it should be noted that 1972 § 9-405 and 1999 § 9-514 provide for the disclosing of an assignment in a financing statement and also provide for the filing of a separate written statement of assignment. Such filings as to an assignment are generally permitted on an optional basis, but are necessary when a continuation statement, statement of release, or termination statement is presented for filing signed by one other than the secured party of record. For discussion of filing when there is an assignment, see Chapter 5, § 9.

§ 10. Time of Perfection

When perfection occurs by possession, the 1972 Code provides that "[a] security interest is perfected by possession from the time possession is taken without relation back and continues only so long as possession is retained, unless otherwise specified in [Article 9]. The security interest may be otherwise perfected as provided in [Article 9] before or after the period of possession by the secured party." 1972 § 9-305.

This rejects the "equitable pledge" theory of relation back under which the taking of possession was deemed to relate back to the date of the original security agreement. The only exception to this rule is the 21-day period of perfection provided in 1972 § 9-304(4) and (5) or 1999 § 9-312(e), (f) and (g), during which a debtor may have possession of specified collateral in which there is a perfected security interest. For discussion of temporary 21-day perfection, see § 3 of this chapter.

The 1999 Code similarly provides that "[i]f perfection of a security interest depends upon possession of the collateral by the secured party, perfection occurs no earlier than the time the secured party takes possession and continues only while the secured party retains possession." 1999 § 9-313(d).

See also 1999 § 9-313(e) as to certificated securities in registered form.

In other instances, under the 1972 Code the time of perfection is determined by the time the security interest attaches and when all of the applicable steps required for perfection have been taken. See 1972 § 9-303(1) and 1999 § 9-308(a). Thus, where a security interest has attached and perfection is by filing, the time of perfection is generally the time of filing. In this connection, 1972 § 9-403(1) states that presentation for filing of a financing statement and tender of the filing fee or acceptance of the statement by the filing officer constitutes filing under Article 9. Similarly, the 1999 Code indicates that communication of a record to a filing office and tender of the filing fee or acceptance of the record by the filing office constitutes filing. 1999 § 9-516(a).

There is also normally no relation back when perfection is by attachment of the security interest followed by filing at a later time, although there is a limited provision applicable to purchase money security interests permitting a ten-day relation back under the 1972 Code, and a 20-day relation back under the 1999 Code, of a filing as against the rights of certain third persons whose interests arise between the time of attachment and the time of filing. See 1972 § 9-301(2) and 1999 § 9-317(e).

If the steps necessary to perfection are taken before the security interest attaches, the security interest is perfected at the time when it attaches. 1972 § 9-303(1) and 1999 § 9-308(a).

Example. Secured party files a financing statement before giving value, before a written security agreement is executed or before the debtor has rights in the collateral. The security interest is perfected automatically when it attaches. See Comment 1 to 1972 § 9-303 and Comment 2 to 1999 § 9-308.

§ 11. Continuity of Perfection

The Code takes the position that perfection is continuous where it occurs through different methods and where there is no intervening period when the perfection is lost. 1972 § 9-303(2) states: "If a security interest is originally perfected in any way permitted under [Article 9] and is subsequently perfected in some other way under [Article 9], without an intermediate period when it was unperfected, the security interest shall be deemed to be perfected continuously for the purposes of this Article." Similarly, in the 1999 Code, see 1999 § 9-308(c).

Example 1. Debtor gives possession of certain

goods to Creditor in pledge (such as in a field warehousing transaction) to secure a loan. Later, Creditor files a financing statement and then relinquishes possession of the goods to Debtor. Creditor's security interest was perfected first by possession and then by filing without an intermediate period when it was unperfected. Creditor's security interest was continuously perfected from the time possession was originally taken.

Example 2. Bank which has issued a letter of credit honors drafts drawn under the credit and receives possession of a negotiable bill of lading covering the goods shipped. Under 1972 §§ 9-304(2) and 9-305 or 1999 §§ 9-312(f) and 9-313, Bank has a perfected security interest in the document and the goods. Bank releases the bill of lading to Debtor for the purpose of the latter procuring the goods from the carrier and selling them. Under 1972 § 9-304(5), Bank continues to have a perfected security interest in the document and goods for 21 days, and under 1999 § 9-312(f), Bank continues to have a perfected security interest in the document or goods for 20 days. Bank files before the expiration of the 21- or 20-day periods. Its security interest continues perfected for as long as the filing is good. When the goods are sold by Debtor, Bank continues to have a security interest in the proceeds of the sale to the extent stated in 1972 § 9-306 and 1999 § 9-315.

§ 12. Methods of Perfection Provided for Only in the 1999 Code

Discussion of perfection methods to this point has focused on perfection methods found only in the 1972 Code or that are common to both the 1972 and 1999 Codes with emphasis placed on any differences between the two versions of the Code as to any particular perfection method. The 1999 Code has added some new perfection methods. Some of the new "methods" actually relate to new forms of collateral that fall within the 1999 Code's scope of application that were not included in the 1972 Code. These new methods of perfecting a security interest are discussed below.

a. Perfection by "Control."

The 1999 Code creates a perfection method based upon the secured party acquiring control of the collateral. The control perfection method applies to collateral that is a deposit account [1999 § 9-102(a)(29)], letter-of-credit right [1999 § 9-102(a)(51)], electronic chattel paper [1999 § 9-102(a)(31)] or investment property [1999 § 9-102(a)(49)]. Specifically, the 1999 Code provides that a security interest in such collateral may be perfected by control of the collateral. 1999 § 9-314(a).

Control of deposit accounts is acquired if the secured party is the bank with which the deposit is maintained or if the debtor, secured party and bank have agreed in an authenticated record that the bank will comply with the secured party's instructions regarding disposition of the account funds, or if the secured party becomes the account holder, that is, the secured party becomes the bank's customer with respect to the account. 1999 § 9-104. Control of electronic chattel paper is acquired essentially by the secured party being identified as the assignee of the chattel paper on the record of the secured party. 1999 § 9-105. As to a letter-of-credit right, the 1999 Code indicates that the secured party has control essentially if the issuer has consented to an assignment of the letter-of-credit proceeds. 1999 § 9-107; see also UCC § 5-114(c). The 1999 Code emphasizes that a security interest perfected by control in these collateral types remains perfected only while the secured party retains control. 1999 § 9-314(a) and (b).

Obtaining control of investment property is treated somewhat differently. For discussion of perfection of security interests in investment property, see § 4b of this chapter and Chapter 1, § 9a(3).

b. *Agricultural Liens*

The 1999 Article 9 includes agricultural liens within its scope of coverage. See 1999 § 9-109(a) (2). "Agricultural lien" is defined in the Code at 1999 § 9-102(a)(5). Essentially, an agricultural lien is an interest other than a security interest in farm products created by statute for one who sells goods or services in the ordinary course of business to a farmer or rents real property to a farmer who uses it in connection with a farming operation. The interest, of course, secures payment of debts the farmer-debtor incurs for the purchase of the goods or services and lease of the real property. To be an "agricultural lien" the 1999 Code also provides that the effectiveness of the lien must not depend on the person's possession of the personal property. Agricultural liens are statutory liens that are drawn in the 1999 Code for perfection and priority purposes. As to perfection of an agricultural lien, the lienor must file a financing statement. 1999 §§ 9-310(a), 9-308(b).

c. "True" Consignments

A significant change regarding consignment transactions has been made under the 1999 version of Article 9. The 1999 Article flatly states that the Article applies to consignments. See 1999 § 9-109(a)(4). The 1999 Article § 9-102(a)(20) defines "consignment" as a transaction, regardless of its form, in which a person delivers goods to a merchant for the purpose of sale. The merchant must deal in goods of this kind under a name other than the name of the person making delivery and must not be an auctioneer and the merchant must not generally be known by its creditors to be substantially engaged in selling goods of others. See 1999 § 9-102(a)(20)(A). The aggregate value of the goods must be $1,000 or more at the time of delivery. See 1999 § 9-102(a)(20)(B). The goods must not be consumer goods immediately before delivery [1999 § 9-102(a)(20)(C)] and the transaction must not create a security interest that secures an obligation [1999 § 9-102(a)(20))(D)].

The gist of the 1999 changes is that some "true" consignments (as described above), that are bailments of goods for the purpose of sale by the bailee, are within the scope of UCC Article 9. In most consignment transactions, the consignor should file a financing statement in order to protect its interest against creditors of the consignee, much as occurs under the 1972 Article 9 and § 2-326(3)(c). See 1999 §§ 9-310(a), 9-102(a)(20), 9-109(a)(4).

d. *Sales and Assignments of Payment Intangibles and Sales of Promissory Notes.*

The 1999 Code also created a new classification of collateral termed "payment intangibles." The 1999 Code defines a payment intangible as meaning a "general intangible" under which the account debtor's principal obligation is a monetary obligation. 1999 § 9-102(a)(61). The term "promissory note" also is defined by the 1999 Code which gives it its ordinary meaning. 1999 § 102(a)(65). As to perfection of security interests in such collateral, the 1999 Code flatly provides that the security interest is automatically perfected when a security interest attaches and the collateral is sold. 1999 § 9-309(3), (4). See also Comment 4, 1999 § 9-309. As to payment intangibles, the 1999 Code also provides that an assignment of a payment intangible which does not by itself or in conjunction with other assignments to the same assignee transfer a significant part of the assignor's payment intangibles is automatically perfected when the security interest attaches. 1999 § 9-309(2). The upshot of all this is that a buyer of payment intangibles or promissory notes, and an assignee of payment intangibles that are not a significant part of the assignor's payment intangibles need not file a financing statement.

e. Commercial Tort Claims

The 1999 Code narrowed the 1972 Code's exclusion from Article 9 of transfers of interests in tort claims. 1972 § 9-104(k). The 1999 Code creates a new category of collateral termed "commercial tort claims," thus including such claims within its scope. A commercial tort claim is a claim that arises out of the debtor's business or profession. It does not include claims for personal injury or death of an individual. See 1999 § 9-102(a)(13). A secured party must file a financing statement to perfect its security interest in such a claim. 1999 § 9-310(a).

f. Supporting Obligations

The 1999 Code adds a new form of collateral termed a "supporting obligation." A "supporting obligation" is defined at 1999 § 9-102(a)(77) to mean a letter-of-credit right or other secondary obligation such as a guaranty that supports payment or performance under an account [1999 § 9-102(a)

(2)], chattel paper [1999 § 9-102(a)(11)], document [1999 § 9-102(a)(30)], general intangible [1999 § 9-102(a)(42)], instrument [1999 § 9-102(a)(47)], or investment property [1999 § 9-102(a)(49)]. A security interest in a support*ed* obligation automatically attaches to the support*ing* obligation; likewise, perfection of a security interest in the support*ed* obligation also perfects the security interest in the support*ing* obligation. 1999 §§ 9-203 (f), 9-308(d). Thus, if a secured party has a perfected security interest in a promissory note which is a type of instrument and that note is supported by a stand-by letter of credit, the secured party automatically has a perfected security interest in the letter-of-credit rights.

g. *Assignment of Health-Care-Insurance Receivables*

The 1999 Code creates a new classification of Article 9 collateral termed "health-care-insurance receivables." The type of collateral consists of interest in or claims under a policy of insurance which is a right to payment of a monetary obligation for health-care goods or services. 1999 § 9-102(a) (46). The 1999 Code provides for automatic perfection of a security interest created by the assignment of the health-care-insurance receivable to the provider of the health-care goods or services. 1999 § 9-309(5).

h. Instruments

An "instrument" is a negotiable promissory note, draft, check or the like. 1999 § 9-102(a)(47). Traditionally, perfection of a security interest in an instrument has occurred only by the secured party taking possession of the instrument. 1972 § 9-304(1). The 1999 Code also permits perfection of a security interest in an instrument to occur by filing a financing statement. 1999 § 9-312(a). This marks a significant change in traditional practices which permit perfection of interests in an instrument only by taking possession of the instrument.

CHAPTER 5

PERFECTION OF SECURITY INTEREST BY FILING

§ 1.   "Notice Filing"

The most common method of perfecting a security interest is by filing a financing statement in a public office. For a general discussion of perfection of a security interest by filing with respect to various kinds of collateral, see Chapter 4, § 5.

Article 9 adopts the system of "notice filing" which proved successful under the Uniform Trust Receipts Act. The basic system is explained in Comment 2 to 1972 § 9-402 as follows:

"What is required to be filed is not, as under chattel mortgage and conditional sales acts, the security agreement itself ["transaction filing"], but only a simple notice [a financing statement] which may be filed before the security interest attaches or thereafter. The notice itself indicates merely that the secured party who has filed may have a security interest in the collateral described. Further inquiry from the parties concerned will be necessary to disclose the complete state of affairs. [This may be accomplished under 1972 § 9-208 or 1999 § 9-210.] Notice filing has proved to be of great use in financing transactions involving inventory, accounts and chattel paper, since it obviates the necessity of re-filing on each of a series of transactions in a continuing arrangement where the collateral changes from day to day. Where other types of collateral are involved, the alternative procedure of filing a signed copy of the security agreement may prove to be the simplest solution. * * *

"However, even in the case of filings that do not necessarily involve a series of transactions the financing statement is effective to encompass transactions under a security agreement not in existence and not contemplated at the time the notice was filed, if the description of collateral in the financing statement is broad enough to encompass them. Similarly, the financing statement is valid to cover after-acquired property and future advances under security agreements whether or not mentioned in the financing statement."

For similar commentary under the 1999 Code, see Comment 2 to 1999 § 9-502.

§ 2. Where to File Under the 1972 Code

The 1972 Code provides each state three alternative approaches that specify where to file a financing statement within the particular state. The 1999 Code does not provide for three alternatives; it requires central filing for most situations. The specifics of the 1972 and 1999 Code place of filing provisions are discussed in this chapter. It should also be noted that some secured transactions involve multiple states. In such a multiple-state transaction, the initial issue is one of determining the state in which to file or otherwise perfect. The multiple-state issue is considered in Chapter 6.

a. *Alternative Code Provisions*

1972 § 9-401(1) is drafted in three alternatives which present various choices between so-called "central" filing at a single public office, such as that of the Secretary of State at a state capital, and so-called "local" filing or filing at a local county or township office where the debtor resides or is located or where the collateral is kept.

All three alternatives contemplate that filing should be in a local office where the collateral consists of fixtures, and also contemplates local filing in certain other secured transactions related to real estate. In other cases, the alternatives present varied choices as to places to file.

The reason for presenting such alternatives is explained in Comment 1 to 1972 § 9-401 which states:

> "Under chattel mortgage acts, the Uniform Conditional Sales Act, and other conditional sales legislation, the geographical unit for filing or recording was local: the county or township in which the mortgagor or vendee resided or in which the goods sold or mortgaged were kept. The Uniform Trust Receipts Act used the state as the geographical filing unit: under that Act statements of trust receipt financing were filed with an official in the state capital and were not filed locally. The state-wide filing system of the Trust Receipts Act has been followed in many accounts receivable and factor's lien acts.

> "Both systems have their advocates and both their own advantages and drawbacks. The principal advantage of state-wide filing is ease of access to the credit information which the files exist to provide. Consider for example the national distributor who wishes to have current information about the credit standing of the

thousands of person he sells to on credit. The more completely the files are centralized on a state-wide basis, the easier and cheaper it becomes to procure credit information; the more the files are scattered in local filing units, the more burdensome and costly. On the other hand, it can be said that most credit inquiries about local businesses, farmers and consumers come from local sources; convenience is served by having the files locally available and there is no great advantage in centralized filing.

"This section [1972 § 9-401] does not attempt to resolve the controversy between the advocates of a completely centralized state-wide filing system and those of a large degree of local autonomy. Instead the section is drafted in a series of alternatives; local considerations of policy will determine the choice to be made."

CAVEAT. In considering problems of where to file, one must consult the version of 1972 § 9-401(1) enacted in the particular state. While the discussion which follows sets forth the highlights of the three alternatives to 1972 § 9-401(1) presented by the Code drafters, *it should be kept in mind that a number of states have enacted versions of 1972 § 9-401(1) which vary from any of the three alternatives.* Moreover, a rather considerable volume of Article 9 litigation has arisen by reason of noncompliance with the "place to file" requirements of 1972 § 9-401(1).

RECOMMENDATION. The general prudential rule might be stated as: "When in doubt, file." Where a question as to the place to file arises, the best solution is to file in all doubtful places. Failure to do this can result in not having a perfected security interest and relegate the secured party to the status of a general creditor of an insolvent debtor. On the other hand, filing in more offices than required merely results in loss of a filing fee in a nominal amount for an "unnecessary" filing.

b. *Farm-related Collateral and Consumer Goods*

The first alternative of 1972 § 9-401(1) contemplates central filing with the Secretary of State or similar state official, for all collateral except certain real-estate-related collateral. Under this alternative, filing is central with respect to all farm-related collateral, including crops, and with respect to consumer goods. See 1972 § 9-401(1)(b) of the first alternative.

Under both the second and third alternatives of 1972 § 9-401(1)(a), filing with respect to all farm-related collateral and consumer goods is local only. That provision, in both alternatives, describes the collateral to be filed locally as follows:

"When the collateral is equipment used in farming operations, or farm products, or accounts or general intangibles arising from or relating to the sale of farm products by a farmer, or consumer goods, then [the proper place to file is] in the office of the [county clerk] in the county of the debtor's residence or if the debtor is not a resident of this state then in the office of the [county clerk] in the county where the goods are kept, and in addition when the collateral is crops growing or to be grown in the office of the [county clerk] in the county where the land is located."

Where the second or third alternative has been enacted, if the collateral is crops and the land where the crops are growing is in one county while the debtor resides in a different county, filing is necessary in both counties. However, it is not necessary to file with respect to crops in the real estate records. See Comment 3 to 1972 § 9-401.

If crops are collateral and the debtor is an incorporated farm, the reference to "residence" is an anomaly. Accordingly, 1972 § 9-401(6) provides that the residence of an organization is its place of business or its chief executive office if it has more than one place of business. Thus, in some instances, double local filing may be necessary where a farm is incorporated and its place of business or chief executive office is elsewhere than in the county where the crops are growing or to be grown.

It should be kept in mind that local filing in the county of the debtor's residence (or where the goods are kept if the debtor is not a resident of the state) is necessary under the second and third alternatives where the collateral is *consumer goods*. While 1972 § 9-301(1)(d) does not require filing for perfection of a purchase money security interest in most consumer goods, filing is necessary where there is a non-purchase money security interest, and filing is also effective to prevent an unauthorized sale of consumer goods free of the security interest to another consumer. See 1972 § 9-307(2).

c. *Fixtures and Other Real-estate-related Collateral*

Under 1972 § 9-401(1) in all alternatives, local filing is prescribed where there is a fixture filing or in the case of certain other real-estate-related collateral. That provision reads:

"When the collateral is timber to be cut or is

minerals or the like (including oil and gas) or accounts [arising from the sale of such minerals, oil and gas at the wellhead or minehead], or when the financing statement is filed as a fixture filing [under 1972 § 9-313] and the collateral is goods which are or are to become fixtures, then [the proper place to file is] in the office where a mortgage on the real estate would be filed or recorded." 1972 § 9-401(1)(a) in the first alternative, 1972 § 9-401(1)(b) in the second and third alternatives.

In other words, 1972 § 9-401(1) requires a local filing in a "mortgage-filing" office (such as a county clerk, register of deeds or the like) where the collateral is timber, oil, gas or minerals or certain accounts arising from the sale of oil, gas or minerals. The same is true where there is a "fixture filing" with respect to fixtures. In this connection, 1972 § 9-403(7) requires the local filing officer to index such filings as if they are real estate mortgages. There is no requirement for an additional filing in the chattel records.

A "fixture filing" is defined in 1972 § 9-313(1)(b) as a "filing in the office where a mortgage on the real estate would be filed or recorded of a financing statement covering goods which are or are to become fixtures and conforming to the requirements of 1972 § 9-402(5)."

It should be kept in mind that 1972 § 9-401(1) does not require a fixture filing as a condition to perfection, even where the collateral is a fixture. Perfection may be made in the same manner as if the collateral were not a fixture (by filing as to equipment or consumer goods, or even without filing if the fixture is consumer goods and there is a purchase money security interest). However, a filing as a fixture filing is necessary to obtain priority over certain real estate interests under 1972 § 9-313.

Where collateral is a fixture and there is a proper fixture filing, no other filing is necessary; the security interest is perfected and is also good against certain real estate interests under 1972 § 9-313. For discussion of priority with respect to real estate interests, see Chapter 7, § 7.

Under the 1972 Code, the only way to perfect a security interest where the collateral is timber to be cut, or minerals, oil and gas and resulting accounts is by filing in a "mortgage-filing" office.

Under the 1972 Code, a filing as a fixture filing will be ineffective if the collateral is not a fixture, but a proper filing as a non-fixture is effective to perfect a security interest even when the collateral is a fixture. However, failure to file as a fixture filing when the collateral is a fixture may result in priority of certain real estate interests over the perfected interest of the secured party, under 1972 § 9-313.

Example 1. Secured party filed a financing statement covering a large factory machine (equipment) as a fixture with the local Register of Deeds, but did not file with the Secretary of State (as required in all alternatives of 1972 § 9-401(1) with respect to non-fixture equipment collateral). The machine could be easily moved and was held to be a non-fixture. The filing is ineffective under the 1972 Code if the filing is as a fixture filing.

Example 2. Secured party filed a financing statement covering a large factory machine (equipment) with the Secretary of State but did not file as a fixture in a local office. The state has the second alternative of 1972 § 9-401(1) which provides that filing as to non-fixture equipment is with the Secretary of State. Since the machine could not be easily moved and was installed by affixation to the floor and walls of the factory building, the machine is a fixture. Under the 1972 Code, the filing is effective to perfect the security interest, but the security interest is inferior to certain real estate interests under 1972 § 9-313. [Note: If the machine is a readily removable factory machine, the security interest is superior to real estate interests under 1972

§ 9-313(4)(c) if the security interest is perfected in any manner.]

d. *Collateral of a Transmitting Utility*

The term "transmitting utility" means "any person primarily engaged in the railroad, street railway or trolley bus business, the electric or electronics communications transmission business, the transmission of goods by pipeline, or the transmission or production of electricity, steam, gas or water, or the provision of sewer service." See 1972 § 9-105(1)(n).

Under 1972 § 9-401(5), the proper place to file in order to perfect a security interest in collateral, including fixtures, of a transmitting utility is in the office of the Secretary of State or similar state official. Such a central filing is effective as a fixture filing with respect to collateral of a transmitting utility that is or becomes fixtures.

e. *Other Collateral*

The first alternative, 1972 § 9-401(1)(b), and the second alternative, 1972 § 9-401(1)(c), declare that the proper place to file "in all other cases" (except with respect to collateral discussed above in this section) is in the office of the Secretary of State or similar state official.

Under the first alternative, all filing except that respecting fixtures or other real-estate-related collateral is central. Under the second alternative, all filing except farm-related collateral, consumer goods and fixtures or other real-estate-related collateral is central.

The third alternative, 1972 § 9-401(1)(c), states that "in all other cases" the proper place to file is in the office of the Secretary of State or similar state official. In addition, if the debtor has a place of business in only one county of this state or if the debtor has no place of business in the state but resides in the state, a local filing in the county where the debtor has his place of business or resides is necessary.

The third alternative requires both central and local filing in most instances, since probably the majority of debtors have their business locations in only one county. Where such dual filing is required, filing in only one of the necessary offices is ineffective to perfect a security interest. A number of decisions have so held.

f. *Effect of Improper Filing*

Where filing is made in an improper place (e.g., a financing statement covering equipment is filed locally when it should have been centrally filed under 1972 § 9-401(1)(c) in the second alternative) or where it is not made in all the places required [e.g., a filing covering equipment of a debtor with a place of business in one county is filed centrally but is not also filed locally as required under 1972 § 9-401(1)(c) in the third alternative], the security interest is not perfected and the improper or insufficient filing is generally ineffective. A number of decisions have so held.

Nevertheless, the improper or insufficient filing may be given effect in certain instances or against certain third persons.

Under 1972 § 9-401(2), a filing which is made in good faith in an improper place or not in all of the places required is nevertheless effective (1) with regard to any collateral as to which the filing complies with the requirements of Article 9, and (2) with regard to collateral covered by the financing statement "against any person who has knowledge of the contents of such financing statement."

The first part of 1972 § 9-401(2) applies where a filing covers different kinds of collateral and is good with respect to some but not all of the collateral covered.

Example. Debtor who lived in King County had a farm in Queen County. Secured party filed a financing statement in King County covering livestock and crops growing on the farm. Under either the second or third alternatives of 1972 § 9-401(1)(a), the filing is effective as to the livestock but is not effective as to the crops, since a second filing in Queen County is also necessary. (Under the first alternative, the filing is completely ineffective, since central filing is necessary.)

The second part of 1972 § 9-401(2) makes the filing effective for all collateral covered by the financing statement against any person "who has knowledge of the contents of such financing statement." This rejects occasional decisions that an improperly filed record is ineffective to give notice even to a person who knows of it. See Comment 5 to 1972 § 9-401.

It would seem that mere knowledge of the existence of a security interest in certain collateral would not, of itself, bring into play the second part of 1972 § 9-401(2). On the other hand, a person who finds and reads the statement which is filed in the "improper place" should be deemed to have knowledge of its contents. Presumably, a person who is shown a copy of the improperly filed statement or who is given accurate details of the filing and of the collateral covered would also be deemed to have knowledge of the contents.

g. *Effect of Change of Debtor's Residence, Place of Business, Location of Collateral or Its Use*

Under 1972 § 9-401(3), a filing which is made in the proper place in the state "continues effective even though the debtor's residence or place of business or the location of the collateral or its use, whichever controlled the original filing, is thereafter changed."

This deals with change of residence or place of business or the location or use of the goods after a proper filing has been made. The provision is important only when local filing is required, and covers only changes between local filing units in the same state. Where the debtor changes location from one state to another state or moves the goods from one state to another state, 1972 § 9-103 comes into play. See Comment 6 to 1972 § 9-401. For discussion of perfection problems when the collateral is moved, see Chapter 6.

An alternative 1972 § 9-401(3), enacted in some states, provides that a filing which is made in the proper county continues effective for four months after a change to another county of the debtor's residence, place of business or location of the collateral, whichever controlled the original filing. After that time, perfection is lost unless a copy of the financing statement signed by the secured party is filed in the new county within the four-month period. A filing in the new county after the four-month period results in reperfection only from the time of such additional filing. However, a change in the use of the collateral does not impair the effectiveness of the original filing.

Example 1. Debtor, a physician with his only office in King County, purchased X-ray equipment on credit from Secured Party. The latter filed centrally and also locally in King County under the third alternative of 1972 § 9-401(1)(c), which was in effect in the state. Later, Debtor moved his office including the equipment to a new location in Queen County. Under the first version of 1972 § 9-401(3), no refiling in Queen County is necessary. Under the alternative 1972 § 9-401(3), Secured Party must refile in Queen County within four months of Debtor's change of location in order to maintain perfection.

Example 2. Debtor, a farmer, purchased a tractor (not a motor vehicle) on credit from Secured Party for use on Debtor's farm. Secured Party filed in King County where Debtor resided and where the farm is located under either the second or third alternative of 1972 § 9-401(1)(a). Later, Debtor sold his farm and purchased a manufacturing business with a single location, also in King County. He took the tractor to that place of business and thereafter used it in his manufacturing operations. Although the use of the collateral, which controlled the original filing, has been changed from equipment used in farming operations to ordinary equipment, no additional filing with the Secretary of State is necessary, under either the first or alternative versions of 1972 § 9-401(3).

§ 3. Where to File Under the 1999 Code

The 1999 Code provides only one approach as to the place of filing of financing statements. The approach requires most filings to occur at a central location except for real-estate-related collateral where local filing will still occur. Comment 2 to 1999 § 9-501 explains the reasoning that led to this change from the 1972 Code:

"Former Article 9 afforded each State three

alternative approaches, depending on the extent
to which the State desires central filing (usually
with the Secretary of State), local filing (usually
with a county office), or both. ... Local filing
increases the net costs of secured transactions ...
by increasing uncertainty and the number of
required filings. Any benefit that local filing may
have had in the 1950's is now insubstantial.
Accordingly, this Article dictates central filing
for most situations, while retaining local filing
for real-estate-related collateral and special filing
provisions for transmitting utilities."

The 1999 Code indicates that the office in which
to file a financing statement to perfect a security
interest or an agricultural lien is the office designated for filing or recording a mortgage on related
real property if the collateral is as-extracted collateral [i.e., oil, gas and minerals, see 1999 § 9-
102(a)(6)] or timber to be cut or the financing
statement is filed as a fixture filing and the collateral
is goods that are or are to become fixtures. 1999
§ 9-501(a)(1). In all other cases filing occurs in a
central location as designated by each State. 1999
§ 9-501 (a)(2). As to debtors that are transmitting
utilities [see § 9-102(a)(80) for the definition of
"transmitting utility"], filing will also occur at a
designated central location, even if the collateral is

fixtures. 1999 § 9-501(b). Apparently because most filings will occur centrally, the 1999 Code has no equivalent to 1972 § 9-401(2) which provides that filing in the wrong location under some circumstances will not be fatal to the effectiveness of the filing. See prior discussion of 1972 § 9-401(2) at § 2f of this chapter.

§ 4.   What to File: Financing Statement

The 1972 and 1999 Code provisions that set forth the requisite form of that which is filed, i.e., the financing statement, differ in some significant respects. The following discussion will describe the form requirements under both the 1972 and 1999 versions of Article 9.

a. Summary of 1972 Code Formal Requirements

The basic requirements of a financing statement under the 1972 Code are set forth in 1972 § 9-402(1). Such requirements are discussed in the lettered subsections which follow but are summarized here:

(1) The financing statement must be signed by the debtor.

(2) The financing statement must name the parties.

(3) The financing statement must give an address of the secured party from which information concerning the security interest may be obtained and give a mailing address of the debtor.

(4) The financing statement must contain a statement indicating the types or describing the items of collateral.

(5) When the financing statement covers fixtures or certain other collateral related to real estate, a description of land is necessary.

While a copy of the security agreement may be filed as a financing statement if it meets the above requirements, the normal practice is to file a simple form containing only the required information. Such a simple statutory form is set forth in 1972 § 9-402(3).

To facilitate filing, "standard" forms have been developed for use in most, if not all, Code jurisdictions which meet the statutory requirements when properly signed and filled in.

In accord with the "notice filing" purpose of Article 9, it is not necessary to give any information in a financing statement other than that sufficient to meet the basic requirements. Thus, it is not necessary to set forth such information as the amount of the debt, interest or finance charges, the maturity of the loan, future advances, or other terms and conditions of the loan or security interest. Neither the statutory form in 1972 § 9-402(3) nor the "standard" forms commonly in use have space for such additional information.

The 1972 Code provides that a financing statement substantially complying with the content requirements, summarized above, is effective even though it contains minor errors that are not seriously misleading. 1972 § 9-402(8).

b. Summary of 1999 Code Formal Requirements

The basic requirements of a financing statement under the 1999 Code are set forth in 1999 § 9-502(a) and (b).

The 1999 Code authorizes electronic filings; that is, the financing statement may be but need not be in tangible form. Under the 1999 Code, a "financing statement" means a record or records composed of an initial financing statement and a filed record relating to the initial financing statement." 1999 § 9-102(a)(39). A "record" means information that is inscribed as a tangible medium or which is stored in an electronic or other medium and is retrievable in perceivable form. 1999 § 9-102(a)(69).

The content requirements of financing statements are discussed in the lettered subsections which follow but are summarized here:

(1) The financing statement must provide the name of the debtor.

(2) The financing statement must provide the name of the secured party or a representative of the secured party.

(3) The financing statement must indicate the collateral covered by the financing statement.

(4) When the financing statement covers fixtures or certain other collateral related to real estate, a description of land is necessary.

(5) The address of the parties and an indication of whether the debtor is an individual or an organization must also be included (note that the addresses and an indication of the individual/organizational status of the debtor are required by the 1999 Code but are not necessary for an initial financing statement to be legally sufficient to perfect a security interest.)

While a copy of the security agreement may be filed as a financing statement if it meets the above requirements, the normal practice is to file a simple form containing only the required information. Such a simple form is set forth in 1999 § 9-521.

The 1999 Code provides that a financing statement substantially satisfying the content requirements, summarized above, is effective even if it has minor errors or omissions, unless the errors or omissions make the financing statement seriously misleading. 1999 § 9-506(a).

c. *Signature Requirement*

(1) 1972 Code General Signature Requirement

Under 1972 § 9-402(1), a *financing statement must be signed by the debtor*, in most instances. The signature of the secured party is not necessary, however.

The form or style of the debtor's signature is discussed below:

(a) No "formal" or "complete" signature of the debtor is necessary. In other words, the debtor need not sign his full name, nor is a handwritten signature of an authorized agent necessary if the debtor is a corporation or other organization. In this connection, it should be noted that the term *signed* includes any symbol executed or adopted by a party with present intention to authenticate a writing. Such authentication may be printed, stamped or written and may be by initials or even thumbprint. No catalog of possible authentications can be complete and the question always is whether the symbol was executed or adopted by the party with present intention to authenticate the writing. See § 1-201(39) and Comment 39 to § 1-201.

(b) No acknowledgment of the signature before a notary is necessary, nor is any sworn affidavit of consideration or the like necessary. A number of pre-Code chattel mortgage statutes required such notarial formalities. The signature also need not be witnessed. Moreover, there is no requirement that the signature be under seal.

(c) If the signature of the debtor is made by an agent, the general common-law concepts of the law of agency determine whether the signature is effective. See § 1-103 which preserves supplementary general principles of law and equity, including the law of principal and agent.

While it would seem that the courts generally take a rather liberal view as to what constitutes a proper or effective signature under Article 9, there may be instances in which a purported "signing" is incomplete and thus is not considered a signature.

Example 1. A financing statement named the debtor corporation and gave its address, but was manually signed by the president who failed to add his title or evidence of authority, although he was authorized to sign. The filing is effective and the individual signer is not personally liable.

Example 2. A financing statement was purportedly "signed" by the use of a stamp naming a corporation followed by the word "by" and a blank space which was not filled in or signed by an authorized individual. The filing is ineffective.

(2) When Secured Party May Sign Alone Under the 1972 Code

In certain instances, a financing statement may be signed by the secured party alone. Such signing is permitted under circumstances where a second filing is made following the commencement of the financing and the original filing, and where the cooperation of the debtor in signing a second financing statement may not always be forthcoming. See Comment 4 to 1972 § 9-402. The secured party alone may sign under the following circumstances:

(a) When collateral subject to a security interest in one state is brought to a second state, necessitating a new filing in the second state. The financing statement must state that the collateral was brought into the second state. 1972 § 9-402(2)(a),

(b) When the debtor's location is changed from one state to a second state necessitating a new filing in the second state. The financing statement must state that the debtor's location was changed to the second state. 1972 § 9-402(2)(a).

(c) When a new filing as to proceeds is necessary, although the security interest in the original collateral is perfected. 1972 § 9-402(2)(b). For discussion of perfection as to proceeds, see § 4h of this chapter and Chapter 4, § 8.

(d) When a filing has lapsed and a new filing is made after the lapse. 1972 § 9-402(2)(c).

(e) When collateral is acquired more than four months after a change of name, identity or corporate structure of the debtor, necessitating a new filing. 1972 § 9-402(2)(d).

(f) When a new filing is necessary under the alternative version of 1972 § 9-401(3) enacted in some states within four months after the debtor has changed residence, place of business or location of the collateral to another county in the same state. See discussion in § 2g of this chapter.

(3) When Both Debtor and Secured Party Must Sign Under the 1972 Code

In one instance under the 1972 Code the signature of both the debtor and the secured party is necessary. Under 1972 § 9-402(4), both parties must sign an amendment to a financing statement. The reason for the requirement is to preclude either party from "adversely affecting the interests of the other." See Comment 4 to 1972 § 9-402.

For other discussion of amendment of a financing statement, see § 6 of this chapter, below.

(4) No Signature Requirement Under the 1999 Code

The 1999 Code does not require the debtor's signature on an initial financing statement. The purpose of eliminating the signature requirement is to accommodate electronic filings. See Comment 3 to 1999 § 9-502. The debtor authorizes filing of an initial financing statement, or an amendment that adds collateral described in the initial financing statement or a new debtor to the initial financing statement, by authenticating the security agreement. 1999 § 9-509 (a), (b). An amendment that adds collateral not covered in the security agreement or adds a new debtor must be authorized in an authenticated record. 1999 § 9-509(a).

Eliminating the debtor signature requirement raised a concern that unauthorized filings might occur. That concern is addressed by the 1999 Code. Any person who files an unauthorized initial financing statement or amendment can be held liable for damages and a statutory penalty of $500. 1999 § 9-625(b), (e)(3). A filing is declared effective only to the extent it is debtor authorized. 1999 § 9-510(a). Finally, a person may file in the filing office a correction statement with respect to a record indexed there under the person's name if the person believes the record is inaccurate or was wrongfully filed. 1999 § 9-518(a). A part of the correction statement must explain the basis of the filing party's belief that the record should be corrected. 1999 § 9-518(b). This, for example, permits a purported debtor to put on public record his belief that a filed financing statement is "bogus" and should be ignored. See Comment 2 to 1999 § 9-518. On the other hand, the filing of a correction statement alone does not affect the validity of the filing it seeks to correct; the filer of the correction statement must use other legal means to affect the filing he seeks to correct. See 1999 § 9-518(c) and Comment 3 to 1999 § 9-518.

d. Naming the Parties

(1) 1972 Code General Requirement of Naming the Parties.

Under 1972 § 9-402(1), a financing statement must give the names of the debtor and the secured party. In this connection, it should be noted that the statutory form of a financing statement set forth in 1972 § 9-402(3) provides space for naming the debtor and the secured party.

Using the correct name of the debtor is quite important because financing statements are filed alphabetically according to the debtor's name. However, in general, minor errors naming the debtor have been overlooked. In this connection, the 1972 Code states:

"A financing statement substantially complying with the requirements of [§ 9-402] is effective even though it contains minor errors which are not seriously misleading." 1972 § 9-402(8).

The intent of this provision is "to discourage the fanatical and impossibly refined reading of [pre-Code] statutory requirements in which courts have occasionally indulged themselves." Comment 9 to 1972 § 9-402.

The likely test in most instances of whether the

misnaming of a party is a substantial or a minor error would seem to depend on whether the error is such as to cause the filing officer to index the statement in such a way as to make it unlikely that one searching the files under the correct name would discover the filing. The following principles may be drawn from case law:

(a) Misspelling of the debtor's first name or initials is a minor error.

(b) Misspelling of the debtor's surname is a substantial error.

(c) Inaccuracy in adding an incorrect trade name following a debtor's correct name is a minor error.

(d) A slight error in naming a corporate debtor (such as naming the debtor as "ABC Corp." when the correct name is "ABC, Inc,") is a minor error.

(e) Naming a corporate debtor by a completely different name is a substantial error (such as naming a debtor as "ABC Corp." when the correct name is "XYZ Corp.").

Some guidance as to the sufficiency of naming the debtor is given in 1972 § 9-402(7). This provides that a financing statement "sufficiently shows the name of the debtor if it gives the individual, partnership or corporate name of the debtor, whether or not it adds other trade names or names of partners."

This contemplates that if the debtor does business under a trade name, filing should be in the debtor's correct name and not the trade name. However, 1972 § 9-403(5) also permits additional indexing of a filing in a trade name if the secured party so desires. If the debtor is a partnership, filing should be in the partnership name and not in the names of any partners nor trade names. See Comment 7 to 1972 § 9-402.

(2) The Effect of Change of Debtor's Name, Identity or Corporate Structure Under the 1972 Code.

1972 § 9-402(7) states:

"Where the debtor so changes his name or in the case of an organization its name, identity or corporate structure that a filed financing statement becomes seriously misleading, the filing is not effective to perfect a security interest in collateral acquired by the debtor more than four months after the change unless a new appropriate financing statement is filed before the expiration of that time."

See also Comment 7 to 1972 § 9-402.

Under the 1972 Code, if a debtor changes his, her or its name substantially, an existing filing would continue to protect collateral acquired before the change or acquired within four months after the change. But a new filing is necessary to cover collateral acquired after four months. Such a new filing may be made by a financing statement signed by the secured party alone, under 1972 § 9-402(2)(d).

(3) The Effect of Sale of Collateral by Debtor Under the 1972 Code

1972 § 9-402(7) also has a sentence reading: "A filed financing statement remains effective with respect to collateral transferred by the debtor even though the secured party knows of or consents to the transfer."

In other words, where a sale of collateral is made by the debtor subject to the security interest, it is not necessary that the secured party file another financing statement naming the buyer of the collateral as a new debtor. The position taken is that any person searching the condition of the ownership of a debtor must make inquiry as to the debtor's source of title and must search in the name of a former owner if circumstances seem to require it. See Comment 8 to 1972 § 9-402.

(4) 1999 Code Requirement of Naming the Parties; Effect of Name Changes and Sale of Collateral

The 1999 Code also requires that the financing statement include the name of the debtor and the name of the secured party or a representative of the secured party. 1999 § 9-502(a)(1), (2). The 1999 Code also requires a financing statement to indicate whether the debtor is an individual or an organization; failure to do so is reason for the filing officer to reject the filing, but if the filing occurs, the absence of this information does not render the financing statement legally insufficient to perfect the security interest. 1999 §§ 9-502(a), 9-516(b)(5).

The 1999 Code indicates that if the debtor is an organization organized under state or federal law that requires maintenance of a public record indicating the organization's existence, i.e., a corporation, the financing statement must reflect the name shown on those records. 1999 §§ 9-503(a)(1), 9-102 (a)(70). There are also rules that specifically deal with naming debtors who are decedent's estates and trusts. See 1999 § 9-503(a)(2), (3).

As to all other debtors who have a name, the financing statement must provide the individual or organizational name of the debtor. 1999 §§ 9-

503(a)(4)(A); 1-201(28). If the debtor does not have a name, the financing statement needs to provide the names of partners, members, associates or others who comprise the debtor. 1999 § 9-503(a)(4)(B).

Under the 1999 Code, a financing statement that includes only a trade name inadequately names the debtor. 1999 § 9-503(c). On the other hand, a financing statement remains valid if it omits a trade name or the names of partners, members, or associates if the debtor has its own name. 1999 § 9-503(b). A financing statement also is effective even if it does not mention the representative capacity of the secured party or the representative of the secured party. 1999 § 9-503(d).

A financing statement that fails sufficiently to provide the name of the debtor in accordance with 1999 § 9-503(a) is deemed seriously misleading. 1999 § 9-506(b). However, if a search of the filing record under the debtor's correct name would disclose a financing statement that fails sufficiently to provide the name of the debtor in accordance with 1999 § 9-503(a), the name provided does not make the financing statement seriously misleading. 1999 § 9-506(c).

With regard to instances in which the debtor's name changes after the filing of an initial financing statement, the 1999 Code takes the same basic approach discussed previously taken by the 1972 Code. The initial filing continues to perfect with respect to the original collateral and collateral acquired by the debtor within four months after the name change. If the name change is seriously misleading, an amendment must be filed within four months after the change to perfect the security interest in any collateral acquired beyond four months of the name change. 1999 § 9-507(c)(2).

The 1999 Code also deals with the effect of a sale of the collateral by the debtor. As is the case under the 1972 Code, a filed financing statement remains effective with respect to collateral transferred by the debtor even if the secured party know of or consents to the transfer. 1999 § 9-507(a). The transferee is bound by the terms of the existing security agreement if the transferee is a "new debtor." 1999 § 9-203(d). Whether one is a "new debtor" depends on the law of contracts and business organizations outside UCC Article 9. 1999 § 9-102(a)(56), (60). If the difference in names between the original and the new debtor is such that the original financing statement is now seriously misleading, the filing is effective as to the collateral transferred and any new collateral acquired during the four months after the new debtor becomes bound. 1999 § 9-508(a), (b)(1), (c). The secured party is unperfected as to new collateral acquired after the expiration of the four-month grace period unless it files an initial financing statement in the name of the new debtor. 1999 § 9-508(b)(2).

e. *Addresses of Parties*

(1) 1972 Code Requirement of Addresses

A financing statement must give "an address of the secured party from which information concerning the security interest may be obtained" and also give "a mailing address of the debtor." 1972 §9-402(1).

While the case law is somewhat inconsistent, it appears to be the general rule that the omission of an address of either party is fatal; the filing is insufficient. A minority of decisions indicate that such an omission is merely a "minor error not seriously misleading." 1972 § 9-402(8). The latter point of view has been taken particularly where the parties did business in a small community and were well-known in that community.

Some cases have also questioned the completeness of an address. Several decisions have held an address insufficient which merely named a city and state, with nothing more. On the other hand, giving an address as a post office box number in a named city and state has been held sufficient.

(2) 1999 Code Requirement of Addresses

The 1999 Code takes a different approach regarding the requirement of including the addresses of both the secured party and the debtor. The addresses of both are required; however, the addresses are not necessary for an initial financing statement to be legally sufficient to perfect a security interest. 1999 §§ 9-502(a); 9-516(b)(4), (5). A filing officer must refuse to accept an initial filing statement that omits addresses. 1999 § 9-520(a), 9-516(b). In other words, if a filing officer mistakenly files a financing statement that lacks the addresses of the parties, the filing is effective to perfect the security interest. On the other hand, if the filing officer does reject a financing statement due to a lack of addresses, perfection has not occurred. 1999 § 9-516(b). In general, see Comment 5 to 1999 § 9-516 which discusses the reasoning of the drafters regarding addresses of the parties.

f. Description of Collateral

(1) 1972 Code Requirement of Description of

Collateral

A financing statement must "contain a statement indicating the types or describing the items of collateral." 1972 § 9-402(1). In certain instances where the collateral is related to real estate, a description of real estate is also necessary. The requirement of real estate description is discussed in § 4g of this chapter, which follows.

Although some description of collateral is necessary, the scheme of "notice filing" in the Code permits broad latitude in description. In this connection, 1972 § 9-110 states that "any description of personal property * * * is sufficient whether or not it is specific if it reasonably identifies what is described."

The test of sufficiency of a description is that it must do the job of making possible the identification of the thing described. Rejected are holdings of some pre-Code chattel mortgage cases that descriptions are insufficient unless they are of the most exact and detailed nature, the so-called "serial number" test. See Comment to 1972 § 9-110.

Some suggestions as to descriptions of collateral are outlined below:

    (a)   In many instances, a general or blanket

description is sufficient. This is often the method used where all the inventory, accounts receivable or equipment is collateral. Examples: "all inventory of debtor," "all automobiles of dealer," "all appliances of dealer," "all accounts," "all equipment in debtor's restaurant."

CAVEAT. While the above rule is generally applicable, there are decisions holding blanket descriptions of collateral as "consumer goods" insufficient, and it is also indicated that blanket descriptions of farm equipment or farm-related collateral might sometimes be open to question. The likely implication of such decisions is to avoid overreaching, or the subjecting of a large number of items of personal property as collateral for a debt incurred in the purchase of a single item or several items. However, an abbreviated description of specific consumer items, such as pieces of furniture, has been held sufficient.

(b)   The description must be reasonably accurate, but need not necessarily be absolutely exact. Thus, a minor error, such as the misstatement of a serial number of an automobile or machine, will generally be regarded as immaterial. On the other hand, a general description of items as part of a greater quantity may fail for indefiniteness.

Example to avoid. A description as "21 head of cattle on Blackacre" fails for indefiniteness if there are more than 21 head of cattle on Blackacre. But a description such as "all cattle on Blackacre bearing the X-X brand" should be sufficient to describe all cattle there which are so branded.

(c)   If a financing statement does not cover all collateral described in the security agreement, the security interest is perfected only as to collateral covered in the financing statement. On the other hand, if the financing statement covers items of collateral not covered in the security agreement, no security interest exists in such items.

(d)   Comment 2 to 1972 § 9-402 and cases indicate that failure specifically to refer to after-acquired property in a financing statement does not preclude perfection as to after-acquired property, if the language of the security agreement and the financing statement make it clear that after-acquired property is covered.

Example. A security agreement covered" all contents of luncheonette including" a number of specific items of equipment, and also referred to after-acquired property. The filed financing statement covered "all contents of luncheonette including" the same specific items of equipment, but did not make an specific reference to after-acquired property. The debtor luncheonette subsequently acquired a cash register. The financing statement covers the cash register and the secured party has a perfected security interest in that item of equipment.

In summary, it might be repeated that all that is necessary is "reasonable identification" in describing the collateral, under 1972 § 9-110. Moreover, 1972 § 9-402(8) states:

"A financing statement substantially complying with the requirements of [§ 9-402] is effective even though it contains minor errors which are not seriously misleading."

(2) 1999 Code Requirement of Description of Collateral

The 1999 Code also requires that the financing statement "indicate" the collateral covered by it. 1999 § 9-502(a)(3). As to the sufficiency of the identification (that is the description) of the collateral, the 1999 Code provides that a financing statement sufficiently describes the collateral if it provides a description that is sufficient for a security agreement. 1999 § 9-504(1). See Chapter 2, § 3c(2), for discussion of the requirement of description of collateral in a security agreement under the 1999 Code. Additionally, the 1999 Code authorizes the use of "super generic" descriptions on the financing statement only. Thus, the 1999 Code authorizes an indication that the financing statement covers "all assets" or "all personal property." 1999 § 9-504(2).

g. *Description of Real Estate*

(1) 1972 Code Requirement of Description of Real Estate

The 1972 Code requires that when a financing statement "covers crops growing or to be grown, the statement must also contain a description of the real estate concerned." 1972 § 9-402(1).

A financing statement covering timber to be cut or covering minerals, oil or gas and resulting accounts, or a financing statement which is filed as a fixture filing (except where the debtor is a transmitting utility) must show that it covers this type of collateral, must recite that it is to be filed in the real estate records and must contain a description of the real estate. If the debtor does not have an interest of record in the real estate, the name of a record owner must be shown. See 1972 § 9-402(1), (5).

An "optional" version of 1972 § 9-402(5) prescribes that such a filing for timber, minerals, oil or gas and resulting accounts and a fixture filing must also recite that it is to be filed "for record." The "optional" version further requires that the description of the real estate be "sufficient if it were contained in a mortgage of the real estate to give constructive notice of the mortgage" under the law of the state.

As to the description of the real estate, "any description of * * * real estate is sufficient whether or not it is specific if it reasonably identifies was is described." 1972 § 9-110. Thus, a description of land by street number or location could be sufficient, although a very loose or indefinite description may be insufficient.

Example 1. A financing statement covered all crops to be grown on Blackacre owned by John Jones, located one mile north of a designated town in a designated county and state. Such description is sufficient.

Example 2. A financing statement referred to "seven acres of cotton" to be grown by the debtor on the land of a named third person in a designated county within the state. Such a description is fatally defective, since it failed to indicate whether the debtor grew exactly seven acres of cotton on the third person's land during the year in question and whether anyone else was also growing cotton on the third person's land.

The same general principles apply under the 1972 Code where crops are collateral; only a general description of land need be given. However, the requirements for description of land where the collateral is timber or minerals, oil or gas or resulting accounts, or where there is a fixture filing, are more stringent under the 1972 Code. The requirement is discussed in Comment 5 to 1972 § 9-402 as follows:

"A description of real estate must be sufficient to identify it. See Section 9-110. This formulation rejects the view that the real estate description must be by metes and bounds, or otherwise conforming to traditional real estate practice in conveyancing, but of course the incorporation of such a description by reference to the recording data of a deed, mortgage or other instrument containing the description should suffice under the most stringent standards. The proper test is that a description of real estate must be sufficient so that the fixture financing statement will fit into the real estate search system and the financing statement be found by a real estate searcher. Optional language has been added by which the test of adequacy of the description is whether it would be adequate in a mortgage of the real estate. [In some states], more detail may be required if there is a tract indexing system or a land registration system."

In certain instances, the debtor may not have an interest of record in the land. Under those circumstances, the financing statement filed under 1972 § 9-402(5) must show the name of a record owner of the land.

Example. Debtor, a builder, has a contract to build a house on the land of John Doe. Debtor purchases a furnace from Secured Party for installation as a fixture in the house. Since Debtor has no interest of record in the land, the financing statement filed as a fixture filing must show the name of Debtor and also name John Doe as the record owner of the land. This enables the filing officer to index the financing statement into the real estate search system. See Comment 5 to 1972 § 9-402.

Sometimes it may be desirable to utilize a combined mortgage covering both real estate and fixtures installed on the real estate. The recording of a real estate mortgage, if it complies with the requirements of a financing statement and properly describes fixtures by item or type, is declared to be effective as a financing statement covering fixtures, as well as real estate (although such a recording will not cover non-fixture collateral). See 1972 § 9-402(6) and Comment 6.

(2) 1999 Code Requirement of Description of Real Estate

In general, the 1999 Code also requires that to be sufficient a financing statement must include a description of real estate when the collateral is real-estate related. Such collateral includes "as-extracted" collateral which essentially is oil, gas, or other minerals or accounts arising out of the sale of such. For a complete definition of "as-extracted" collateral, see 1999 § 9-102(a)(6). A real estate description also is required for timber to be cut. Finally, if the financing statement is filed as a fixture filing and covers goods that are or are to become fixtures, a real estate description is required. The 1999 Code eliminates the 1972 Code requirement of a real estate description for a financing statement covering crops. As to the requirement of a real estate description for as-extracted collateral, timber to be cut, and fixtures, see 1999 § 9-502(b)(3).

The required description of real estate is adequate if it reasonably identifies what is described although a particular state enactment can require a description that would be sufficient to give constructive notice of a mortgage, i.e., a complete "legal" description. 1999 §§ 9-502(b)(3), 9-108.

As to collateral for which a description of real estate is required, the 1999 Code also requires the financing statement to satisfy the content requirements of any financing statement. See 1999 § 9-502(a), (b). Additionally, the financing statement must indicate that it covers the type of collateral; that it is to be filed in the real property records; and if the debtor does not have an interest of record in the real property, the financing statement must include the name of a record owner. 1999 § 9-502(b)(1), (2), (4). The 1999 Code also permits use of a mortgage in lieu of a financing statement if filed as a fixture filing or as a financing statement covering as-extracted collateral or timber to be cut. However, the mortgage must indicate the goods or accounts it covers and otherwise satisfy the requirements of a financing statement. 1999 § 9-502(c).

h. *Reference to Proceeds or Products of Collateral*

Under 1972 § 9-402(3) and 1999 § 9-521(a), no reference to "proceeds" need be made on a financing statement. The reason is that, in most instances, perfection as to collateral under 1972 § 9-306(3) and

1999 § 9-315(c) automatically perfects as to proceeds. See discussion in Chapter 4, § 8.

Where perfection as to proceeds is not automatic under the 1972 Code, perfection lapses after 10 days, and a new filing is necessary to cover proceeds. 1972 § 9-306(3). Such a filing may be by a statement signed only by the secured party under 1972 § 9-402(2)(b), but it should describe the proceeds sufficiently to comply with the requirements of 1972 § 9-306(3).

Where perfection as to proceeds is not automatic under the 1999 Code, perfection lapses after the twenty-first day after the security interest attaches to the proceeds, and a new filing is necessary to cover proceeds. 1999 § 9-315(d). Because the debtor's signature is not required on a financing statement under the 1999 Code, no signature of the debtor is required with regard to a financing statement filed when necessary to continue perfection in proceeds. See prior discussion in this chapter at § 4c(4).

The statutory form of 1972 § 9-402(3) contains the statement: "products of the collateral are also covered." Standard forms of financing statements contain a box making the above statement; all that need be done is to check such a "products" box. The 1999 statutory form of § 9-521 does not contain such a statement related to products of collateral.

Under the 1972 Code, the basic reason for claiming "products" is to follow a security interest into finished goods when a portion of a manufacturing process is being financed. Under 1972 § 9-315(1)(b), if a financing statement covering the original goods also covers the product into which the goods have been manufactured, processed or assembled, the security interest continues in the product or mass. Under the 1999 Code, the security interest continues in the product or mass without regard to any mention of products on the financing statement. 1999 § 9-336.

i. *Security Agreement or Reproduction as Financing Statement*

Under 1972 § 9-402(1), a copy of the security agreement is sufficient as a financing statement if it contains the information required in a financing statement (as discussed in previous parts of this section) and is properly signed.

This permits the filing of a chattel mortgage, conditional sales agreement or other traditional form of security agreement if it meets the requirements for a financing statement and is properly signed.

Under the 1972 Code, such a security agreement filed as a financing statement need only be signed by the debtor.

The 1972 § 9-402(1) states:

"A carbon, photographic or other reproduction of a security agreement or a financing statement is sufficient as a financing statement if the security agreement so provides or if the original has been filed in this state."

The 1999 Code has deleted any reference to filing a security agreement in lieu of a financing statement. The drafters of the 1999 Code concluded that the 1972 provision was unnecessary and unwise. See Comment 4 to 1999 § 9-502. Even so, it would seem that if a security agreement satisfies all of the form requirements of a financing statement set forth at 1999 § 9-502, the security agreement could be filed and would effectively perfect the security interest.

§ 5. Time of Filing

Article 9 has no provision, as existed in some pre-Code statutes, requiring a filing within a specified period of time after the debtor receives the collateral.

Although there is no prescribed time within which to file under the Code, delayed filing may result in subordination of the security interest to the claim of a third person. Moreover, if filing is delayed and is not made until within 90 days of bankruptcy of the debtor, the delayed filing might be set aside as a preferential transfer. See Chapter 8, § 5a.

It is not necessary to delay filing until a security agreement is made or until a security interest attaches. "A financing statement may be filed before a security agreement is made or a security interest otherwise attaches." 1972 § 9-402(1). See also the similar 1999 § 9-502(d). However, where filing is premature, perfection does not take place until the security interest attaches. As to attachment of a security interest, see Chapter 3, § 1.

The time of filing is determined by 1972 § 9-403(1) which reads:

"Presentation for filing of a financing statement and tender of the filing fee or acceptance of the statement by the filing officer constitutes filing under [Article 9]."

Under the above provision, if a filing officer mistakenly refuses to accept for filing a financing statement in proper form and accompanied by the proper fee, the statement is deemed nonetheless to have been filed. As to the effect of a mistake by the filing officer, see § 13b(1) of this chapter.

The time of filing is determined in a similar manner by 1999 § 9-516(a) which reads:

> "Except as otherwise provided in subsection (b), communication of a record to a filing office and tender of the filing fee or acceptance of the record by the filing office constitutes filing."

The 1999 Code specifies that filing does not occur with respect to a record that a filing office refuses to accept for reasons enumerated by the 1999 Code at 1999 § 9-516(b). A record that is communicated to the filing office with tender of the filing fee that the filing officer refuses to accept for any other reason is deemed effective or filed except against a purchaser of the collateral which gives value in reasonable reliance upon the absence of a filed record. 1999 § 9-516(d). Again, as to the effect of a mistake by the filing officer, see § 13b(2) of this chapter.

§ 6. Amendment to Financing Statement

Sometimes, an amendment to a financing statement may be filed. However, if any amendment adds collateral, it is effective as to the added collateral only from the filing date of the amendment. See 1972 § 9-402(4), 1999 § 9-512(c).

The 1972 Code makes it clear that an amendment to a financing statement must be signed by both the debtor and the secured party. 1972 § 9-402(4). The 1972 Code also makes it clear that an amendment does not extend the period of effectiveness of a financing statement. 1972 § 9-402(4). A continuation statement should be filed when the effectiveness of a filing is to be extended. See § 8 of this chapter.

The 1999 Code permits secured parties of record to amend a filed financing statement without the need to obtain the debtor's signature. See Comment 3 to 1999 § 9-512. However, if the amendment adds collateral or adds a debtor, the debtor must have authorized the amendment or it will not be effective. 1999 §§ 9-509(a), 9-510(a). The 1999 Code also makes it clear that an amendment does not extend the period of effectiveness of a financing statement. 1999 § 9-512(b). A continuation statement should be filed when the effectiveness of a financing statement is to be extended. See § 8 of this chapter.

Normally, an amendment is filed when items or types of collateral are added which are not covered in the original financing statement. However, a security interest in additional units of a type of collateral already described in a filed financing statement can be created under an after-acquired property clause of a security agreement or a new security agreement; no amendment is necessary. See 1972 § 9-204(1), (2) and Comment 4 to 1972 § 9-402; see also 1999 § 9-204(a), (b).

Example. A filed financing statement covers all radios as inventory in the hands of debtor retailer, under a security agreement covering "all present and future radios as inventory." Debtor who had been handling the X make of radio also takes on the Y make of radio. No new filing is necessary. But if debtor decides to handle refrigerators under financing by the secured party, a new security agreement is necessary and an amendment to the financing statement referring to refrigerators as inventory should be filed.

§ 7. Duration of Filing; Lapse

1972 § 9-403(2) and 1999 § 9-515(a) flatly declare that a filed financing statement is good for five years. A special provision is added by the 1999 Code that applies to financing statements filed in connection with a public-finance transaction or a manufactured-home transaction which indicates such filings are effective for 30 years after the date of filing. 1999 § 9-515(b). Several exceptions to the five-year period exist, however:

a. Under the 1972 Code, if the filing is effective when insolvency proceedings are commenced by or against the debtor, the duration of the filing is extended until the termination of the insolvency proceedings plus 60 days, if that date is later than the end of the five-year period of the original filing. See 1972 § 9-403(2). This provision is deleted in the 1999 Code. See Comment 4 to 1999 § 9-515.

b. A filing stating that the debtor is a transmitting utility under 1972 § 9-401(5) is good until a termination statement is filed. See 1972 § 9-403(6). The 1999 Code is in accord. See 1999 § 9-515(f).

c. A real estate mortgage effective as a fixture filing under 1972 § 9-402(6) is good until the mortgage is released or satisfied as of record or its effectiveness otherwise terminates as to the real estate. See 1972 § 9-403(6). The 1999 Code is in accord. See 1999 § 9-515(g).

The effectiveness of a filed financing statement lapses at the expiration of the five-year or other period of duration, under 1972 § 9-403(2) and 1999 § 9-515(c), unless a continuation statement is filed prior to the lapse. Upon such lapse, the security interest becomes unperfected. It is made clear that there is no lapse if the security interest is perfected in some other way (as where the secured party repossesses the collateral just before the end of the five-year period of the filing).

Under 1972 § 9-403(2), it is clear that if the security interest becomes unperfected upon lapse, it is deemed unperfected "as against a person who became a purchaser or lien creditor before lapse." Under 1999 § 9-515(c), it is clear that if the security interest becomes unperfected upon lapse, it is deemed never to have been perfected "as against a purchaser of the collateral for value." Note that this provision of the 1999 Code does not apply to lien creditors. See Comment 3 to 1999 § 9-515.

Example. A and B both made nonpurchase money advances against the same collateral, and both perfected security interests by filing. A who filed first is entitled to priority under 1972 § 9-312(5) or 1999 § 9-322(a)(1). But if no continuation statement is filed, A's filing may lapse first. So long as B's interest remains perfected thereafter, he is entitled to priority over A's unperfected interest. This rule avoids a circular priority under some prior statutes, under which A was subordinate to the debtor's trustee in bankruptcy, with A retaining priority over B and B having priority over the trustee in bankruptcy. See Comment 3 to 1972 § 9-403.

§ 8. Continuation Statement

When the period of a filing is about to expire, the secured party may extend the time of perfection by filing a continuation statement. The continuation statement may be filed within six months prior to the expiration of the five-year period of the original filing. 1972 § 9-403(3), 1999 § 9-515(d). A special provision is added by the 1999 Code that applies to financing statements filed in connection with public-finance transactions or manufactured-home transactions which indicates that a continuation statement may be filed only within six months before the expiration of the 30-year effective period specified in 1999 § 9-515(b).

The time within which to file a continuation statement is absolute; filing more than six months before the end of the five-year period of the original filing is ineffective. Moreover, if a filing has lapsed and no continuation statement is filed prior to lapse, a subsequently-filed continuation statement is ineffective. In that case, a new financing statement must be filed to revive perfection. Under 1972 § 9-402(2)(c), such a new filing need be signed only by the secured party. 1999 Article 9 has no equivalent provision because even the signature of the debtor is not required on a initial financing statement.

Under the 1972 Code, a continuation statement must be signed by the secured party, but the debtor need not sign. Again, 1999 Article 9 has no equivalent requirement because even the signature of the debtor is not required on the initial financing statement.

Under the 1972 Code, the continuation statement must identify the original statement by file number and state that the original statement is still effective. See 1972 § 9-403(3). If the continuation statement is signed by a person other than the secured party of record, it must be accompanied by a separate written statement of assignment signed by the secured party of record and meeting the requirements of 1972 § 9–405(2).

Under the 1999 Code, the required contents of a continuation statement are set forth in the definition of "continuation statement." 1999 § 9-102(a)(27). The continuation statement must identify the initial financing statement and indicate that it is a continuation statement for the identified financing statement.

Upon timely filing of a continuation statement, the effectiveness of the original filing is extended for five years after the last date to which the filing was effective. Succeeding continuation statements may be filed to extend the period for additional five-year periods. See 1972 § 9-403(3) and 1999 § 9-515(e).

No continuation statement is necessary where the debtor is a transmitting utility, nor is it necessary where a real estate mortgage is effective as a fixture filing. See 1972 § 9-403(6) and 1999 § 9-515(f), (g).

§ 9. Assignment of Security Interest

1972 § 9-405 deals with filing when a security interest is assigned. In this regard, 1972 § 9-405(1) recognizes that an original financing statement filed may disclose an assignment by indicating the name and address of the assignee, or by setting forth the assignment itself, or by including a copy thereof on the face or back of the statement. This permits an initial filing in the name of the assignee as secured party. 1999 § 9-514(a) similarly permits an original filing to disclose an assignment.

Example.   Seller takes a security interest in widgets sold on credit to Buyer and at once assigns the security interest to Financer. Seller files a financing statement naming Financer as assignee.

Another provision, 1972 § 9-405(2), deals with filing when the security interest is assigned following the original filing. This permits the filing of a separate written statement of assignment, which must be signed by the secured party of record (the assignor), set forth the names of the secured party of record and the debtor, the file number and date of the original filing, the name and address of the assignee and a description of the collateral assigned. A copy of the assignment itself is sufficient if it complies with the above requirements. 1999 § 9-514(b) similarly provides that assignments of security interest that occur after the initial filing can be filed.

1972 § 9-405(2) and 1999 § 9-514(c) make it clear that an assignment of a security interest in a fixture set forth in a mortgage effective as a fixture filing under 1972 § 9-402(6) and 1999 § 9-502(c) may be made only by an assignment of the mortgage under the law governing mortgages.

Where an assignment of a security interest is disclosed in a filing or filed separately, the assignee becomes the secured party of record. See 1972 § 9-405(3); c.f. 1999 § 9-514.

It should be kept in mind that if a secured party assigns a perfected security interest, no filing under Article 9 is necessary to continue the perfected status of the security interest against creditors of and transferees from the original debtor. See 1972 § 9-

302(2) and 1999 § 9-310(c) and discussion in Chapter 4, § 9.

Thus, filing of an assignment is optional in most instances under the 1972 and 1999 Codes. However, under the 1972 Code, a separate statement of assignment must be filed in the following instances:

(1) If a continuation statement is signed by one other than the secured party of record. 1972 § 9-403(3).

(2) If a statement of release is signed by one other than the secured party of record. 1972 § 9-406.

(3) If a termination statement is signed by one other than the secured party of record. 1972 § 9-403(1).

These provisions are omitted in the 1999 Code.

§ 10. Statement of Release

An optional filing provided for in 1972 § 9-406 is a statement of release which may be filed when all or a part of any collateral described in a filed financing statement is to be released under the 1972 Code. The same purpose of releasing collateral can be evidenced by filing an "amendment" of a financing statement under 1999 § 9-512. A statement of release must contain a description of the collateral being released, the names and addresses of the debtor and the secured party and the file number of the financing statement and must be signed by the secured party. The 1972 Code expressly declares that if the statement of release is signed by a person other than the secured party of record, it must be accompanied by a separate written statement of assignment signed by the secured party of record and meeting the requirements of 1972 § 9-405(2). The required contents of an amendment releasing collateral under the 1999 Code are similar except that no signatures are required. 1999 § 9-512.

Normally, a statement of release is used when there is a partial release of collateral. It may also be used when all the collateral is released but where the financing is to be continued, with other collateral substituted either at the time of release or at a later time. Upon substitution of other collateral, an amendment to the financing statement should be filed.

A statement of release should not be used when the secured transaction is ended. A termination statement should be used. See § 11 of this chapter which follows.

§ 11. Termination Statement

a. 1972 Code Provisions Related to Termination Statement

(1) Collateral Other Than Consumer Goods

Whenever there is no outstanding secured obligation and no commitment to make advances, incur obligations or otherwise give value, the secured party must on written demand by the debtor send the debtor a termination statement to the effect that the secured party no longer claims a security interest under the financing statement, which shall be identified by file number. 1972 § 9-404(1). The 1972 Code makes it clear that such a termination statement must be sent for each filing officer with whom the financing statement was filed.

It is also stated in 1972 § 9-404(1) that if a termination statement is signed by a person other than the secured party of record, it must be accompanied by a separate written statement of assignment signed by the secured party of record and meeting the requirements of 1972 § 9-405(2).

The requirement of a termination statement is explained in Comment 2 to 1972 § 9-404 as follows:

"This section adds to the usual provisions one covering the problem which arises because a

secured party under a notice filing system may
file notice of an intention to make advances
which never may be made. Under this section, a
debtor may require a secured party to send a
termination statement when there is no outstanding obligation and no commitment to make future
advances."

Since most financing statements expire in five
years, no compulsion is placed on the secured party
to file a termination statement, except in the case of
consumer goods under the 1972 Code. All that the
secured party need do is send the termination statement to the debtor, except where consumer goods
are involved. See Comment 1 to 1972 § 9-404.

(2) Consumer Goods

A special requirement found in 1972 § 9-404(1)
is applicable to consumer goods. If a financing
statement covering consumer goods has been filed,
then within one month (or within 10 days following
written demand by the debtor) after there is no
outstanding secured obligation and no commitment
to make advances, incur obligations or otherwise
give value, the secured party must file with each
filing officer with whom the financing statement
was filed, a termination statement to the effect that
he no longer claims a security interest under the

financing statement, which shall be identified by file number. See 1972 § 9-404(1).

This provision requires filing of a termination statement by the secured party in the case of consumer goods even without a demand by the consumer. The reason is that many consumers will not realize the importance of clearing the situation as it appears on file. Where motor vehicles as consumer goods are involved, a certificate of title law may control the filing and release, instead of the provisions of Article 9. See Comment 1 to 1972 § 9-404.

It should be noted that many purchase money security interests in consumer goods other than motor vehicles will not be filed, in view of 1972 § 9-302(1)(d). No termination statement is necessary in such a situation.

(3) Failure to Send or File Termination Statement

If the secured party fails to file a termination statement relating to consumer goods or fails to send a termination statement to the debtor in other cases within 10 days after proper demand therefor, the secured party shall be liable to the debtor for $100 and in addition for any loss caused to the debtor by such failure. See 1972 § 9-404(1).

This is one of the few instances in Article 9 where a statutory "rule of thumb" penalty of a minimum amount is permitted, in favor of the debtor and against the secured party, for failure of the latter to perform a duty required under Article 9. the provision should be read along with "penalty" provisions set forth in statutes outside the Code affecting consumer credit, retail installment sales and like matters.

b. 1999 Code Provisions Related to Termination Statement

The 1999 Code for the most part has not significantly changed the 1972 Code provisions regarding termination statements.   Non-consumer goods collateral and consumer goods transactions are treated differently just as they are under the above-described 1972 Code except that the compliance period following a demand for a termination statement is increased from ten to twenty days. 1999 § 9-513.

If the secured party fails to file a required termination statement in the case of consumer goods, or send a required termination statement in the other cases, the statement can be filed without the secured party's authorization.   1999 § 9-509(d)(2).   A secured party who improperly fails to file or provide a termination statement is liable for a $500 fine plus damages. 1999 § 9-625(b), (e)(4).

The 1999 Code treats a termination statement as an amendment to a filed financing statement. Thus, the termination statement must identify by file number the initial financing statement and indicate either that it is a termination statement or that the filed financing statement is no longer effective. 1999 § 9-102(a)(79).

§ 12. Filing Where There Is Consignment or Lease

In certain instances, it may be desirable to file under Article 9 with respect to a lease or consignment of personal property, even where the lease or consignment is not intended to confer a security interest. For discussion of leases or consignments as secured transactions, see Chapter 2, § 6d and e.

1972 § 9-408 and 1999 § 9-505 permit a filing covering consigned or leased goods. This permits a consignor or lessor to file a financing statement using the terms "consignor," "consignee," "lessor," "lessee" or the like, instead of the terms "debtor" and "secured party" used in 1972 § 9-402(1) and

1999 § 9-502(a). The Article 9 provisions relating to the place of filing and the form of a financing statement apply as appropriate to such a financing statement. However, such a filing is not of itself a factor in determining whether or not the consignment or lease is intended as security. If it is determined that a consignment or lease is intended for security, a security interest of the consignor or lessor which attaches to the consigned or leased goods is perfected by such a filing.

This sets forth a special method of filing where a consignor desires to file under § 2-326(3)(c) or where a lessor desires to file without such a filing itself indicating an intent that the transaction be a secured transaction. In other words, a consignor or lessor may make a precautionary filing, although he may have good reason (such as a "tax" reason) to desire the transaction not be a secured transaction within Article 9. See Comments 1 and 2 to 1972 § 9-408 and Comment 2 to 1999 § 9-505. It should be noted that 1999 § 9-505 is an expanded version of 1972 § 9-408. The 1999 Code provision "embrace[s] more generally other bailments and transactions" than just consignments and leases.

§ 13. Duties of Filing Officers

a. *General Duties*

Various duties of a filing officer (such as the Secretary of State, a county clerk or various employees) are spelled out in Article 9. Such duties are summarized as follows:

(1) Financing statements and other filings are to be marked with a file number and the date and hour of filing and are to be available for public inspection. They are to be indexed in the name of the debtor. 1972 § 9-403(4); 1999 § 9-519.

(2) A financing statement covering timber to be cut or minerals or the like (including oil and gas) or accounts resulting from the sale of minerals (including oil and gas) at the wellhead or minehead, or a statement filed as a fixture filing is to be indexed under the name of the debtor and any owner of record shown on the statement in the same fashion as with respect to real estate mortgages. Optional language also specifies that the statement is to be filed for record. 1972 § 9-403(7); 1999 § 9-519(d), (e).

(3) Rules are set forth as to removal and destruction of lapsed statements. 1972 § 9-403(3); 1999 § 9-522.

(4) Procedures are set forth as to the marking and indexing of a filed statement of assignment, 1972 § 9-405(2) and 1999 § 9-514, and a statement of release of collateral, 1972 § 9-406 and 1999 § 9-512.

(5) Procedures are set forth as to the handling of termination statements which are filed. 1972 § 9-404(2); 1999 § 9-513.

(6) Schedules of various filing fees are set forth with respect to financing and other statements filed and increased fees are permitted where nonstandard forms are filed. 1972 §§ 9-403(5), 9-404(3), 9-405(1) and (2); 1999 § 9-525.

b. *Effect of Mistake of Filing Officer*

(1) 1972 Provisions Related to Effect of Mistake of Filling Officer

The text of the 1972 Code does not explicitly deal with the question whether a mistake made by the filing officer in connection with a financing statement received for filing causes the invalidation of the filing.

However, 1972 § 9-403(1) has the effect of making a filing good as of the time it is tendered for filing. The draftsmen of the Code take the position that, under 1972 § 9-403(1), the secured party does not bear the risk that the filing officer will not properly perform his duties. The secured party is deemed to have complied with the filing requirements when he presents his financing statement for filing and the filing fee has been tendered or the statement accepted by the filing officer. See Comment 1 to 1972 § 9-407.

Mistakes by a filing officer may consist of such acts as improperly refusing to take a statement presented for filing or improperly indexing a filed statement. The filing is good notwithstanding any such mistake, provided that it is in proper form and presented to the proper filing office, accompanied by the proper fee.

Since the secured party does not bear the risk of a mistake on the part of the filing officer, a loss resulting from such a mistake may be borne by a third person, such as one who checked the filings, failed to discover the particular filing because of the mistake, and extended credit to the debtor in reliance on the absence of a filing. In some states, a third person who has such a loss might have a remedy against the filing officer himself on his official bond for improper performance of his duties, but such a remedy is dependent on local statutes outside the

Code.

Example 1. A financing statement in proper form was mailed from out-of-state to the proper county clerk accompanied by the proper filing fee. The county clerk mistakenly returned the financing statement with a note stating that a notarial certificate of the type used in real estate mortgages was necessary for secured transactions affecting out-of-state parties. The notarial certificate was obtained and the filing was sent a second time and accepted by the clerk. The filing was considered to have been made when the first rejected filing was received by the county clerk.

Example 2. A financing statement in proper form was mailed from out-of-state but incorrectly addressed. It reached the county clerk of a different county than where the debtor was located. The filing was returned to the sender, who then mailed it to the proper county clerk. The first filing was ineffective because the mistake was that of the secured party.

Example 3. A secured party filed a financing statement in proper form, accompanied by the proper filing fee, in the proper office. The filing officer erroneously indexed the statement in the records by showing the secured party as the debtor and the debtor as the secured party. The filing is effective.

Example 4. P, a prospective purchaser of equipment from L, made inquiry of a filing officer as to filings on L as Debtor and was informed that no such filings existed. The information was erroneous. In reliance on the information erroneously given, P made the purchase from L. P then lost the purchased equipment to the secured party of L who had perfected a security interest. The act of the filing officer in furnishing the erroneous information was held to be ministerial and not discretionary, and subjected the filing officer to a possible claim for damages under local statutory law.

(2)   1999 Provisions Related to Effect of Mistake of Filing Officer

The 1999 Code specifies that communication of a record to a filing office and tender of the filing fee or acceptance of the record by the filing office constitutes filing. 1999 § 9-516(a). Thus, as is the case under the 1972 Code, the filing secured party does not bear the risk of a filing officer's error, assuming the filing is "communicated" to the filing office with the filing fee or is otherwise accepted by the filing officer. Additionally, the 1999 Code specifically indicates that the failure of a filing officer to index or record correctly does not affect the effectiveness of the filed record. 1999 § 9-517.

The 1999 Code does provide an exclusive list of reasons for which a filing officer must reject the filing and further provides that refusal to accept for any of these reasons means filing does not occur. 1999 § 9-516(b). If the filing officer mistakenly rejects the filing for some other reason, the filing is effective except as against a purchaser of collateral which gives value in reasonable reliance upon the absence of the record from the files. 1999 § 9-516(d).

c. Information as to Filing

An "optional" 1972 provision adopted in most Code jurisdictions, 1972 § 9-407, carries out a function of "notice filing" by specifying means of obtaining information as to a filing made from the filing officer. A non-optional provision carries out the same function under the 1999 Code. 1999 § 9-523.

The filing officer shall, upon the request of the person who files, return to that person (normally the secured party) a copy of the statement filed bearing a notation of the file number and the date and hour of the filing. This applies to any statement filed. See 1972 § 9-407(1) and Comment 1 and 1999 § 9-523(a), (b) and Comment 3. See also 1972 § 9-403(5), which permits the stamping of a copy of a financing statement or continuation statement with filing information.

A search procedure is set forth in 1972 § 9-407(2) which requires a filing officer upon request to issue to any person who has tendered the proper fee his certificate as to what filings have been made against any particular debtor and to furnish copies of such filed financing statements or statements of assignment at a fee based on the number of pages involved. This search procedure may be utilized by anyone, and is of obvious utility to prospective creditors and others who need to ascertain what collateral of a particular debtor is subject to a security interest. The 1999 Code has a substantially similar provision providing for a search procedure. See 1999 § 9-523(c)-(e).

A person who searches the files and discovers a filing may obtain further details of the transaction by utilizing (within the cooperation of the debtor) the procedure set forth in 1972 § 9-208 and 1999 § 9-210. See discussion in Chapter 3, § 6.

CHAPTER 6

CHOICE OF LAW AND PERFECTION IN MULTIPLE STATE TRANSACTIONS

§ 1. General Principles

A general choice-of-law rule is set forth in § 1-105 applicable to various commercial relationships arising under different Articles of the Uniform Commercial Code. That general rule applies to secured transactions, at least as between the debtor and the secured party. See Comment 1 to 1972 § 9-103 and Comment 2 to 1999 § 9-301. Under § 1-105(1), the parties may by agreement determine the law that governs their relationship, so long as the transaction "bears a reasonable relation" to the jurisdiction the law of which is selected. Failing such specification of the law of a particular state by agreement, a court in a Code state may apply its own law (the Code) to transactions "bearing an appropriate relation" to the state. This suggests the likelihood that, in the absence of an agreement specifying the state whose law shall govern, a court will follow general conflict-of-laws principles and apply the law of the state having the most significant relationship with the transaction.

Governing law, as between the parties in the absence of agreement, will thus often be determined by the law of the place of contracting or the law of the place of performance. Moreover, the law of the place of location of the collateral will likely be applied where the question is the effect of some act affecting the collateral, such as the propriety of repossession or of sale of the collateral by the secured party following repossession.

Although general choice-of-law principles in commercial transactions are governed by § 1-105, that provision has but limited application with respect to secured transactions. The reason is that most secured transactions questions do not settle rights as between the debtor and the secured party, but instead litigate claims to the collateral as between the secured party and third persons. Choice-of- law problems where the rights of third persons are at issue frequently involve the perfection of the security interest in multiple state transactions, or what law governs the effect of perfection or non-perfection. See § 1-105(2).

Accordingly, the balance of this chapter deals with the question of the state in which the security interest is to be perfected, in a multi-state transaction. Such rules are set forth in 1972 § 9-103 and 1999 §§ 9-301–9-307, 9-316, and 9-337. In addition, rules are set forth to determine the effect on perfection in one jurisdiction when the collateral is moved to a second jurisdiction.

§ 2. Where to Perfect a Security Interest in a Multiple State Transaction

Problems of conflict of laws or choice of law in commercial transactions should often be minimal where a uniform statute such as the Uniform Commercial Code is widely adopted. Nevertheless, a significant choice-of-law problem may arise where the question is in what state to file or take other action to perfect a security interest. Such a problem may also arise where collateral subject to a perfected security interest in one state is moved to another state, and no action is taken to perfect in the second state.

The problems covered in the balance of this chapter might be summarized to some extent in the following hypothetical example:

Debtor, incorporated in State A with its chief executive office in State B, grants a security interest in goods located in State C to X who is located in State D. Some of the goods are then sold by Debtor to Buyer and shipped to him in State E. An account due from Buyer to Debtor arises, which is assigned by Debtor to Y in another secured transaction. Y is located in State F. Debtor keeps his account records in State G. Debtor then moves other goods to State H and there gives Z a security interest in those goods. What law governs the perfection of the various security interests?

These questions are answered by1972 § 9-103 and 1999 §§ 9-301–9-307, 9-316, and 9-337 which are concerned with the place to perfect the security interest and the effect of perfection or non-perfection. Other conflict-of-law problems not involving perfection are dealt with in § 1-105.

§ 3.   Governing Law Based on Location of Collateral

a. Ordinary Goods, Documents, Instruments and Investment Property Under 1972 Code.

With respect to ordinary goods, the general rule under the 1972 Code is that the state in which to perfect a security interest by filing or otherwise is that of the *location of the collateral*. That is the rule under 1972 § 9-103(1)(b). The 1972 Code declares that the controlling law as to perfection and the effect of perfection or non-perfection of a security interest is the law of the jurisdiction "where the collateral is when the last event occurs on which is based the assertion that the security interest is perfected or unperfected."

This rule applies to ordinary goods, but special rules apply to goods covered by a certificate of title, mobile goods and minerals or the like (including oil and gas). Special rules also apply where goods are moved from one state to another state. See discussion in subsequent sections of this chapter.

The place of location of the collateral also applies where the collateral is of a "semi-intangible" nature such as documents and instruments. Under 1972 § 9-103(1)(b), the place to perfect by taking possession or by filing where effective, or to perfect for a temporary period under 1972 § 9-304(4) or (5), is the place of location of the documents or instruments. Other rules sometimes apply, however, where an instrument is part of chattel paper. See discussion as to chattel paper immediately below.

1972 § 9-103(6)(c) as amended declares that perfection of a security interest in uncertificated securities is governed by the law of the jurisdiction of organization of the issuer. See also § 8-110(d). This does not affect certificated securities; the law of location of the certificate governs perfection. 1972 § 9-103(6)(b). See also § 8-110(c). Other provisions of 1972 § 9-103(6) deal with the question of where to perfect a security interest in a security entitlement or account [1972 § 9-103(6)(d)] and a commodity contract or account [1972 § 9-103(6)(e)]. For general discussion of security interests in investment property, see Chapter 4, § 4b and Chapter 1, § 9a(3).

b. *Chattel Paper Under 1972 Code*

Where the collateral is chattel paper under the 1972 Code, several rules are given. Where there is a possessory security interest in chattel paper, the law of the place of location governs perfection. But where there is a non-possessory security interest, the law of the place of the debtor's location (residence, place of business or chief executive office if there is more than one place of business) governs. Thus, if perfection as to chattel paper is by filing rather than by taking possession, the place to perfect is the jurisdiction where the debtor is located. See 1972 § 9-103(4).

c. *Security Interest in Goods to be Kept in Another State Under 1972 Code*

The 1972 Code sets forth a rule to cover the situation where goods are bought in one state subject to a purchase money security interest at the time of sale, but where it is understood by the parties to the secured transaction that the goods are to be kept in a different state. Under this rule, which might be termed the "30-day" rule, the law of the state to which the goods are removed, rather than the law of the state of purchase, governs perfection. However, the goods must be taken to the "removal" state within 30 days.

Under 1972 § 9-103(1)(c), in the case of a purchase money security interest in ordinary goods, where it is understood by the parties at the time the security interest attaches that the goods will be kept in another state, the law of that state governs perfection and the effect of perfection or non-perfection from the time the security interest attaches until 30 days after the debtor receives possession of the goods, and thereafter if the goods are removed to that state before the end of the 30-day period.

Example. Seller in State X agrees to sell equipment on a purchase money secured basis to Buyer in State Y. The equipment is promptly shipped from

State X to State Y. The law of State Y governs perfection and the effect of perfection or non-perfection.

It should be noted that the 30-day rule applies only where the parties to the secured transaction understand *at the time the security interest attaches* that the goods are to be kept in another state. The provision does not apply where the goods are delivered to the debtor in one state and he thereafter moves the goods to another state, in the absence of prior understanding between the parties.

The 30-day rule applies, under the 1972 Code, only where there is a purchase money security interest in ordinary goods which are to be moved; it does not apply where the collateral is mobile goods (see § 4b of this chapter), nor where a certificate of title is obtained (see § 7a of this chapter), nor where the collateral is minerals, including oil and gas (see § 5 of this chapter).

The 1999 Code has no equivalent provision because as to non-possessory security interests, that is where the secured party does not take possession of the collateral, the creditor must perfect in the state in which the debtor is located. 1999 § 9-301(1). Thus, the location of the collateral is irrelevant where the debtor maintains possession of the collateral.

d. Removal of Goods Subject to Security Interest in One State to Another State Under 1972 Code

Under the 1972 Code, the question of continuance of perfection may arise where goods which are subject to a perfected security interest in one state are subsequently taken to another state. This is due to the fact that an initial filing under the 1972 Code must occur where the collateral is located. 1972 § 9-103(1)(b). This problem does not occur under the 1999 Code where filing as to non-possessory security interests, that is where the secured party does not take possession of the collateral, occurs in the state of the debtor's location. 1999 § 9-301(1).

Under pre-Code law, the general rule was that perfection with respect to a chattel mortgage or conditional sale covering goods in one state continued even after the goods were removed to another state. Some courts followed a contrary rule and held that perfection in the first state was lost after the goods were moved to another state.

The 1972 version of the Code essentially requires that reperfection of the security interest in the state of removal is necessary within four months after the goods are removed. After that time, the security interest perfected in the original state becomes unperfected.

Under 1972 § 9-103(1)(d), a secured party who files in one state to perfect his security interest while the goods are there, and then files again in the state of removal within the four-month period has a continuously perfected security interest. In this connection, it should be noted that 1972 § 9-402(2)(a) permits a secured party alone to sign a financing statement to be filed in the state of removal.

Also, if the secured party fails to file in the state of removal within four months, the perfection of the security interest in the original state is lost. It makes no difference whether the secured party knows of the removal or not; failure to file within four months of removal results in loss of perfection.

The above rules apply to collateral as to which the place to perfect is in the state where the collateral is located. But the rules do not apply to collateral where perfection is effected under a certificate of title law.

Some specific provisions in the 1972 Code are summarized below:

a. The four-month grace period following

removal of the goods may be shortened if the five-year period of the original filing lapses in less than four months. In such case, the secured party must perfect in the state of removal before lapse of the filing in the original state.

Example 1. Debtor gave a security interest in goods located in State A to Secured Party who filed in State A on March 1, 1995. On February 1, 2000, Debtor moved the goods to State B. Under the 1972 Code, Secured Party has only until March 1, 2000 (five years after the original filing in State A) to perfect in State B. But if the goods had been moved to State B on February 1, 1999, Secured Party would have four months from that date to perfect in State B.

b. Under the 1972 Code, if no action is taken to perfect in the state of removal within the four-month (or lesser) grace period, the security interest not only becomes unperfected, but it is deemed to have been unperfected as against a person who became a "purchaser" [defined in § 1-201(32) and (33)] after removal. In other words, under the 1972 Code, a loss of perfection by failure to file within the four-month period is retroactive to the time of removal of the goods.

Example 2. X purchased goods in State A.

Bank perfected a security interest in the goods by filing in State A. X then moved the goods to State B and sold them to Y within four months of removal. Y resold the goods to Z during the four-month period. Bank did not file in State B or take other action to perfect either during or after the four-month period. Under the 1972 Code, Y would not be liable in conversion unless Bank perfected in State B before the end of the four-month period.

c. The 1972 Code makes it clear that a secured party who has a purchase money security interest in consumer goods may protect himself against an unauthorized sale of the goods to another consumer after the goods have been taken to another state only by filing in the state of removal within four months. This rule applies whether the secured party had filed in the first state before removal or had a perfected security interest without filing under 1972 § 9-302(1)(d). But filing is not necessary in the state of removal in order to maintain perfection otherwise, since the perfection is automatic. As to automatic perfection where there is a purchase money security interest in consumer goods, see Chapter 4, § 2a.

Example 3. Debtor gave Secured Party a purchase money security interest in consumer goods in State A. Secured Party did not file in State A and had an automatically-perfected security interest under 1972 § 9-302(1)(d). Debtor removed the goods to State B. No action is necessary at any time to continue perfection in State B. But if Secured Party does not file in State B within four months, Debtor can give good title to another consumer by sale of the goods under 1972 § 9-307(2).

e. *Governing Law Based on Location of Collateral Under 1999 Code*

The 1999 Code provides that where the creditor has possession of the collateral, a so-called "possessory security interest," the law governing perfection and the priority of a security interest is the law of the jurisdiction in which the collateral is located. 1999 § 9-301(2). Since in most secured transactions the creditor does not take possession of the collateral, this rule will infrequently apply. A significantly different rule applies if the creditor is not in possession of the collateral. See subsequent discussion at § 4d of this chapter. It should be noted that the 1999 Code treats certificate-of-title collateral separately. See 1999 § 9-303 and later discussion in this chapter at § 7b.

The law of the jurisdiction in which the collateral is located also governs perfection and priority issues if a fixture filing is involved or the collateral is timber to be cut. 1999 § 9-301(3). Similarly, if the collateral is "as-extracted" collateral, i.e., oil or gas and minerals [1999 § 9-102(a)(6)], the law of the jurisdiction in which the wellhead or minehead is located governs perfection and priority issues. 1999 § 9-301(4).

Because agricultural liens are within the scope of the 1999 UCC Article 9, a rule was necessary to designate which state in which the lien should be filed. While farm products are located in a particular state, the local law of that state governs the perfection and priority of agricultural liens in the farm products. 1999 § 9-302.

The 1999 place-of-perfection rules regarding investment property are not significantly changed. As to uncertificated securities, perfection of a security interest is governed by the law of the jurisdiction of the issuer. 1999 § 9-305(a)(2). See also § 8-110(d). For certificated securities, the law of the state in which the certificate is located governs. 1999 § 9-305(a)(1). See also § 8-110(c). Other rules apply to all others forms of investment property. As to where to perfect a security interest in a security entitlement or a securities account, see 1999 § 9-305(a)(3); as to a commodity contract or commodity account, see 1999 § 9-305(a)(4). For general discussion of security interests in investment property, see Chapter 4, § 4b and Chapter 1, § 9b(3).

§ 4.　Governing Law Based on Debtor's Location

a. *Accounts and General Intangibles Under the 1972 Code*

The 1972 Code provides at § 9-103(3) that the state in which to perfect a security interest where accounts or general intangibles are collateral is where the debtor is located. The debtor is deemed to be located at his residence, place of business or chief executive office if he has more than one place of business. In this connection, a corporate debtor is not necessarily located in the state of incorporation. For example, a debtor incorporated in Delaware with its chief executive office in Illinois is deemed located in the latter state. If the debtor is a foreign air carrier, it is deemed located at the designated office of the agent upon whom service of process may be made. See 1972 § 9-103(3)(b) and (d).

A special rule applies under 1972 § 9-103(3) if the debtor is located in a foreign country which has no provision of law for filing or recording a security interest. In such event, the law of the place in the United States where the debtor has its major executive office governs perfection through filing. Alternatively, perfection is permitted by notification to the account debtor if the debtor is not located in the United States or Canada. See 1972 § 9-103(3)(c).

There is one category of accounts to which the rule of 1972 § 9-103(3) does not apply: accounts resulting from the sale of minerals (including oil and gas) at the wellhead or minehead. In such case, the law of the state where the minehead or wellhead is located applies. See § 5 of this chapter.

Where perfection of a security interest in chattel paper is by filing, the state in which to file is that of the debtor's location. But when perfection is by possession, the place of location of the chattel paper itself is where to perfect. See § 3b of this chapter, above.

b. *Mobile Goods Under the 1972 Code*

The term "mobile goods" is defined in 1972 § 9-103(3)(a) as goods "which are of a type normally used in more than one jurisdiction, such as motor vehicles, trailers, rolling stock, airplanes, shipping containers, road building and construction machinery and commercial harvesting machinery and the like, if the goods are equipment or are inventory leased or held for lease by the debtor to others, and are not covered by a certificate of title * * *"

In 1972 § 9-103(3), the state in which to perfect a security interest where mobile goods are collateral is where the debtor is located. The rules as to where the debtor is located are the same under the 1972 Code as where the collateral is accounts or general intangibles. See discussion in § 4a of this chapter.

A different rule applies where mobile goods are covered by a certificate of title. See § 7a of this chapter.

c. *Where Debtor Changes Location to Another State Under the 1972 Code*

Where the state in which to perfect a security interest is that of the location of the debtor, with respect to accounts, general intangibles and mobile goods, a rule is set forth in 1972 § 9-103(3)(e) to cover the case where the debtor changes location (moves his residence, office or chief executive office to another state). Under that provision, if the debtor changes location to another state, a security interest perfected in the former state of location remains perfected normally for four months after the debtor moves. After that time, the security interest becomes unperfected unless action has been taken to perfect in the state of removal.

In other words, under the 1972 Code, if the debtor moves to another state, the secured party must act to perfect the security interest in the second state within four months, if the collateral is accounts, general intangibles or mobile goods. However, a financing statement filed in the second state may be signed by the secured party alone. See Chapter 5, § 4c(2).

The four-month grace period following removal may be shortened if the five-year period of the original filing lapses in less than four months. In such case, the secured party must perfect in the state of removal before lapse of the filing in the original state.

d. *Governing Law Based on Debtor's Location Under the 1999 Code*

(1) General Rule under 1999 Code

For most secured transactions under the 1999 Code, the law governing perfection and priority issues will be the law of the location of the debtor. Specifically, in most transactions in which the secured creditor is not in possession of the collateral, a so-called "non-possessory" security interest, the law of the jurisdiction in which the debtor is located governs. 1999 § 9-301(1). The exceptions to the debtor-location rule for non-possessory security interests include fixture filings, timber to be cut, and as-extracted collateral. 1999 § 9-301(3), (4). See discussion at § 5 of this chapter. Additionally, certificate-of-title collateral (1999 § 9-303), deposit accounts (1999 § 9-304), investment property (1999 § 9-305) and letter-of-credit rights (1999 § 9-306) are given separate treatment. As to investment property, see § 6 of this chapter; as to deposit accounts and letter-of-credit rights, see § 8 of this chapter.

The 1999 Code specifies where the debtor is located at 1999 § 9-307. If the debtor is an individual, the debtor is located at the debtor's principal residence. 1999 § 9-307(b)(1). Debtors that are "organizations" are treated differently. An "organization" includes a corporation, estate, trust, and a partnership. For a complete definition of "organization" see § 1-201(28). A debtor that is an organization and has only one place of business is located at its place of business [1999 § 9-307(b)(2)]; if it has more than one place of business, it is located at its chief executive office [1999 § 9-307(b)(1)].

However, a "registered organization" that is

organized under the law of a state is located in that state of organization. 1999 § 9-307(e). A "registered organization" usually means an organization organized under the law of a single state as to which the state must maintain a public record showing the organization to have been organized. 1999 § 9-102(a)(70). In other words, a registered organization will be a debtor that is incorporated.

Example. Acme, Inc. obtains a loan from Big Bank and grants Big Bank a security interest in all of Acme, Inc.'s inventory and equipment. Big Bank is located in California; Acme, Inc. only does business in California. All of the collateral is located in California. However, Acme, Inc. is incorporated under the laws of Delaware. Big Bank must file its financing statement in Delaware.

The 1999 Code has separate debtor location rules for federally registered organizations which essentially require filings to be made in the District of Columbia. 1999 § 9-307(f), (h).

(2) Effect of Change of Location of Debtor Under 1999 Code

The 1999 Code deals with issues that arise when the debtor changes location to a new state after an initial filing. A security interest remains perfected until the *earliest* of the time perfection would have ceased under the law of the state in which perfection initially occurred; the expiration of four months after a change of the debtor's location to a new state; or the expiration of one year after a transfer of the collateral to a person that becomes a debtor and is located in another jurisdiction.   1999 § 9-316(a). Using the four-month portion of the above rule, this means the secured party must perfect, i.e., file a financing statement, in the new state within the four months after the change of the debtor's location to a new state; if the secured party fails to do so, the security interest becomes unperfected and is deemed never to have been perfected as against a purchaser of the collateral for value. 1999 § 9-316(b).

Example. Using the immediately prior example, assume Big Bank filed a financing statement in State B. Subsequently, Acme, Inc. reincorporated in State C. Big Bank must file a financing statement in State C within four months after the reorganization in State C to maintain perfection. If the debtor, Acme, Inc., sold collateral to a purchaser for value within the four-month period, or thereafter, the buyer would take free of the security interest if Big Bank fails to file in State C within the four-month period.

§ 5. Collateral Related to Real Property

Some Article 9 collateral bears a close relationship to real property.   Such collateral includes minerals, oil, gas and resulting accounts; timber to be cut; and fixtures. Additionally, agricultural liens which fall within the scope of the 1999 Code relate to real property.

Under 1972 § 9-103(5), the place to perfect a security interest in minerals (including oil and gas) which attaches upon extraction is at the wellhead or minehead. The same rule governs with respect to accounts resulting from the sale of such items at the wellhead or minehead. The 1999 Code is in accord. See 1999 § 9-301(4).

When the collateral is timber to be cut, the 1972 and 1999 Codes require perfection in the state in which the timber is located.   1972 § 9-103(1)(b); 1999 § 9-301(3)(B). The same rules apply to fixtures under both Codes. 1972 § 9-103(1)(b); 1999 § 9-301(3)(A).

The 1999 Code includes agricultural liens within its scope. It provides that while farm products are located within the state, that state governs perfection and priority issues related to the farm products. 1999 § 9-302.

§ 6. Investment Property

With regard to investment property, recall that there are two methods by which a security interest may be perfected: by filing or by "control." See discussion at Chapter 4, §§ 4b, 12a. As to the multistate perfection issue, the 1972 Code as amended at § 9-103(6)(c) states that the law of the jurisdiction of organization of the issuer governs the perfection and the effect of perfection or non-perfection of a security interest in uncertificated securities. See also § 8-110(d). For example, if the issuer of stock that is uncertificated is incorporated in Delaware, but has its principal office in New York, and if the owner living in Pennsylvania grants a security interest to a lender located in New Jersey, the law of Delaware governs the perfection or non-perfection of a security interest. However, a court should resort not only to the law of Delaware, but also to the conflict of laws rules of that state.

With respect to certificated securities, the law of location of the certificate governs perfection. 1972 § 9-103(6)(b). Other provisions of 1972 § 9-103(6) deal with the question of where to perfect a security interest in a security entitlement or account [1972 § 9-103(6)(d)] and a commodity contract or account [1972 § 9-103(6)(e)].

The 1999 Code provisions related to investment property essentially are in accord with the 1972 Code. See 1999 §§ 9-305, 9-316(f).

For general discussion of security interests in investment property, see Chapter 4 § 4b and Chapter 1, § 9a(3)..

§ 7. Removal of Goods Where a Certificate of Title Exists

The 1972 and 1999 Codes both treat multi-state issues separately where a certificate of title exists. The provisions of the two versions of Article 9 differ to some extent. As a result, the following discussion will separately cover the 1972 and 1999 Code provisions in point.

a. Removal of Goods Where a Certificate of Title Exists under the 1972 Code.

1972 § 9-103(2) applies "to goods covered by a certificate of title issued under a statute of this state or of another jurisdiction under the law of which indication of a security interest on the certificate is required as a condition of perfection." 1972 § 9-103(2)(a). This provision of the 1972 Code is summarized as follows:

(1) Where a security interest is perfected by notation by a motor vehicle department or agency on a certificate of title of one state and the vehicle or other property is then removed to another state, the security interest remains perfected without time limit if the certificate of title is not surrendered and the vehicle is not registered in the other state. 1972 § 9-103(2)(b).

Note: 1972 § 9-103(2)(b) among other things states that perfection is lost upon "surrender of the certificate." The Code does not define the word "surrender." Comment 4(c) to 1972 § 9-103 indicates that ordinarily the secured party is in possession of the certificate that notes the security interest. It should follow that "surrender" would not ordinarily occur without some action by the secured party. However, the language of 1972 § 9-103(2)(b) indicates that perfection is lost if surrender is by anyone, including the debtor. Thus, if the secured party releases the certificate to the debtor for some reason, the debtor is in a position to "surrender" it. Moreover, in some states, the debtor is allowed under local "title" laws to retain the certificate even if a security interest is noted thereon. The debtor would thus be in a position to "surrender" the certificate and obtain (perhaps fraudulently) a new "clean" certificate. The Code also does not specify to where the certificate of title must be delivered to constitute a "surrender." Local certificate of title statutes might provide an answer.

(2) Where a security interest is perfected by notation on a certificate of title in one state and the vehicle or other property is then moved to another stated and registered there, the perfection on the certificate is lost after four months following removal. But the secured party is protected if he takes action within four months to perfect in the second state. 1972 § 9-103(2)(b). See Comment 4(c) to 1972 § 9-103.

(3) Where a security interest is perfected other than by notation on a certificate of title in a "non-title" state (as by filing there) and the vehicle or other property is then moved to another state and thereafter covered by a "clean" certificate of title issued by that state, the perfection in the original state is lost after four months following removal. But the secured party is protected if he takes action within four months to perfect in the second state. 1972 § 9-103(2)(c). See Comment 4(c) to 1972 § 9-103.

(4) Where a security interest is perfected in any manner (by notation on a certificate of title or by

filing) in one state and the vehicle or other property is then moved to another state and thereafter covered by a "clean" certificate of title issued by that state which does not show the security interest, the security interest is subordinate to the rights of a "nonprofessional" buyer (i.e., a person who is not a dealer) who gives value and buys on the basis of the latter "clean" certificate of title without knowledge of the security interest. This rule applies without regard to the four-month period. 1972 § 9-103(2)(d). See Comment 4(e) to 1972 § 9-103.

(5) The rule of item (4) above does not apply if the buyer is a "professional" (i.e., a dealer). In such case, the four-month rule applies and the taking of action to perfect in the state of removal within four months is effective. 1972 § 9-103(2)(d). See Comment 4(e) to 1972 § 9-103.

(6) The rule of item (4) above also does not apply if the certificate of title issued by the state of removal bears on it a notation that the vehicle or other property "may be subject to security interests not shown on the certificate." In such case, the four-month rule applies and the taking of action to perfect in the state of removal within four months is effective. 1972 § 9-103(2)(d). See Comment 4(e) to 1972 § 9-103.

(7) Where, under any of the above situations, a "clean" certificate of title is issued by the state of removal, it is unlikely that the secured party can reperfect by having the security interest noted on the certificate of title, absent cooperation from the debtor. However, the secured party may perfect within the four-month period by repossessing the vehicle or other property. See Comment 4(e) to 1972 § 9-103.

The following examples illustrate some of the problems that have arisen with respect to motor vehicles where a certificate of title is involved:

Example 1. A car was purchased in State A subject to a security interest noted on a certificate of title issued by that state. The car was taken to State B but no action was taken to register the car there or obtain a new certificate of title there. The security interest noted on the certificate of title of State A is effective without time limit, under the 1972 Code.

Example 2. A car was purchased in State A subject to a security interest noted on a certificate of title issued by that state. The car was taken to State B, a "non-title" state and registered there. Under the 1972 Code, the four-month rule would apply and the security interest would become unperfected if no filing is made or other action is taken to perfect in the second state within that period.

Example 3. A car was purchased in State A, a "non-title" state, subject to a security interest perfected by filing there. The car was taken to State B where a "clean" certificate of title was fraudulently obtained. Under the 1972 Code, the four-month rule would apply and the security interest would become unperfected if no action is taken to perfect in the second state within that period. But if a "nonprofessional" innocent buyer for value purchased the car in the second state on the basis of the "clean" certificate of title, the buyer would prevail without regard to the four-month period.

Example 4. A car was purchased in State A subject to a security interest noted on a certificate of title issued by that state. The car was taken to State B where a "clean" certificate of title was fraudulently obtained. Under the 1972 Code, the four-month rule would apply and the security interest would become unperfected if no action is taken to perfect in the second state within that period. But if a "nonprofessional" innocent buyer for value purchased the car in the second state on the basis of the "clean" certificate of title, that buyer would prevail without regard to the four-month period.

b. *Removal of Goods Where a Certificate of Title Exists Under the 1999 Code*

1999 § 9-303 applies to goods covered by a certificate of title. The section applies even if there is no other relationship between the jurisdiction under whose certificate of title the goods are covered and the goods or the debtor. 1999 § 9-303(a). The lack of a requirement of a relationship between the state that issues a certificate of title to the goods or the debtor is in accord with cases that have considered the matter under 1972 § 9-103(2). See Comment 2 to 1999 § 9-303.

1999 § 9-303 and related sections are summarized as follows:

(1) 1999 § 9-303(b) indicates when goods are covered by a certificate of title. Goods first become covered by a certificate of title when a valid application for the title and the application fee are delivered to the appropriate authority, such as a state department of motor vehicles. Such goods cease to be covered by a certificate of title in two situations. First, if the certificate of title ceases to be effective under the law of the issuing jurisdiction, the goods obviously are no longer subject to the certificate of title. The second situation arises when the goods become covered subsequently by a certificate of title

issued by another jurisdiction. Unlike the former 1972 § 9-103(2)(b), the 1999 Code eliminates the concept of "surrender" as an event that results in the law of the state that issued the certificate of title not to apply. See Comment 3 to 1999 § 9-303. If, however, the certificate of title is surrendered to an appropriate authority in another state with a valid application and fee for a new title, the law of the state that originally issued the certificate of title ceases to apply.

(2) 1999 § 9-303(c) provides that the law of the jurisdiction under whose certificate of title the goods are covered governs perfection and priority issues related to the security interest in the goods. That law governs until the goods cease to be covered by the certificate of title.

(3) 1999 § 9-316 deals with situations in which the goods cease to be covered by the certificate of title. The fact that the law of one jurisdiction ceases to apply under § 9-303(b) does not mean that a security interest perfected under that law becomes unperfected automatically. See Comment 4 to 1999 § 9-303. The gist of 1999 § 9-316(d) and (e) is that in most cases the security interest will remain perfected.

1999 § 9-316(d) indicates that a security interest

in goods covered by a certificate of title, which is perfected by any method under the law of another jurisdiction when the goods become covered by a certificate of title in another state, remains perfected until the security interest would have become unperfected under the law of the other (former) jurisdiction had the goods not become so covered. However, 1999 § 9-316(e) provides an exception to this continuity of perfection rule. The security interest becomes unperfected as against a purchaser of goods for value and is deemed never to have been perfected against such a purchaser if the applicable requirements for perfection are not satisfied before the earlier of either the time the security interest would have become unperfected under the law of the other jurisdiction had the goods not become covered by a certificate of title in the new state, or the expiration of four months after the goods have become so covered.

Example. Debtor grants a security interest to Big Bank on an automobile which is covered by a certificate of title issued by State A. Big Bank perfects the security interest by complying with State A's certificate-of-title statute. Debtor moves to State B and applies for a certificate of title in State B. One year later, Creditor obtains a judicial lien on the car. State A ceases to govern perfection once Debtor delivers the application and fee to State B authorities, at which time State B law governs. 1999 § 9-303(b). But, State B's 1999 § 9-316(d) provides that Big Bank's security interest remains perfected until it would become unperfected under State A's law had no certificate been issued by State B. Thus, Big Bank's security interest remains perfected and is senior to Creditor's judicial lien. See Comment 5 to 1999 § 9-316.

Example. Assume the same facts as described in the previous example except that after four months from the time Debtor applied for the State B certificate of title, Debtor sells the car to Buyer. Under these circumstances, Buyer takes free of Big Bank's security interest. Lender did not reperfect within four months after the car became covered by the State B certificate of title. Thus, under 1999 § 9-316(e), Big Bank's security interest is deemed never to have been perfected against Buyer. See also 1999 § 9-317(b) and Comment 5 to 1999 § 9-316.

The 1999 Code adds one more section that must be considered when analyzing perfection and priority issues in certificate-of-title collateral when more than one state is involved. 1999 § 9-337 provides for priority for certain parties if, while a security interest in goods is perfected under the law of another state, a second state issues a certificate of title that does not show the goods are or may be subject to a security interest. Under these circumstances, a "nonprofessional buyer" takes free of the security interest if he gives value and does not know of the security interest. 1999 § 9-337(1). A "nonprofessional buyer" is a person not in the business of selling goods of the kind. Additionally, the security interest is subordinate to a conflicting security interest in the goods that attaches and is perfected after the issuance of a certificate and without the conflicting secured party's knowledge of the security interest. 1999 § 9-337(2).

§ 8. Multistate Perfection Under 1999 Code for Deposit Accounts and Letter-of-Credit Rights

The 1999 Code brings within its scope collateral in the form of some deposit accounts and letter-of-credit rights. 1999 §§ 9-109(a)(1), 9-102(a)(29), (51). See also discussion of these collateral types as falling within UCC Article 9's scope at Chapter 1, § 7e and Chapter 7, §§ 12 and 13. Secured transactions involving such collateral fell outside the scope of the 1972 Code. The inclusion of these types of collateral necessitated some new provisions applicable to multistate transactions in which deposit accounts and letter-of-credit rights serve as the collateral.

As to deposit accounts, the law of the bank's jurisdiction governs perfection and priority issues related to security interests in a deposit account maintained with that bank. 1999 § 9-304(a). The 1999 Code provides rules that determine a bank's jurisdiction [1999 § 9-304(b)] and rules that deal with situations in which the depositary bank changes jurisdictions. 1999 § 9-316(f).

As to letter-of-credit rights, the general rule is that the law of the jurisdiction of the party who issued the letter of credit governs perfection and priority issues related to security interests in letter-of-credit rights. The 1999 Code provides a rule that determines the jurisdiction of the issuer [1999 § 9-306(b)] and rules that deal with situations in which the issuer changes jurisdictions. 1999 § 9-316(f).

CHAPTER 7

PRIORITIES OF SECURED PARTIES AND OTHERS

§ 1. Introduction

As stated in the Comment to 1972 § 9-101, the rules set out in Article 9 "are principally concerned with the limits of the secured party's protection against purchasers from and creditors of the debtor." See also Comment 1 to 1999 § 9-101 which states that "[f]or the most part [1999 Article 9] follows the general approach and retains much of the terminology of former [1972] Article 9."

The extent of protection of the secured party from claims of third persons with respect to the collateral depends in many instances on whether the security interest is perfected or not. The extent of such protection when the security interest is perfected is summarized in Comment 1 to 1972 § 9-303, which reads in part as follows:

"A perfected security interest may still be or become subordinate to other interests * * * but in general after perfection the secured party is protected against creditors and transferees of the debtor and in particular against any representative of creditors in insolvency proceedings instituted by or against the debtor."

Similarly, see Comment 2 to 1999 § 9-308.

While a perfected security interest is protected against most third-party claims, even an unperfected security interest has limited protection against certain third persons. See discussion in § 2b of this chapter.

The interests of third persons which compete with the interest of the secured party in the collateral fall into two basic classes: purchasers of the collateral and other creditors of the debtor. Note that if the debtor files bankruptcy, the trustee, as a representative of the debtor's creditors, also can become a competitor. Bankruptcy is considered in Chapter 8 of this Nutshell.

Such third-party competitors of the secured party for the collateral may be further broken down as follows:

a. Buyers or transferees of the collateral

b. Other secured parties.

c. General or unsecured creditors.

d. Creditors who have obtained a lien on the collateral by attachment, levy or the like.

e. Representatives of creditors, such as an assignee for the benefit of creditors, a trustee in bankruptcy or a receiver, who have the status of lien creditors.

f. Persons who have liens on the collateral by operation of law, such as the possessory lien of a repairman.

g. Governmental units having liens by statute, such as the United States with a Federal tax lien.

For each priority dispute, there is a specific rule to determine which claimant has priority. Thus, it is important to identify carefully the basis of both parties' claims. Armed with that information, one is able to select the applicable priority rule. Otherwise stated, a single "first-in-time, first-in-right" rule will not suffice to resolve all priority disputes.

§ 2.   Priority When Security Interest is Unperfected

a. Priority Over Unperfected Security Interest

Both the 1972 and 1999 Codes have provisions

that set forth the classes of persons who have priority with respect to collateral over the holder of an unperfected security interest. (It should be noted that the 1999 Code provisions also apply to unperfected agricultural liens. See § 14 of this chapter that discusses the priority of agricultural liens under the 1999 Code.)

The classes of persons who have priority with respect to the collateral over the holder of an unperfected security interest are listed in 1972 § 9-301(1) and 1999 § 9-317, and include the following:

(1) Persons entitled to priority under 1972 § 9-312 or 1999 § 9-322. Those provisions allow priority to particular kinds of secured parties with perfected security interests over a secured party with another perfected security interest. Thus, by implication an unperfected security interest is subordinate to another secured party's perfected security interest. This is clearly implied under 1972 §§ 9-301(1)(a) and 9-312(5)(a). Similarly, see 1999 §§ 9-317(a)(1) and 9-322(a)(1). In short, priority is given to the first to file or otherwise perfect a security interest under both 1972 § 9-312(5)(a) and 1999 § 9-322(a)(1). See § 4a of this chapter.

(2) A person who becomes a lien creditor before the security interest is perfected. 1972 § 9-301(1)(b)

or 1999 § 9-317(a)(2). Under both the 1972 and 1999 versions of Article 9, *it is necessary that the lien be obtained by legal proceedings before the security interest is perfected.* See Comment 3 to 1972 § 9-301. The same is general true under the 1999 Code. See Comment 4 to 1999 § 9-317.

Example. Secured Party took a security interest in certain equipment but failed to file a financing statement and had an unperfected security interest. A judgment creditor of debtor had the sheriff levy on the equipment, thereby acquiring a lien. Under the 1972 and 1999 Codes, the judgment creditor has priority over the unperfected interest of Secured Party.

Note: A "lien creditor" is defined as "a creditor who has acquired a lien on the property involved by attachment, levy or the like and includes an assignee for the benefit of creditors from the time of assignment, and a trustee in bankruptcy from the date of the filing of the petition or a receiver in equity from the time of appointment." 1972 § 9-301(3) and 1999 § 9-102(a)(52).

(3) Certain buyers of tangible or semi-intangible collateral [goods, instruments, documents or chattel paper under the 1972 Code; the 1999 Code adds a security certificate defined in § 8-102(a)(16) as a

"certificate representing a security" and, as to chattel paper, limits application of the rule to tangible chattel paper]. This includes a person who is not a secured party and who is a transferee in bulk or other buyer not in the ordinary course of business. Such a buyer has to give value and receive delivery of the collateral *without knowledge of the security interest* and before it is perfected. See 1972 § 9-301(1)(c) and 1999 § 9-317(b). The 1972 version also includes in the class of protected buyers a buyer of farm products in ordinary course of business. [Other buyers in ordinary course of business take free of even perfected security interests under 1972 § 9-307(1) and thus have priority over unperfected security interests.] The 1999 Code also gives lessees priority that receive delivery of collateral subject to an unperfected security interest. 1999 § 9-317(c).

(4) Certain transferees of intangible collateral (accounts and general intangibles). This includes a transferee who is not a secured party and who gives value *without knowledge of the security interest* and before it is perfected. See 1972 § 9-301(1)(d). The 1999 Code has a similar provision that applies to a licensee of a general intangible or a buyer of accounts, general intangibles, electronic chattel paper, and investment property other than certificated

securities. 1999 § 9-317(d).

b. *Priority of Unperfected Interest Over Others*

By a converse reading of 1972 § 9-301(1) and 1999 § 9-317, which are discussed immediately above, certain classes of third-person claimants have rights in the collateral subordinate even to an unperfected security interest. These include:

(1) General creditors of the debtor who have no liens on the collateral. However, it should be noted that a representative of general creditors (such as an assignee for the benefit of creditors, a trustee in bankruptcy, or a receiver) would have priority as a lien creditor under 1972 § 9-301(3) and 1999 §§ 9-317(a)(2) and 9-102(a)(52).

(2) Certain buyers of goods, instruments, documents and chattel paper who have knowledge of the security interest. 1972 § 9-301(1)(c) and 1999 § 9-317(b). As to lessees who take delivery with knowledge of an unperfected security interest, the lessee takes subject to the security interest under the 1999 Code. 1999 § 9-317(c).

(3) Certain transferees of accounts and general intangibles who have knowledge of the security interest. 1972 § 9-301(1)(d). Similarly, see 1999

§ 9-317(d).

(4) A secured party with an unperfected security interest also has rights superior to those of a second secured party with an unperfected security interest whose security interest attaches at a time later than when the first security interest attaches. See 1972 § 9-312(5)(b) and 1999 § 9-322(a)(3).

c. *Grace Period for Filing Purchase Money Security Interest*

Ordinarily when a filing is made after the time the security interest attaches while otherwise unperfected, the filing is effective to perfect the security interest only from the time it is made. See 1972 §§ 9-303(1), 9-403(1) and 1999 §§ 9-308(a), 9-516(a). In other words, there is ordinarily no relation back of a filing, or grace period within which a filing may be made, except as set forth below. See Comment 5 to 1972 § 9-301 and, c.f., Comment 8 to 1999 § 9-318.

A limited 10-day grace period is given in 1972 § 9-301(2) with respect to a *purchase money security interest*. Under the 1972 Code, the period is 10 days after the debtor receives possession of the collateral, and this can cut off the interests only of intervening lien creditors or bulk purchasers of the collateral (but not the interests of purchasers other than bulk purchasers). See Comment 5 to 1972 § 9-301. A number of states under the 1972 Code have extended the grace period to 20 days or some other period by non-uniform amendment to 1972 § 9-301(2). Under the 1999 Code, the period is 20 days after the debtor receives delivery of the collateral, and this can cut off interests only of intervening buyers, lessees, or lien creditors. 1999 § 9-317(e).

Example 1. Debtor gives Secured Party a purchase money security interest in widgets which are delivered to Debtor on April 1. Secured Party files on April 10. The filing within 10 days is sufficient to give Secured Party priority over Creditor who obtained a judgment lien on the collateral on April 3.

Example 2. Debtor gives Secured Party a non-purchase money security interest in widgets on April 1. Secured Party files on April 10. The filing is ineffective as to any of the conflicting claimants described in 1972 § 9-301(1) and 1999 § 9-317(a) who obtained their rights in the collateral prior to the filing.

Note the similar 10-day grace period under 1972 § 9-312(4) and 20-day grace period under 1999 § 9-

324(a) for protection of the purchase money secured party against another secured party (except as to inventory collateral). See § 4b of this chapter.

§ 3. Priority When Collateral Is Sold or Transferred

a. *Unauthorized Sale*

"Except where [Article 9] otherwise provides, a security interest continues in collateral notwithstanding sale, exchange or other disposition thereof unless the disposition was authorized by the secured party in the security agreement or otherwise, and also continues in any identifiable proceeds including collections received by the debtor." 1972 § 9-306(2). The 1999 Code has a nearly identical provision, except that it also applies to agricultural liens. 1999 § 9-315(a)(1).

Under 1972 § 9-306(2) and 1999 § 9-315(a)(1), if the debtor makes an unauthorized sale of the collateral, the security interest continues in the collateral in the hands of the buyer, unless the buyer takes free of the security interest under some other provision of Article 9. The security interest also attaches to the proceeds of the sale. 1972 § 9-306(2), 1999 § 9-315(a)(2). The secured party may claim both the original collateral and proceeds, but may of course have only one satisfaction.   See Comment 3 to 1972 § 9-306 and Comment 3 to 1999 § 9-315.

It should be noted that 1972 § 9-311 and 1999 § 9-401 recognize that a debtor's equity in the collateral may be sold or transferred involuntarily, whether or not the secured party consents, but such transfer is subject to the security interest.   See discussion in Chapter 3, § 9.

The above does not mean that all buyers of the collateral take subject to the security interest when the collateral is sold without the consent of the secured party. Certain classes of buyers take free of even a perfected security interest and additional classes take free of an unperfected security interest.

Buyers or other transferees who take the collateral free of even a perfected security interest, in the event of an unauthorized sale, include the following:

(1) A buyer in ordinary course of business. 1972 § 9-307(1) and 1999 § 9-320(a).

(2) A consumer-buyer of consumer goods from another consumer, where the secured party has perfected without filing. 1972 § 9-307(2) and 1999 § 9-320(b).

(3) A buyer of the collateral with respect to certain future advances made after sale of the collateral. 1972 § 9-307(3). Similarly, as to buyers and lessees with regard to the priority of future advances, see 1999 § 9-323(c)-(f).

(4) Certain purchasers of chattel paper and instruments who give new value and take possession. 1972 § 9-308 and 1999 § 9-330.

(5) Persons who have the status of holder in due course or like status with respect to a negotiable instrument, a negotiable document of title or a security. 1972 § 9-309 and 1999 § 9-331.

The above group of buyers and transferees also takes free of an unperfected security interest. See discussion of each such group later in this section of the chapter.

Certain additional classes of buyers take free of an unperfected security interest. For discussion, see § 2a of this chapter.

b. *Sale With Consent of Secured Party*

1972 § 9-306(2) and 1999 § 9-315(a)(1) make it clear that a security interest in collateral is lost where its sale or disposition is *authorized by the secured party* in the security agreement or otherwise. Obviously, a secured party may expressly authorize the sale of the collateral by the debtor. The sale may also be impliedly authorized through conduct on the part of the secured party, as where the debtor repeatedly on prior occasions made sales of the same kind of collateral which were known to the secured party and to which no objection was voiced. In some instances, the secured party may expressly or by conduct be deemed to have waived a term in the security agreement which prohibits sale by the debtor. Consent to a sale may also be implied through the common-law concepts of waiver and estoppel. See § 1-103.

1972 § 9-402(7) has a sentence reading: "A filed financing statement remains effective with respect to collateral transferred by the debtor even though the secured party knows of or consents to the transfer."

That sentence of 1972 § 9-402(7) appears inconsistent with the provision of 1972 § 9-306(2) that declares a sale of the collateral free of the security interest if consented to by the secured party. Presumably, the two provisions might be reconciled by reading 1972 § 9-402(7) as applying where a secured party consents to a sale of the collateral subject to the security interest or where the buyer from the debtor knowingly buys subject to the security interest. In such case, the secured party does not have to file again after the collateral is sold, and does not have to name the buyer as a new debtor in a filed financing statement. See UCC Permanent Editorial Board Commentary No. 3, which takes that position. Note that the 1999 Code has clarified this apparent inconsistency in this manner. See 1999 § 9-507(a) and Comment 3 to 1999 § 9-507.

c. *Buyer in Ordinary Course of Business*

(1) General Rule

A buyer in ordinary course of business "takes free of a security interest created by his seller even though the security interest is perfected and even though the buyer knows of its existence." 1972 § 9-307(1). Similarly, see 1999 § 9-320(a). However, this rule does not apply to a person buying farm products from a person engaged in farming operations. See § 3c(2) of this chapter.

A lengthy definition of the term "buyer in ordinary course of business" is set forth in § 1-201(9). That definition should be read with 1972 § 9-307(1) and 1999 § 9-320(a) in determining whether a particular buyer of collateral takes free of a perfected security interest. The following is a summary of different applications or non-applications of the "buyer in ordinary course of business" rule:

(a) The rule applies whether the security interest is perfected or unperfected. Note that where the security interest is unperfected, other classes of buyers also take free of the security interest, under 1972 § 9-301(1)(c) and 1999 § 9-317(b), (c). See § 2 of this chapter.

(b) The rule applies where the sale is unauthorized by the secured party. If the secured party has authorized the sale in the security agreement or otherwise, the buyer takes free of the security interest without regard to the limitations of 1972 § 9-307(1) or 1999 § 9-320(a). See Comment 2 to 1972 § 9-307. Note that 1972 § 9-306(2) and 1999 § 9-315(a)(1) permit a buyer to take free of a security interest where the sale is authorized by the secured party. See § 3b of this chapter.

(c) The definition of "buyer in ordinary course of business" in § 1-201(9) is restricted to a buyer (except a pawnbroker) "from a person in the business of selling goods of that kind." Thus, the rule of 1972 § 9-307(1) and 1999 § 9-320(a) *applies primarily to a buyer of inventory.*

Example 1. A buyer of a car from an automobile dealer is a buyer in ordinary course of business and takes free of a security interest given by the dealer. The same rule may apply where one dealer buys a car from another dealer, since dealers frequently sell cars to other dealers.

Example 2. A buyer of goods which are not inventory is not ordinarily regarded as a buyer in ordinary course of business and thus takes subject to a perfected security interest created by the seller of the goods. This principle has been applied to a buyer of an automobile used as equipment by a car repair garage which was not an auto dealer. It has also been applied where the seller is a company in the business of renting cars, even though the company from time to time replaces its stock of cars available for rental and sells the replaced cars. There is a contrary case authority, holding that a car-leasing company which from time to time sells leased cars is in the business of selling cars and can confer title free of a security interest on a buyer in ordinary course of business.

(d) A buyer in ordinary course of business is one who buys "in good faith and without knowledge that the sale to him is in violation of the ownership rights or the security interest of a third party." Section 1-201(9). This means that the buyer takes free of the security interest if he merely knows that there is a security interest which covers the goods; but he takes subject to that interest if he knows, in addition, that the sale is in violation of some term in the security agreement not waived by the words or conduct of the secured party. See Comment 2 to 1972 § 9-307. There is no equivalent Comment to 1999 § 9-320.

Example 3. Retailer gave a security interest in inventory to manufacturer. The security agreement prohibited sales by Retailer to other persons in the retail business who might buy for the purpose of selling the items at discount. Buyer, another retailer, knew of this prohibition in the security agreement, but nonetheless bought some of the inventory covered by the security agreement from Retailer. Buyer takes subject to the security interest.

(e) A buyer in ordinary course of business may buy for cash or by exchange of other property (e.g., by a trade-in) or on secured or unsecured credit, and may receive goods or documents of title under a pre-existing contract for sale. However, there can be no buyer in ordinary course of business where there is a transfer in bulk (as where a business is sold to another) or where there is a transfer as security for or in total or partial satisfaction of a money debt. See § 1-201(9). In other words, a person taking a security interest is not a buyer in ordinary course of business. Also, a person who takes collateral in satisfaction of a debt is not a buyer in ordinary course of business.

Example 4. Seller-Dealer owed money to Contractor arising from prior transactions between the two parties. Seller-Dealer transferred a truck to Contractor in satisfaction of the debt. Contractor is not a buyer in ordinary course of business and takes the truck subject to a security interest perfected by Creditor. But where Contractor purchased a truck from Seller-Dealer partly for cash, partly through trade-in of an older truck and partly by cancellation of a debt owed Contractor by Seller-Dealer, Contractor is a buyer in ordinary course of business.

Note: Although a person taking a security interest is not himself a buyer in ordinary course of business, a person taking a security interest in collateral purchased by a buyer in ordinary course of business takes free of any other security interest which is cut off by the buyer in ordinary course of business.

(f) A buyer in ordinary course of business takes free of a security interest only if it was *created by his seller*. 1972 § 9-307(1) and 1999 § 9-320(a).

Example 5. A bought a car from dealer X and gave a security interest in the car to Bank M. Without authority from M, A sold the car to dealer

Y. Dealer Y then sold the car to B who gave a security interest to Bank N. Although B is a buyer in ordinary course of business, he (and N) take subject to the security interest of M since that had not been created by Y who sold the car to B, but had been created by an earlier owner of the car, A.

(g) A buyer of minerals or the like (including oil and gas) at the wellhead or minehead may be considered a buyer in ordinary course of business. See § 1-201(9).

(2) Buyer of Farm Products

An exception to the rule permitting a buyer in ordinary course of business to take free of a security interest created by his seller is made where the buyer is "a person buying farm products from a person engaged in farming operations." 1972 § 9-307(1) and 1999 § 9-320(a).

Although this special rule has been criticized in a number of quarters, it exists in both the 1972 and 1999 Codes. The rule has been applied where a farmer or rancher obtains a loan and grants a security interest in crops or livestock. Under 1972 § 9-307(1) and 1999 § 9-320(a), the secured party in such case may follow the security interest into the hands of a buyer of the crops, such as a grain elevator or food processor, or into the hands of a buyer of livestock.

The "farm products" exception usually applies only where the secured party has a perfected security interest. If the secured party has an unperfected security interest, the buyer may take free of the security interest under 1972 § 9-301(1)(c) and 1999 § 9-317(b). The "farm products" exception does not apply where the farmer himself processes the crop into something else and then sells the resulting product.

Example 1. A farmer gave a security interest in a crop of peanuts to an agency of the United States government which filed a financing statement. The farmer then sold his crop to a company that buys and sells farm products. The company took the crop subject to the security interest and was liable to the United States for conversion when it resold the crop.

Example 2. A farmer gave a security interest in a crop of cotton to an agency of the United States government which filed a financing statement. The farmer ginned the cotton in his own ginning mill and then sold the product. Since the cotton had ceased to be "farm products" after ginning, the buyer took free of the security interest.

In response to criticism of the farm products exception, Congress enacted preemptive legislation as a part of the Food Security Act of 1985. See 7 U.S.C.A. § 1631. This federal statute provides that, regardless of 1972 § 9-307(1) or 1999 § 9-320(a), farm product buyers take free of security interests in farm products created by their seller. However, the statute does set forth two exceptions under which the buyer takes subject to the security interest.

The first exception is a "prenotification" exception under which the buyer will take subject to the perfected security interest if within one year before the sale the buyer has received written notice of the security interest from either the secured party or the debtor. The federal statute contemplates that the debtor will provide the secured party with a list of buyers to whom to give notice. In order to "encourage" the debtor to do so, the statute provides that if the farmer-debtor sells farm products to someone not on the list, the debtor is subject to civil penalty as set forth in the statute.

The second exception arises if a state has established a special "central filing system." The federal legislation in effect encourages states to do so. If a state has established such a central filing system, the secured creditor must file an "effective financing statement" in this central filing system, a system that is established and maintained separately from a UCC Article 9 central filing system. Farm product buyers also would be required to register with the same central filing office. That office would then compile a master list organized by type of farm product and by the county where each product is produced. The filing office then will distribute the master list of security interests to registered buyers. Thus, theoretically the buyer would receive notice of a security interest in a particular seller's farm products and would take subject to the security interest should he choose to buy from that farmer-seller.

d. Buyer Where Purchase Money Security Interest Is Automatically Perfected in Consumer Goods

"In the case of consumer goods, a buyer takes free of a security interest even though perfected if he buys without knowledge of the security interest, for value and for his own personal, family or household purposes unless prior to the purchase the secured party has filed a financing statement covering such goods." 1972 § 9-307(2). Similarly, see 1999 § 9-320(b).

Under 1972 § 9-302(1)(d) and 1999 § 9-309(1), no filing is required to perfect a purchase money security interest in consumer goods except motor vehicles required to be registered and where a fixture filing is necessary to obtain priority over conflicting interests in fixtures under 1972 § 9-313 and 1999 § 9-334. Even though the security interest is perfected automatically upon attachment in such case, a buyer meeting the conditions of 1972 § 9-307(2) or 1999 § 9-320(b) takes free of the perfected security interest. But if the purchase money secured party files, any buyer takes the consumer goods subject to the security interest.

To come within this provision, a buyer must buy (a) without knowledge of the security interest, (b) for value, and (c) for "consumer" purposes. In other words, the rule applies only to a consumer buying consumer goods from another consumer. The purchase must be made before a financing statement is filed.

For discussion of 1972 § 9-302(1)(d) and 1999 § 9-309(1) permitting perfection automatically upon attachment of a purchase money security interest in consumer goods, see Chapter 4, § 2a.

Example 1. Jones bought a deep freeze for use in his home from Appliance Company and gave Appliance a purchase money security interest in the deep freeze for the unpaid price. Appliance did not file a financing statement. Six months later, Jones sold the deep freeze to his next door neighbor, Smith, who bought it for use in his home. Although Appliance has a perfected security interest, the sale is free of that interest if Smith bought for value and without knowledge of the security interest. But if Appliance had filed, Smith's purchase would be subject to the security interest.

Example 2. Jones bought a deep freeze for use in his home from Appliance Company and gave Appliance a purchase money security interest in the deep freeze for the unpaid price. Appliance did not file a financing statement. Six months later, Jones traded in the deep freeze to Frosty, another dealer in deep freezes, for a more expensive model. Even though Appliance did not file, it has a security interest superior to the rights of Frosty, since the latter did not buy for personal, family or household purposes.

e. *Where Future Advances Are Made After Sale of the Collateral*

Under 1972 § 9-307(3) and 1999 § 9-323(d), (f), a buyer, even though he may otherwise purchase collateral subject to a security interest, takes free of that security interest "to the extent that it secures future advances made after the secured party acquires knowledge of the purchase, or more than 45 days after the purchase, whichever first occurs." Under the 1972 Code, this rule does not apply if the advance is made pursuant to a commitment entered into without knowledge of the purchase and before the expiration of the 45-day period. The same is true under the 1999 Code. See 1999 § 9-323(e), (g).

Example 1. Jones, a retailer, gave Secured Party a security interest in his inventory under a security agreement permitting Secured Party at its option to make future advances to enable Jones to acquire additional inventory. Secured Party promptly filed a financing statement. More than six months later, on March 1, Jones sold his business to Smith without the knowledge or consent of Secured Party. On April 1, Jones borrowed $10,000 from Secured Party on the representation that he was buying more inventory. On May 1, Jones borrowed another $10,000 on a like representation. Secured Party learned of the sale to Smith on June 1. Under 1972 § 9-307(3) and 1999 § 9-323(d), Secured Party has a security interest in the inventory transferred from Jones to Smith which is good against Smith to the extent of any indebtedness of Jones prior to March 1 and also to the extent of the April 1 advance. But Secured Party's interest is not good against Smith as respects the May 1 advance, which was made more than 45 days after the sale to Smith.

Note: In the above example, if Secured Party on April 1 (less than 45 days after the sale) had made a binding commitment to advance $10,000 on May 1, Secured Party's interest would have been good against Smith as respects the $10,000 advanced on May 1 to Jones.

Example 2. Debtor S gave lender L a purchase money security interest in a boat in April, 2000, which security interest was promptly perfected. In August, 2000, S sold the boat to R. In June, 2001, S borrowed additional sums from L, part of which was used to pay off the balance due on the former loan and part of which was used for other purposes. Since the additional borrowing was more than 45 days after the sale of the boat, the additional sum loaned is a future advance. Moreover, the entire new loan is a future advance if the former loan is extinguished. The result is that R takes the boat free of the security interest to the extent that it secures such future advances.

f. Purchaser of Chattel Paper or Instrument

When a security interest is taken in inventory, proceeds of the sale of inventory are also subject to the security interest. In some instances, the proceeds may consist of chattel paper or instruments. For example, a secured party may finance an inventory of automobiles or appliances in the hands of a dealer. A credit buyer of a car or appliance from the dealer may sign a promissory note and grant a security interest by way of a security agreement (chattel paper) for the unpaid price, or he may just sign a promissory note (instrument) for the price.

A security interest in chattel paper may be perfected either by the secured party taking possession, 1972 §§ 9-302(1)(a) and 9-305 and 1999 §§ 9-310 (b)(6) and 9-313(a), or by filing, 1972 § 9-304(1) and 1999 § 9-312(a). It may also be perfected where the chattel paper is proceeds if the security interest in the inventory giving rise to the proceeds is perfected. See 1972 § 9-306(3) and 1999 § 9-315(c)-(e).

A security interest in an instrument under the 1972 Code is normally perfected by the secured party taking possession and cannot be perfected by filing, 1972 § 9-304(1). Although it is possible to perfect a security interest in an instrument by filing under the 1999 Code [1999 § 9-312(a)], normally perfection will still occur by taking possession. The security interest may be temporarily perfected for not over 21 days without possession under 1972 § 9-304(4) and (5), or for not over 20 days without possession under 1999 § 9-312(e) and (f). It may also be perfected where the instrument is proceeds if the security interest in the inventory giving rise to the proceeds is perfected, 1972 § 9-306(3) and 1999 § 9-315(c)-(e).

Where a secured party has a perfected security interest in chattel paper or an instrument without being in possession, the debtor who remains in possession may transfer the chattel paper or instrument to a third person who takes possession. That third person then has an interest as a purchaser (or a security interest perfected through possession) in conflict with the nonpossessory but perfected interest of the secured party. 1972 § 9-308 and 1999 § 9-330 set forth circumstances under which the purchaser of chattel paper or an instrument may take possession and acquire rights superior to those of the secured party with the nonpossessory perfected security interest.

1972 § 9-308 gives priority to a purchaser of chattel paper or an instrument, *who gives new value and takes possession of it in the ordinary course of his business*, over a nonpossessory security interest in such collateral under the following circumstances:

(1) If the nonpossessory secured party has a perfected security interest by filing or a temporary

perfected interest under 1972 § 9-304, or a perfected interest in proceeds under 1972 § 9-306, provided that the purchaser acts without knowledge that the specific chattel paper or instrument is subject to the security interest; or

(2) If the nonpossessory secured party claims the chattel paper or instrument as proceeds of inventory subject to a security interest under 1972 § 9-306, whether or not the purchaser knows that the specific chattel paper or instrument is subject to the security interest.

Note: See the Comments to 1972 § 9-308, which detail the typical inventory sales transactions that may bring about a conflict between a purchaser in possession of chattel paper or an instrument and a secured party with a perfected nonpossessory interest in the same chattel paper or instrument.

Example. Dealer gave financer A a security interest in its inventory of automobiles and in proceeds of the sale of inventory which A perfected. Dealer sold a car to Buyer who executed a security agreement (chattel paper) on the car for the unpaid purchase price. Dealer then physically transferred the security agreement to financer B which acquired the paper for value, and which regularly acquired such security agreements representing sales of automobiles from Dealer. Even though B knew that A was financing Dealer's acquisition of inventory, B has priority as to Buyer's security agreement over the claim of A to that agreement as proceeds of inventory. The only claim of A is to the subsequent proceeds arising from the sale by Dealer of the chattel paper to B.

1999 § 9-330 is very similar to 1972 § 9-308. As to chattel paper, a purchaser of it has priority over a security interest in it which is claimed merely as proceeds of inventory subject to a security interest if the purchaser, in good faith and in the ordinary course of the purchaser's business, gives new value and takes possession or obtains control of the chattel paper and the paper does not indicate it has been assigned to one other than the purchaser. 1999 § 9-330(a); see also, 1999 § 9-105. As to any other security interest in the chattel paper, the purchaser takes free of the security interest if he gave value and took possession or control of the paper in good faith and in the ordinary course of the purchaser's business and if the purchaser had no knowledge that the purchaser was violating the rights of a secured party. 1999 § 9-330(b).

As to instruments, 1999 § 9-330(d) gives a purchaser of an instrument priority over a security interest in the instrument perfected by a method other than possession. To obtain this priority, the purchaser must give value and take possession in good faith and without knowledge that the purchaser is violating the rights of the secured party.

g. *Purchaser of Instrument or Document With Holder in Due Course or Like Status*

Under 1972 § 9-309 and 1999 § 9-331, a purchaser of paper which is negotiable, including negotiable instruments, negotiable documents and investment securities, who has the status of holder in due course (or analogous status with respect to a negotiable document or an investment security), has priority over an earlier security interest even though perfected. Filing under Article 9 does not constitute notice of such earlier security interest to any holder or purchaser.

Example. Secured Party filed a financing statement covering all accounts due or to become due Debtor. Account Debtor, who owed money to Debtor on an account, mailed a check to Debtor in payment. Debtor indorsed and delivered the check to Creditor to whom Debtor also owed money. If Creditor takes the check as holder in due course under Article 3 of the Code (which includes taking without knowledge of Secured Party's interest),

Creditor has priority over Secured Party with respect to the check. The filing gave no notice of the security interest to Creditor.

§ 4. Priority Between Secured Parties

a. The "First-to-File-or-Perfect" Rule

(1) Generally

1972 § 9-312 sets forth a number of rules governing priority between conflicting security interests in the same collateral. Special rules exist with respect to conflicting security interests in crops, conflicting security interests in inventory where one of the interests is a purchase money interest, and conflicting interests in other collateral where one of the interests is a purchase money interest. See 1972 § 9-312(2), (3) and (4), discussed in §§ 4b(1)and (2) of this chapter. Similar provisions are found in the 1999 Code at 1999 §§ 9-322 through 9-324.

The general rule governing priority between perfected security interests in the same collateral (in the absence of a special rule) is stated in 1972 § 9-312(5)(a) as follows:

"Conflicting security interests rank according to priority in time of filing or perfection. Priority dates from the time a filing is first made covering the collateral or the time the security interest is first perfected, whichever is earlier, provided that there is no period thereafter when there is neither filing nor perfection."

The same rule, although worded somewhat differently, is found at 1999 § 9-322(a)(1). The rule also applies to agricultural liens under the 1999 provision. As to agricultural lien priority, see also 1999 § 9-322(a)(2) and (3). The priority of agricultural liens under the 1999 Code is also discussed at § 14 of this chapter.

This rule gives special effect to filing, which may take place even before the security interest attaches (and accordingly before it is perfected). The rule also recognizes that perfection may take place in one way and then in another way (as where the secured party is in possession, then releases the collateral to the debtor but has temporary perfection under 1972 § 9-304(4) or (5), or 1999 § 9-312(e) or (f), and then files before the end of the period of temporary perfection). If perfection remains continuous, the time of initial perfection is determinative.

Note that if the conflicting security interests are both unperfected, the first to attach has priority. See 1972 § 9-312(5)(b) and 1999 § 9-322(a)(3).

Application of the general "priority" rules between conflicting security interests is illustrated by the following examples, taken from Comment 5 to 1972 § 9-312 (see also Comment 4 to 1999 § 9-322):

Example 1. A files against X (debtor) on February 1. B files against X on March 1. B makes a non-purchase money advance against certain collateral on May 1. A has priority even though B's advance was made earlier and was perfected when made. It makes no difference whether or not A knew of B's interest when he made his advance.

Example 2. A and B make non-purchase money advances against the same collateral. The collateral is in the debtor's possession and neither interest is perfected when the second advance is made. Whichever secured party first perfects his interest (by taking possession of the collateral or by filing) takes priority and it makes no difference whether or not he knows of the other interest at the time he perfects his own.

Example 3. A has a temporarily perfected (21 day) security interest, unfiled, in a negotiable document in the debtor's possession under 1972 § 9-304(4) or (5), or 1999 § 9-312(e) or (f). On the fifth day B files and thus perfects a security interest in the same document. On the tenth day A files. A has priority, whether or not he knows of B's interest when he files, because he perfected first and has maintained continuous perfection or filing.

(2) Where Future Advances Are Made

If future advances are made while a security interest is perfected by filing or the taking of possession, the security interest with priority under the "first to file or perfect" rule of 1972 § 9-312(5)(a) and 1999 § 9-323(a) has the same priority with respect to the future advances. "If a commitment is made before or while the security interest is so perfected, the security interest has the same priority with respect to advances made pursuant thereto. In other cases a perfected security interest has priority from the date the advance is made." 1972 § 9-312(7).   Similarly, see 1999 § 9-323(a) and Comment 3 to 1999 § 9-323.

This rule is explained in Comment 7 to 1972 § 9-312 as follows:

"The application of the priority rules to future advances is complicated. In general, since any secured party must operate in reference to the Code's system of notice, he takes subject to future advances under a priority security interest while it is perfected through filing or possession, whether the advances are committed or non-committed, and to any advances subsequently made 'pursuant to commitment' * * * during that period. In the rare case when a future advance is made without commitment while the security interest is perfected temporarily without either filing or possession, the future advance has priority from the date it is made * * *."

See also Comment 5 to 1972 § 9-312 which states in part:

"The justification for the rule lies in the necessity of protecting the filing system—that is, of allowing the secured party who has first filed to make subsequent advances without each time having, as a condition for perfection, to check for later filings than his."

Comment 3 to 1999 § 9-323 similarly expresses the reasoning underlying the priority given to future advances by 1999 § 9-323(a) when the conflicting claimants are both asserting security interests in the same collateral.

Example. On February 1 A makes an advance against machinery in the debtor's possession and files his financing statement. On March 1 B makes an advance against the same machinery and files his financing statement. On April 1 A makes a further advance, under the original security agreement, against the same machinery (which is covered by the original financing statement and thus perfected when made). A has priority over B both as to the February 1 and as to the April 1 advance and it makes no difference whether or not A knows of B's intervening advance when he makes his second advance. A wins, as to the April 1 advance, because he first filed even though B's interest attached, and indeed was perfected, before the April 1 advance. The same rule would apply if either A or B had perfected through possession. The same result would be reached even though A's April 1 advance was not under the original security agreement but was under a new security agreement under A's same financing statement or during the continuation of A's possession. See Comment 7 to 1972 § 9-312 and Comment 3 to 1999 § 9-323.

b. *Where There Is Purchase Money Security Interest*

(1) Non-inventory Collateral

"A purchase money security interest in collateral other than inventory has priority over a conflicting security interest in the same collateral or its proceeds if the purchase money security interest is perfected at the time the debtor receives possession of the collateral or within ten days thereafter." 1972 § 9-312(4). The 1999 Code has the same provision except that it permits perfection within 20 days after the debtor receives possession of the collateral. 1999 § 9-324(a). For discussion of priority as to proceeds, see § 4d of this chapter.

1972 § 9-312(4) and 1999 § 9-324(a) are summarized as follows:

(a) Both sections state a general rule applicable to all kinds of collateral except inventory and give the holder of a purchase money security interest priority in such collateral as equipment, if the purchase money security interest is perfected when the debtor receives possession of the collateral or within 10 days thereafter under the 1972 Code, or within 20 days thereafter under the 1999 Code. This means that the purchase money secured party either has filed a financing statement before the end of 10 days under the 1972 Code or 20 days under the 1999 Code or has a temporarily perfected security interest in goods covered by documents under 1972 § 9-304(4) or (5), or 1999 § 9-312(e) or (f), which is continued in a perfected status before the expiration of the 21-day period there specified in the 1972 Code or the 20-day period there specified in the 1999 Code. There is no requirement that the purchase money secured party be without notice or knowledge of the other security interest; he takes priority although he knows of the other interest or that interest has been filed.

(b) The 1972 Code provision allows a 10-day grace period for filing by the purchase money secured party after the debtor receives possession of the collateral for protection against any other secured party. A number of states under the 1972 Code have extended the period to 20 days or some other period, by non-uniform amendment to 1972 § 9-312(4). The 1999 Code has provided for a 20-day period as well. 1999 § 9-324(a). Note the similar 10-day grace period under 1972 § 9-301(2) and a 20-day grace period under 1999 § 9-317(e) for protection of the purchase money secured party against a transferee in bulk (under the 1972 Code) or a lien creditor. See § 2c of this chapter.

Example 1. On February 1 A makes advances to X under a security agreement which covers "all the machinery in X's plant" and contains an after-acquired property clause. A promptly files his financing statement. On March 1 X acquires a new machine, B makes an advance against it and files his financing statement. On April 1 A, under the original security agreement, makes an advance against the machine acquired March 1. If B's advance creates a purchase money security interest, he has priority (provided he filed before X received possession of the machine or within 10 days thereafter under the 1972 Code or within 20 days under the 1999 Code). If B's advance, although he gave new value, did not create a purchase money interest, A has priority as to both of his advances by virtue of his priority in filing, although the parties perfected simultaneously on March 1 as to the new machine.

(c) Where a purchase money secured party fails to file or perfect before the debtor receives possession of the collateral or within 10 days thereafter under the 1972 Code or 20 days thereafter under the 1999 Code, his priority is governed by the "first to file or perfect" rule of 1972 § 9-312(5)(a) and 1999 § 9-322(a), and not by 1972 § 9-312(4) or 1999 § 9-324(a). For discussion of the "first to file or perfect" rule, see § 4a of this chapter.

(d) Where there are two conflicting security interests which are both purchase money security interests under the 1972 Code, probably the "first to file or perfect" rule of 1972 § 9-312(5) Code governs priority. However, under the 1972 Code, if both purchase money secured parties file before the debtor receives the collateral or within 10 days thereafter, it would seem that they rank equally in priority in proportion to the amount of debt owed to each under 1972 § 9-312(4). The 1999 Code con tains a provision that determines priority between two conflicting purchase money security interests. 1999 § 9-324(g). It grants priority to a purchase money security interest created in favor of a seller over a purchase money security interest held by a third-party lender. Otherwise, the first-to-file-or-perfect rule of 1999 § 9-322(a) applies.

(e) It should be noted that the 1999 Code has some special provisions regarding purchase money security interest priority in livestock [1999 § 9-324(d), (e)] and software [1999 § 9-324(f)].

(2) Inventory Collateral

Where the collateral is inventory and there are conflicting security interests, under both the 1972 and 1999 Codes the holder of a purchase money interest is favored over other secured parties, but he must perfect his interest before the debtor receives the inventory and must also take certain other steps. The 1972 and 1999 Code provisions in point vary only slightly from each other.

Under 1972 § 9-312(3) and 1999 § 9-324(b), the purchase money secured party with an interest in inventory has priority over a conflicting security interest in the same inventory if:

(a) The purchase money security interest is

perfected at the time the debtor receives possession of the inventory. In other words, there is no 1972 Code 10-day or 1999 Code 20-day grace period as exists with respect to other kinds of collateral.

(b) The purchase money secured party gives notification to the holder of the conflicting security interest if the holder had filed a financing statement covering the same types of inventory before the date of the filing made by the purchase money secured party (or before the beginning of the period of temporary perfection under 1972 § 9-304(5) and 1999 § 9-312(f). The notice under the 1972 Code provision must be in writing; under the 1999 Code, the notice must be an "authenticated notification" which includes both a signed, written notice or an electronic notice with an encrypted signature.

(c) The holder of the conflicting security interest receives the notification within five years before the debtor receives possession of the inventory.

(d) The notification states that the person giving the notice has or expects to acquire a purchase money security interest in inventory of the debtor, describing such inventory by item or type.

Note that it is not necessary that the purchase money secured party obtain the consent of the other secured party who has filed.

The reason for the different requirements for priority as respects a purchase money security interest in inventory from the simpler rule covering other collateral in 1972 § 9-312(4) is explained in Comment 3 to 1972 § 9-312 as follows:

"Under [1972 § 9-312(3)] the same rule of priority, but without the ten day grace period for filing, applies to a purchase money security interest in inventory, with the additional requirement that the purchase money secured party give notification, as stated in subsection (3), to any other secured party who filed earlier for the same item or type of inventory. The reason for the additional requirement of notification is that typically the arrangement between an inventory secured party and his debtor will require the secured party to make periodic advances against incoming inventory or periodic releases of old inventory as new inventory is received.   A fraudulent debtor may apply to the secured party for advances even though he has already given a security interest in the inventory to another secured party.   The notification requirement protects the inventory financer in such a situation: if he has received notification, he will presumably not make an advance; if he has not received notification (or if the other interest does not qualify as a purchase money interest), any advance he may make will have priority. Since an arrangement for periodic advances against incoming property is unusual outside the inventory field, no notification requirement is included in [1972 § 9-312(4)]."

For a similar discussion in the 1999 Code Comments, see Comment 4 to 1999 § 9-324.

Example. Bank made a loan to Debtor, appliance dealer, secured by all inventory now owned or hereafter acquired. Bank filed a financing statement. One month later, Finance Company advanced money to Debtor to permit acquisition for resale of inventory manufactured by X. A financing statement covering such X inventory was filed. An officer of Finance Company then telephoned the loan officer of Bank and informed the latter that Finance Company intended to "floor plan" certain X merchandise for Debtor on a "secured money interest." This all took place before any X inventory was delivered to Debtor. Written notice would be necessary under the 1972 Code and written or electronic notice would be necessary under the 1999 Code, but the contents of the notice described above should be sufficient.

It should be noted that the 1999 Code has some

special provisions regarding purchase money security interest priority in livestock [1999 § 9-324(d), (e)] and software [1999 § 9-324(f)].

c. *Crops as Collateral*

1972 § 9-312(2) gives priority to a perfected security interest for new value in crops based on a current crop production loan over an earlier perfected security interest in the crops which secures obligations (such as rent, interest or mortgage principal amortization) due more than six months before the crops become growing crops. The new value must be given not more than three months before the crops become growing crops by planting or otherwise. See Comment 2 to 1972 § 9-312.

This rule enables a farmer to borrow money to plant current crops without regard to the existence of debt obligations secured by future growing crops due more than six months earlier. It makes no difference whether the current crop financer knows of the earlier security interest when he makes the loan.

Where two or more perfected security interests in crops do not fall within the pattern of 1972 § 9-312(2), priority is governed by the "first to file or perfect" rule of 1972 § 9-312(5)(a). Priority with respect to other agricultural collateral (such as livestock) is also governed by the "first to file or perfect" rule of 1972 § 9-312(5)(a), except where the "purchase money security interest" rule of 1972 § 9-312(4) might apply.

The 1999 Code has no equivalent to 1972 § 9-312(2). The drafters did include some suggested "model provisions" but made no recommendation on whether these model provisions should be enacted. See Appendix II, 1999 § 9-324A, to 1999 UCC Article 9 and Comment e to 1999 § 9-101 and Comment 2 to § 9-324.

d. Accounts and Proceeds

(1) Purchase Money Security Interest in Inventory

A priority problem may arise where one person takes a security interest in present and future accounts of a debtor and a different person takes a purchase money security interest in inventory of the same debtor. When the inventory is sold by the debtor, some form of proceeds results from the sale, which may consist of accounts, chattel paper or payment in the form of cash or checks. Which secured party, the account financer or the inventory purchase money financer, has priority?

1972 § 9-312(3) resolves the issue by giving the inventory purchase money secured party priority (if he takes the proper steps prescribed in that provision) restricted only to "identifiable cash proceeds received on or before the delivery of the inventory to a buyer." 1999 § 9-324(b) resolves the issue by giving the inventory purchase money secured party priority (if he takes the proper steps prescribed in that provision) in chattel paper or instruments constituting proceeds of the inventory; in proceeds of the chattel paper; and in identifiable cash proceeds of the inventory.

In other words, under the 1972 Code the inventory financer, having purchase money priority, obtains such priority over the financer of accounts who filed earlier only with respect to identifiable cash proceeds described in 1972 § 9-306(1), consisting of money, checks, deposit accounts and the like. Other proceeds from the sale of inventory, such as accounts and proceeds of accounts go to the financer of the accounts who filed earlier.

Stated another way, under the 1972 Code if the debtor sells inventory for cash or checks which can be identified as proceeds resulting from such sale, or if such proceeds are deposited in an earmarked bank account, the inventory financer has priority. But if the debtor sells the inventory and creates an account, the financer of the debtor's accounts who filed earlier has priority. He likewise has priority with respect to proceeds resulting when the account debtor makes payment of the account, even where these are cash proceeds. The reason is that the cash proceeds are "proceeds of proceeds" and do not arise directly from the sale of inventory to a buyer. The 1999 Code as described above would extend the priority of the purchase money secured party to proceeds of inventory that are chattel paper or instruments or proceeds of the chattel paper as well as to identifiable cash proceeds. 1999 § 9-324(b).

Except where the purchase money inventory financer has priority with respect to proceeds under the 1972 and 1999 Codes, priority as to proceeds is governed by the "first to file or perfect" rule. See § 4a(1) of this chapter.

(2) Purchase Money Security Interest in Other Collateral

A purchase money security interest in collateral other than inventory has priority over a conflicting security interest in the same collateral if the purchase money security interest is perfected at the time the debtor receives possession of the collateral or within 10 days thereafter under the 1972 Code and within 20 days thereafter under the 1999 Code. 1972 § 9-312(4) and 1999 § 9-324(a).

When under these rules the purchase money secured party has priority over another secured party, there is a question whether this priority extends to the proceeds of the original non-inventory collateral. The 1972 and 1999 Codes give the purchase money secured party priority as to proceeds (whether they are cash or non-cash proceeds), on the basis that there is ordinarily no expectation that such non-inventory collateral will be sold.

Note that a purchase money secured party with priority as to inventory under 1972 § 9-312(3) of the 1972 Code has priority only as to identifiable cash proceeds arising from the sale of the inventory.

(3) The "First to File or Perfect" Rule

In cases where a purchase money secured party in inventory or other collateral does not obtain priority with respect to proceeds under the rules of 1972 § 9-312(3) or (4) or 1999 § 9-324(a) or (b), priority as to proceeds is governed by the "first to file or perfect" rule, described in § 4a(1) of this chapter. This is made clear in 1972 § 9-312(6) and 1999 § 9-322(b) which state that for the purposes of the "first to file or perfect" rule of 1972 § 9-312(5) and 1999 § 9-322(a), a date of filing or perfection as to collateral is also a date of filing or perfection as to proceeds. The 1999 Code does add some special rules in this regard applicable to certain types of collateral. See 1999 § 9-322(c) - (e).

The application of this rule under the 1972 Code is illustrated in examples set forth in Comment 8 to 1972 § 9-312, which are also set forth in edited form below. Although these examples do not necessarily appear in the 1999 Code Comments, the same result would occur under the 1999 Code.

Example 1. A files a financing statement covering a described type of inventory then owned or thereafter acquired. B subsequently takes a purchase money security interest in certain inventory also described in A's financing statement and achieves priority under 1972 § 9-312(3) or 1999 § 9-324(b) as to that inventory. The inventory is then sold producing proceeds. If the proceeds are instruments or chattel paper, the rights of A and B and of any other claimant are governed by 1972 §§ 9-308 and 9-309 or 1999 §§ 9-330 and 9-331. If the proceeds are cash, B has priority. 1972 § 9-312(3) or 1999 § 9-324(b). But if the proceeds are accounts, the priorities as to the original collateral do not control the priority as to the accounts. Under 1972 §§ 9-306 and 9-312(6) or 1999 §§ 9-315 and 9-322(b)(1), A's first filing as to the inventory constitutes a first filing as to the accounts, provided that the same filing office would be appropriate for filing as to accounts under 1972 § 9-306(3) or 1999 § 9-315(d). A has priority as to the accounts.

Example 2. A files a financing statement covering a described type of inventory then owned or thereafter acquired. B subsequently takes a purchase money security interest in certain inventory also described in A's financing statement and achieves priority under 1972 § 9-312(3) or 1999 § 9-324(b) as to that inventory. The inventory is then sold and proceeds consisting of accounts are created. If B had filed directly as to accounts, the date of that filing would be compared to the date of A's filing as to the inventory, and the first-to-file rule would prevail. This assumes that A's filing as to inventory is effective to cover accounts as proceeds under 1972 § 9-306(3) or 1999 § 9-315(d). For discussion of perfection as to proceeds, see Chapter 4, § 8 and Chapter 5, § 4g.

Example 3. C files a financing statement covering all accounts of Debtor. A and B then file as to inventory in the manner and order described in Example 1, above. C's first filing as to accounts has priority over the filings of A and B which would cover the accounts as proceeds of inventory. But if either A or B filed as to inventory before C filed and such filing is good as to accounts as proceeds, the filing preceding C's direct filing as to accounts would prevail.

e. *Where There Is A Consignment*

In most instances, a person who consigns merchandise to another person for resale by the latter runs the risk of losing the consigned goods to the creditors of the consignee, unless the consignor takes one of the steps outlined in § 2-326(3). Generally, the safest course for the consignor to take is to file under Article 9. See § 2-326(3)(c). Additionally, because the 1999 Article 9 includes consignments within its scope [see 1999 § 9-109(a)(4)], this also emphasizes the need for the consignor to file a financing statement to protect his interest in the consigned goods from creditors of the consignee. For discussion of consignments in the light of Article 9, see Chapter 2, § 6e. For discussion of filing where there is a consignment, see Chapter 5, § 12.

In some instances, a consignment may be a secured transaction in the form of inventory financing and thus subject to Article 9 generally. Filing by such a consignor gives him a perfected security interest. Since the consignor has a purchase money security interest in the consigned goods as inventory in the hands of the consignee, he may protect himself against claims of other secured parties with perfected security interests in the consignee's inventory by taking the steps outlined in 1972 § 9-312(3) and 1999 § 9-324(b), that is, by filing before the consignee receives the consigned goods and by giving appropriate notice to other inventory secured parties who have filed. See § 4b(2) of this chapter.

In some other instances, a "true consignment" is not intended as a secured transaction, although the consignor may still file under Article 9 in order to protect his interest against creditors of the consignee. What are the rights of such a consignor who files, as against another person who has a perfected security interest in the inventory of the consignee, which inventory includes the consigned goods?

Third persons, such as other secured parties or creditors of the consignee are in much the same position, whether a consignment is intended as a secured transaction or not. Accordingly, 1972 § 9-114 and 1999 §§ 9-103(d) and 9-324(b) set forth additional steps to be taken by a consignor in a true consignment transaction which is not a secured transaction, in order to obtain priority over a secured party who has filed with respect to inventory, including the consigned goods. The steps to be taken are the same as those required of a secured party with a purchase money security interest in inventory under 1972 § 9-312(3) and 1999 § 9-324(b). In other words, the consignor must file before the consignee receives possession of the goods, and must give written notification to any other secured party who has filed. The notification must state that the consignor expects to deliver goods on consignment to the consignee, and describe the goods by item or type. The notification must be given within five years before the consignee receives the goods.

f. Other Priority Rules

1972 § 9-312(1) declares that the rules of priority stated in other sections of Part 3 of Article 9 (1972 §§ 9-301 through 9-318) shall govern where applicable. Such priority rules are discussed at various places in this chapter.

There are also cross references in 1972 § 9-312(1) to certain other Code provisions which govern priority when applicable.

(1) Reference is made to § 4-210, which states

that the security interest obtained by a bank in an item and accompanying documents handled by the bank for collection has priority over conflicting perfected security interests.

(2) Reference is made to 1972 § 9-103 on security interests related to multi-state transactions, which sets forth rules as to where to perfect and the effect of moving collateral from one jurisdiction to another. For discussion, see Chapter 6.

(3) Reference is made to 1972 § 9-114 governing priority with respect to consignments. See § 4e of this chapter.

1999 § 9-322(f) makes cross references as well, indicating that Part 3 of 1999 Article 9 otherwise sets forth the priority rules that govern security interests.

(1) Reference is made to § 9-322(g) which gives preemptive effect to separate statutory law from UCC Article 9 that governs priority of agricultural liens.

(2) Reference is made to § 4-210 described above.

(3) Reference is made to § 5-118 which is given effect with respect to the security interest of an issuer of a letter of credit or a nominated person.

§ 5-118 is added by the 1999 Code and gives a security interest to an issuer of a letter of credit in a document presented under the letter of credit to the extent that the issuer honors or gives value for the presentation.

(4) Reference is made to 1999 § 9-110 with respect to security interests arising under UCC Article 2 or 2A. See discussion of 1999 § 9-110 in the next section of this chapter.

§ 5.   Unpaid Seller of Goods

In certain instances, an unpaid seller of goods may have a claim to the goods against one who has a perfected security interest extending to such goods, which interest is given by the buyer. The controversy may arise where a buyer of goods has granted a security interest to a lender in all of the buyer's inventory and all after-acquired inventory and where either of the following two situations occurs: (1) a seller sells goods that become part of the buyer's inventory for cash and is paid by the buyer's check which is dishonored for insufficient funds, or (2) a seller sells the goods that become part of the buyer's inventory on credit but discovers that the buyer is insolvent.

The first situation is a cash sale. The buyer's right as against the seller to retain or dispose of the goods is conditional upon his making the payment due, under § 2-507(2). Payment by check is conditional and is defeated as between the parties by dishonor of the check on due presentment, under § 2-511(3).

The second situation is a sale on credit. Under § 2-702(2) and (3), the seller has a right to reclaim the goods upon discovering the insolvency of the buyer on credit, but the seller must normally act within 10 days of receipt by the buyer of the goods.

The 1972 Code does not have a clear answer as to whether the unpaid seller's interest has priority over a security interest granted by the buyer in after-acquired property. In either of the above situations, it would seem that the cash or credit seller should be able to get the goods back against the claim of a secured party of the buyer who has a perfected security interest in the goods as after-acquired property. In particular, it would seem that the seller should prevail if a demand for them is made within 10 days of receipt by the buyer. See § 2-702(2) and Comment 3 to § 2-507, indicating that the 10-day rule also applies in the case of a cash sale, as well as a credit sale. However, case law has generally favored the buyer's secured party in such a situation.

For a leading case, see In re Samuels & Co., Inc. 526 F.2d 1238 (5th Cir. 1976), applying Texas law.

The 1999 Code also does not provide a clear answer to this priority problem. Code Comments appear to reject the case law that gives Article 9 secured parties priority over the unpaid seller's claim to the goods. See Comment 5 to 1999 § 9-110.

For discussion of the right of the unpaid seller for cash or on credit as against the buyer's trustee in bankruptcy, see Chapter 8, § 10.

§ 6. Priority Between Secured Party and Lien Creditor

a. General Rule

The Code does not expressly deal with priority between a secured party with a perfected security interest and a creditor who has subsequently obtained a lien on the collateral by attachment, garnishment, levy or the like. However, it is clearly implied that the secured party with a prior perfected interest should prevail over a subsequent lien creditor, since 1972 § 9-301(1)(b) and 1999 § 9-317(a)(2) make an unperfected security interest subordinate to the rights of a person who becomes a lien creditor before the security interest is perfected. See discussion in § 2a of this chapter.

In other words, if the secured party files or otherwise perfects before the creditor obtains a lien, the secured party has priority. On the other hand, if the creditor obtains a lien before the secured party files or otherwise perfects, the creditor has priority.

CAVEAT. Some state statutes outside the Uniform Commercial Code set forth liens of various kinds which take priority over even an earlier, perfected security interest. Statutes of that nature are varied in scope from state to state.

Note: Federal tax liens can also have priority in certain instances over prior perfected security interests. In addition, some perfected security interests can be set aside in a federal bankruptcy proceeding. For discussion of federal tax liens, see § 6c of this chapter. For discussion of the effect of bankruptcy on a security interest, see Chapter 8 generally.

b. *Future Advances by Secured Party*

The 1972 and 1999 Codes give priority to a subsequent lien creditor against a prior perfected security interest to the extent of certain future advances made by the secured party. Specifically, both versions of Article 9 provide that a person who becomes a lien creditor while a security interest is perfected takes subject to the security interest only to the extent that it secures advances made before he became a lien creditor or within 45 days thereafter or made without knowledge of the lien or pursuant to a commitment entered into without knowledge of the lien. 1972 § 9-301(4) and 1999 § 9-323(b).

Comment 7 to 1972 § 9-301 and Comment 4 to 1999 § 9-323 point out that the purpose of 1972 § 9-301(4) and 1999 § 9-323(b) is to give a perfected security interest priority with respect to future advances for 45 days after a lien is obtained on the collateral, without regard to knowledge of the lien on the part of the secured party. Even after 45 days, the secured party has priority if he makes the advance without knowledge of the lien. Presumably, actual knowledge is necessary; knowledge should not be imputed by reason of the filing of a judgment lien or the like.

These provisions of the 1972 and 1999 Codes dovetail with the 45-day provision of the Federal Tax Lien Act, which is discussed immediately below.

c. Federal Tax Lien

If any person liable to pay any tax to the United States neglects or refuses to pay the same after demand, the amount (including interest and other additions) shall be a lien in favor of the United States upon all property belonging to such person. The lien arises at the time the assessment is made, demand for payment of the tax occurs, and the taxpayer fails to pay the taxes. 26 U.S.C.A. § 6321. The priority of the lien as against third-party claims generally, relates back to the time of assessment of the tax. 26 U.S.C.A. § 6322. However, the lien is not valid as against the holder of a security interest until appropriate notice of the lien is filed. See 26 U.S.C.A. 6323(a).

Filing of a federal tax lien may be made in any place designated by the law of the state where the property subject to the lien is situated, or with the clerk of the local United States District Court if no such state law exists. See 26 U.S.C.A. § 6323(f). Most states have statutes permitting the filing of a federal tax lien in some state, county or other local office.

The federal tax lien is declared in 26 U.S.C.A. § 6323(a) to be inferior to the interest of any purchaser, holder of a security interest, mechanic's lienor or judgment lien creditor until notice of the tax lien has been filed. In other words, if an Article 9 security interest is perfected on a taxpayer's property prior to the time the notice of tax lien is filed, the security interest is given priority over the tax lien.

26 U.S.C.A. § 6323(c) limits priority of the security interest with regard to collateral acquired after the notice of tax lien is filed that becomes subject to a secured party's UCC Article 9 security interest because of an after-acquired property clause in the security agreement. As to such after-acquired collateral, 26 U.S.C.A. § 6323(c) provides for priority of the security interest only if the secured party perfected its security interest prior to the filing of the federal tax lien and made any loans to the taxpayer without knowledge of the tax lien; the collateral must be "commercial financing security," i.e., accounts, chattel paper or instruments; and the collateral must have been acquired within 45 days of the filing of the notice of the federal tax lien.

26 U.S.C.A. § 6323(d) further limits priority of the security interest as to future advances made by the secured party after notice of the tax lien has been filed. In order to have priority as to such advances, the secured party must have perfected its security interest prior to the filing of the notice of the tax lien

and the advance must have been made within 45 days after the filing of the notice of the tax lien or before the secured party obtained knowledge of the federal tax lien filing, which ever first occurs.

d. Artisan's or Repairman's Lien

"When a person in the ordinary course of his business furnishes services or materials with respect to goods subject to a security interest, a lien upon goods in the possession of such person given by statute or rule of law for such materials or services takes priority over a perfected security interest unless the lien is statutory and the statute expressly provides otherwise." 1972 § 9-310. The 1999 Code has reworded this provision but has not changed its substance. 1999 § 9-333.

The above Code provisions recognize that most states have so-called "artisan's lien" statutes which accord to a repairman a lien on goods in his possession for the cost of repairs made or materials used in making repairs. The repairman has a right to payment before being required to surrender the goods to the owner.

1972 § 9-310 and 1999 § 9-333 give the repairman's lien priority over even a perfected security

interest, in the absence of a statute expressly making
the repairman's lien subordinate. The reason for the
Code provisions is that such liens deserve priority,
since the repairman's work has enhanced or preserved the value of the collateral. See Comment 1 to
1972 § 9-310.

There is no requirement of consent on the part of
the secured party that the repairs be made. However, the superiority of the lien over the security
interest depends on possession of the goods by the
repairman; if he surrenders possession before he is
paid, his lien is subordinate to the perfected security
interest.

§ 7. Priority of Security Interest in Fixtures

Significant issues related to priority of claims in
fixtures are dealt with in the 1972 and 1999 Codes.
See 1972 § 9-313 and 1999 § 9-334. These issues
involve the relative priority between a person with
a security interest in fixtures and one or more competing real estate interests. Such real estate interests
might include the interest of an owner of the real
estate (other than the debtor) where the fixtures are
installed, the interest of a mortgagee of the real
estate, the interest of one who has a judgment lien
on the real estate or the interest of a subsequent

purchaser of the real estate. For a definition of "fixtures," see Chapter 1, § 7a(5).

The 1972 and 1999 Codes make it clear in the "filing provisions" of the Codes (1972 §§ 9-401 et seq. and 1999 §§ 9-501 et seq.) that a fixture filing must be made not only at the office where a mortgage on the real estate would be filed or recorded, but also that the filing must be made in the real estate records of that office in such a way as to permit one searching the real estate title to locate the filing.

The provisions of the 1972 and 1999 Codes relating to priority are summarized as follows:

(1) In general, priority over real estate interests is largely governed by fixture filing, or in some instances by perfection in some other manner.

(2) A purchase money security interest in fixtures has priority over the conflicting interest of an encumbrancer or owner arising before the goods become fixtures, if the security interest is perfected by a fixture filing before the goods become fixtures or within 10 days thereafter under the 1972 Code and within 20 days thereafter under the 1999 Code. 1972 § 9-313(4)(a), 1999 § 9-334(d). Even under the 1972 Code, a few states have extended the time period, e.g., to 20 days, by non-uniform amend-

ments to 1972 § 9-313. The debtor must either have an interest of record in the real estate or be in possession.

In other words, the holder of a purchase money security interest (which most security interests in fixtures would be) has a 10-day/ 20-day grace period after installation of the fixture within which to make an effective fixture filing. The requirement that the debtor have an interest of record in the real estate or be in possession makes it clear that a fixture secured party may not defeat real estate interests by taking a security interest against a contractor who has no interest of record or is not in possession. On the other hand, a fixture filing may be made where the debtor is a lessee in possession of the real estate if the name of a record owner is given in the filing. See 1972 § 9-402(5) and Comment 5 to 1972 § 9-313; see also 1999 § 9-502(b)(4).

(3) A security interest in fixtures has priority if it is perfected by a fixture filing before the interest of the encumbrancer or owner is of record, the security interest has priority over any conflicting interest of a predecessor in title of the encumbrancer or owner, and the debtor has an interest of record or is in possession of the real estate. This rule basically gives priority according to the usual priority rule of real estate conveyancing, that is, the first to file or

record prevails. The apparent limitation that the secured party must have priority over any interest of a predecessor in title of the conflicting interest is merely an expression of the usual rule that a person must be entitled to transfer what he has. See 1972 § 9-313(4)(b) and Comment 4(b) to 1972 § 9-313; 1999 § 9-334(e)(1).

Example 1. A purchase money security interest is not filed as a fixture filing within 10 days (under the 1972 Code) or within 20 days (under the 1999 Code) after the fixture is installed. It is thus subordinate to the interest of a prior recorded mortgage. It is also subordinate to the interest of an assignee of the mortgage even though the assignment is recorded after the fixture filing is made.

Example 2. A purchase money security interest is filed as a fixture filing within 10 days (under the 1972 Code) or within 20 days (under the 1999 Code) after the fixture is installed. It is thus superior to the interest of a prior recorded mortgage. It is also superior to the interest of an assignee of the mortgage or to the interest of any subsequent mortgagee or purchaser of the real estate, which interest is recorded after the fixture filing is made.

(4) A security interest has priority if the fixtures are readily removable factory or office machines or

readily removable replacements of domestic appliances which are consumer goods, and before the goods become fixtures, the security interest is perfected by any method permitted under Article 9. 1972 § 9-313(4)(c), 1999 § 9-334(e)(2)(A), (C). In other words, a secured party need not file a fixture filing with respect to readily removable factory or office machines to have priority, but may file with respect to ordinary equipment as a chattel filing. Under 1999 § 9-334 (e)(2)(B) the same rule applies to equipment that is not primarily used or leased for use in the operation of the real property. Where the replacements of domestic appliances are consumer goods, a secured party need not file at all, since perfection takes place automatically upon attachment of the security interest under 1972 § 9-302(1)(d), 1999 § 9-309(1).

(5) A security interest in fixtures has priority if the conflicting interest is a lien on the real estate obtained by legal or equitable proceedings after the security interest was perfected by any method permitted under Article 9, i.e., filing a financing statement or filing a fixture filing. 1972 § 9-313(4)(d), 1999 § 9-334(e)(3). This recognizes that a judgment lien creditor is not a "reliance creditor" who would have searched records. Moreover, the provision is intended to make certain that a security

interest in a fixture which is perfected in any manner should be considered as perfected in the event of subsequent bankruptcy of the debtor. See Comment 4(c) to 1972 § 9-313 and Comment 9 to 1999 § 9-334. This should protect a perfected security interest from a claim under the "strong-arm" clause of the Bankruptcy Code, no matter how the interest was perfected. For discussion of the "strong-arm" clause, see Chapter 8, § 4.

Example 3. Debtor purchases a new heating/air-conditioning unit for installation on his business premises. Although the unit is a fixture, Secured Party who has a purchase money security interest in the unit files in the office or offices where a filing should be made on ordinary chattels as equipment. Creditor subsequently obtains a judgment lien on the real estate where the unit is installed. Although Secured Party did not make a fixture filing, he has a perfected security interest good against Creditor. Note that if the unit had been installed as a replacement of a similar unit in a home, the security interest could be perfected without filing and would be good against any encumbrancer or owner of the home.

(6) A security interest in fixtures, whether or not perfected, has priority over the conflicting interest of an encumbrancer or owner who has consented in writing to the security interest or has disclaimed an

interest in the goods as fixtures. The security interest also has priority if the debtor has a right to remove the goods as against the encumbrancer or owner. 1972 § 9-313(5), 1999 § 9-334(f). This latter provision should apply in a case where the fixture is installed on land leased by the debtor and where the lease permits the debtor to remove the fixture. Examples are mobile homes or prefabricated buildings placed on leased land. See Comment 2 to 1972 § 9-313.

(7) A purchase money security interest in fixtures is subordinate to a construction mortgage which is recorded before the goods become fixtures if the goods become fixtures before completion of the construction. A subsequent mortgage given to refinance the construction mortgage has the same priority. 1972 § 9-313(6), 1999 § 9-334(h). The reason for giving priority to the construction mortgagee is to prevent the double-financing of fixtures where funds to purchase the goods are obtained from the mortgagee and the fixtures are then purchased on credit from a supplier. The latter who sells on credit for installation in a house or building under construction should protect himself by checking the real estate records before allowing the credit sale. Note that this rule does not apply where additions are made to a building after completion of the improve-

ment and are financed under an "open-end" clause of a construction mortgage or refinancing mortgage. See Comment 4(e) to 1972 § 9-313 and Comment 11 to 1999 § 9-334.

(8) In any case not specified above, a security interest in fixtures is subordinate to the conflicting interest of an encumbrancer or owner of the related real estate who is not the debtor. 1972 § 9-313(7), 1999 § 9-334(c).

(9) Article 9 does not prevent creation of an encumbrance upon fixtures pursuant to real estate law. 1972 § 9-313(3), 1999 § 9-334(b). However, note that a recorded real estate mortgage is ineffective to cover nonfixture personal property on the mortgaged premises, as against the interest of a secured party. A mortgagee desiring to cover such nonfixture property should take action to perfect his interest under Article 9, as by filing in the chattel records.

The 1999 Code adds special provisions dealing with manufactured homes. Generally, a security interest in a manufactured home has priority over an encumbrancer or owner if the security interest is created pursuant to statutory law separate from the Code. See 1999 §§ 9-334(e)(4); 9-311(a)(2); 9-102(a)(53), (54).

The 1999 Code also indicates that a perfected security interest in crops growing on real property has priority over a conflicting interest of an encumbrancer or owner of the real property if the debtor has an interest of record or is in possession of the real property. 1999 § 9-334(i).

§ 8. Priority of Security Interest in Accessions

In certain instances, a security interest may be taken in goods which are installed or affixed to other goods, which are called "accessions," such as a new motor installed in an automobile. Another person may have a competing claim to the whole of the goods in which the accession is installed, such as a person with a security interest in the automobile in which the new motor is installed. The treatment of such priority issues related to accessions varies significantly between the 1972 and 1999 Codes.

a. Priority in Accessions Under the 1972 Code

1972 § 9-314 sets forth rules of priority between a secured party with an interest in an accession and a competing claim to the whole of the goods.

Essentially, a person with a perfected security

interest in an accession has priority with respect to the accession over all competing interests in the whole of the goods. A secured party who does not perfect but whose interest attaches before the goods become part of the whole has priority over the existing claims of all others to the whole, but not over a person acquiring a subsequent interest in the whole without knowledge of the security interest and before perfection. Such a secured party also does not have priority over a prior perfected security interest in the whole to the extent of subsequent advances made before the "accession" secured party perfects his interest.

An "accession" secured party whose interest attaches after the accession becomes part of the whole generally does not have priority over competing existing interests in the whole and also does not have priority over subsequent interests in the whole if the interest of the "accession" secured party is not perfected.

The rules relating to security interests in accessions under 1972 § 9-314 are expressly made subject to the rules of 1972 § 9-315, governing security interests in raw materials or components which are processed into finished goods.

b. Priority in Accessions Under the 1999 Code

1999 § 9-335 sets forth rules of priority between a secured party with an interest in an accession and a competing claim to the whole goods. Unlike the 1972 Code, the 1999 Code provides a definition of "accession." Accordingly, an accession means goods that are physically united with other goods in such an manner that the identity of the original goods is not lost. 1999 § 9-102(a)(1). A good is an accession regardless of the cost or difficulty of removing the accession from the other goods and regardless of whether the original goods have come to form an integral part of the other goods; however, if the identity of the goods is lost, the good is not an accession and 1999 § 9-335 is inapplicable. See Comment 2 to § 9-335. If a security interest is perfected in goods when the goods become an accession, the security interest remains perfected thereafter. 1999 § 9-335(a), (b).

Subject to only one exception, the 1999 Code indicates that the priority rules governing priority of a security interest found in other provisions of Part 3 of 1999 Article 9 will apply. Thus, for example, when appropriate, the first-to-file-or-perfect rule of 1999 § 9-322(a)(1) or the purchase money security rule of 1999 § 9-324(a) will apply. The one exception involves certificate-of-title collateral. A security interest in an accession is subordinate to a security interest in the whole which is perfected by compliance with certificate-of-title statutes. 1999 §§ 9-335(d), 9-311(b).

§ 9. Priority When Goods are Commingled or Processed

If a secured party claims an interest in the "products" of collateral under the 1972 Code, he may do so by checking a box in a standard form of financing statement reading "Products of the collateral are also covered." The reason for claiming "products" of collateral is to follow a security interest into finished goods when the secured party finances a part of a manufacturing process. This is unnecessary under the 1999 Code because the security interest automatically attaches to the product. 1999 § 9-336(c).

Under 1972 § 9-315(1), if a security interest in goods was perfected and the goods become part of a product or mass, the security interest continues in the product or mass if (a) the goods are so commingled into the product or mass that their identity is lost, or (b) the financing statement covering the original goods also covers the product. Where the financing statement covers the product of collateral, no separate security interest may be claimed under

1972 § 9-314 dealing with accessions.

Under 1999 § 9-336(a)-(d), a security interest does not exist in commingled goods but does attach to a product or mass when goods are physically united with other goods in a manner that their identity is lost in the product or mass; if the security interest was perfected in goods before commingling, the security interest remains perfected in the product or mass.

Where "more than one security interest attaches to the product or mass, they rank equally according to the ratio that the cost of the goods to which each interest originally attached bears to the cost of the total product or mass." 1972 § 9-315(2), 1999 § 9-336(f)(2).

The above rules apply not only to processing where raw materials lose their identity when processed into finished goods, but also where components are assembled into a machine. See Comment 3 to 1972 § 9-315. Similarly, see Comment 2 to 1999 § 9-336, which gives as an example ball bearings in a machine.

§ 10. Priority When Goods are Returned or Repossessed

A priority problem may sometimes arise where there are conflicting security interests with respect to returned or repossessed goods. In some instances, a seller of goods may finance his inventory with one secured party. When he sells an item of inventory other than for cash, an account may arise or chattel paper may be given by the debtor to the seller. The seller may then assign the account or chattel paper to a second secured party. If the goods are later returned to the seller by the buyer voluntarily for any reason or are repossessed by the seller (which he may do under 1972 and 1999 §§ 9-205 if he handles his own collections), a conflict may arise between the inventory secured party and the secured party taking the assignment of the account or chattel paper.

The 1972 Code deals with such conflicting security interests in 1972 § 9-306(5) and Comment 4, which may be summarized as follows:

a. The inventory secured party with a security interest in the goods before sale automatically has a security interest in the returned goods if the original debt is unpaid. If the security interest had been perfected at the time of sale by a still-effective filing, it remains perfected automatically upon return of the goods; otherwise, the secured party must take possession of the returned goods or must file.

b. An unpaid transferee of chattel paper taken when the goods were sold has priority with respect to the returned goods over the inventory secured party if the chattel paper transferee had priority over the inventory secured party with respect to the chattel paper itself under 1972 § 9-308. For discussion of priority under 1972 § 9-308, see §3f of this chapter.

c. An unpaid transferee of an account arising after the sale of the goods has a security interest in the returned goods subordinate to the interest of the inventory secured party, if the latter's security interest is perfected.

d. An unpaid transferee of chattel paper or an account must perfect his security interest in the returned goods for protection against creditors of the seller-transferor and purchasers of the returned or repossessed goods. In other words, the unpaid transferee must file or take possession of the returned goods; his security interest does not automatically carry over to the returned goods as does the security interest of the inventory secured party.

Note however that if the seller again sells the

returned goods to a second buyer who is a buyer in the ordinary course of business, the buyer is fully protected against either the inventory secured party or the secured party having an interest in the chattel paper or account. See Comment 4 to 1972 § 9-306.

The 1999 Code deals with such conflicting security interests in 1999 § 9-330. See Comments 9-11 to 1999 § 9-330. However, the 1999 Code actually has no exact equivalent to 1972 § 9-306(5), discussed immediately above. See Comment 8 to 1999 § 9-315. Even so, according to the Comments 9-11 of 1999 § 9-330, the priority rules regarding returned or repossessed goods have not been changed by the 1999 Code.

§ 11. Investment Property

The 1972 Code (as revised) provides special priority rules when the collateral is investment property. For a general discussion of investment property and perfection of security interests therein, see Chapter 4, § 4b and Chapter 1, § 9a(3).

1972 § 9-115(5)(a) provides that a security interest that is perfected by "control" over the investment property has priority over a security interest of another secured party who does not have control. Perfection by control is considered in Chapter 4, § 4b and Chapter 5, § 12a. If the conflicting security interests are both perfected by control, they rank equally, subject to two exceptions. 1972 § 9-115(5) (b). The exceptions are set forth in 1972 § 9-115(5) (c), (d). In all other cases, i.e., where neither secured party has "control," the usual priority rules applicable to perfected security interests apply to investment property. 1972 § 9-115(5)(f); see also 1972 § 9-312(5), (6) and (7).

The 1999 Code rules regarding priority of security interests in investment property are very similar to the 1972 provisions just discussed. 1999 § 9-328. However, there is at least one significant difference. When conflicting security interests are both perfected by control, the priority of the security interest is determined on the basis of which party first obtained control; that party is given priority, unlike the 1972 Code which ranks security interests in investment property perfected by control equally. Compare 1972 § 9-115(5)(b) to 1999 § 9-328(2)(A).

§ 12. Deposit Accounts Under the 1999 Code

The 1999 Code governs secured transactions when the collateral is a non-consumer deposit account. See 1999 §§ 9-109(a), (d)(13); 9-102(a)

(29) and discussion at Chapter 1, § 7. As a result, priority rules were added to deal with priority disputes involving deposit accounts. Such rules were not included in the 1972 Code because secured transactions in deposit accounts were not included within the scope of the 1972 Code unless proceeds from other collateral were deposited into an account.

A security interest perfected by control of a deposit account has priority over a conflicting security interest of another secured party who does not have control. 1999 § 9-327(1). Perfection by control is considered in Chapter 4, § 12a. If both security interests are perfected by control, they rank according to priority in time of obtaining control. 1999 § 9-327(2). On the other hand, a security interest held by the bank at which the account is maintained has priority over another secured party's security interest unless that secured party perfected it's security interest by control, in which case that security interest is given priority. 1999 § 9-327(3), (4). If funds are transferred from a deposit account, usually the transferee will take free of the security interest in the account. 1999 § 9-332(b).

A separate priority issue involving deposit accounts arises when a secured party has a security interest in a debtor's account or can trace proceeds from other collateral into the account. If the depositary bank has made a loan to the debtor-account holder and that loan is in default, the bank has a common-law right to set off the loan against the account. The issue arises as to who has priority in the account—the bank asserting its setoff right or the UCC Article 9 secured party. The 1999 Code provides that the bank has priority unless the secured party has perfected its security interest by control, in which case the secured party is given priority. 1999 § 9-340. See also related 1999 §§ 9-341, 9-342.

§ 13. Letter-of-Credit Rights Under the 1999 Code

The 1999 Code governs secured transactions when the collateral is a letter-of-credit right. See 1999 §§ 9-109(a), 9-102(a)(51), and discussion at Chapter 1, § 7 and Chapter 4, § 12a. As a result, priority rules were added to deal with priority disputes over letter-of-credit rights. Such rules were not included in the 1972 Code because secured transactions in letter-of-credit rights were not included within the scope of the 1972 Code. It should be noted that even the 1999 Code is inapplicable to the extent that the rights of a transferee beneficiary or nominated person under a letter of credit are independent and superior under § 5-114.

A security interest perfected by control of a letter-of-credit right has priority over a conflicting interest of another secured party who does not have control. 1999 § 9-329(1). Perfection by control is considered in Chapter 4, § 12a. If both security interests are perfected by control, they rank according to priority in time of obtaining control. 1999 § 9-329(2).

§ 14. Agricultural Liens Under the 1999 Code

The 1999 Code has included agricultural liens within its scope. 1999 §§ 9-109(a)(2), 9-102(a)(5). Such liens were beyond the scope of the 1972 Code. For discussion of agricultural liens as included within the scope of the 1999 Code, see Chapter 1, § 3 and Chapter 4, § 12b.

The inclusion of agricultural liens within 1999 Article 9 necessitated inclusion of priority rules applicable to such liens. For the most part, the priority rules applicable to unperfected and perfected security interests also apply to agricultural liens. For example, such rules include the first-to-file-or-perfect rule of 1999 § 9-322(a). For discussion of this rule, see § 4a(1) of this chapter. However, 1999 § 9-322(g) provides that a perfected agricultural lien on collateral has priority over a security interest in or agricultural lien on the same collateral if the statute creating the agricultural lien so provides. In other words, the statute creating the agricultural lien can preempt application of the usual Code priority rules. See also Comment 12 to 1999 § 9-322.

§ 15. "Double Debtor Problem" Under 1999 Code

Sometimes a debtor acquires property that is subject to a security interest created by another debtor.

Example. Adams owns an item of equipment subject to a security interest he granted to Old Bank. Adams sells the equipment to Baker, the latter taking the equipment subject to Old Bank's security interest. Baker then grants a security interest to New Bank. Who has priority to the equipment—Old Bank or New Bank?

The 1972 Code did not have a provision directly on point. The 1999 Code would usually give priority to Old Bank. 1999 § 9-325(a) gives Old Bank priority as long as Old Bank's security interest was perfected when Baker acquired the equipment and remained perfected subsequently. There are some exceptions to this priority rule but those exceptions apply only in unusual situations. See 1999 § 9-325(b) and Comment 6 to 1999 § 9-325.

§ 16. Priority of Security Interests Created by A "New Debtor" Under 1999 Code

The 1999 Code addresses the priority issues that arise when a new debtor becomes bound by a security agreement of an original debtor but where each debtor has a secured creditor.

Example. Old Bank has acquired a security interest in Adams' existing and after-acquired inventory. Old Bank perfected by filing a financing statement. New Bank has acquired a perfected security interest in Baker's existing and after-acquired inventory. New Bank perfected by filing a financing statement. Baker later becomes bound as debtor by Adams' security agreement because Baker has acquired Adams' business and has assumed Adams' debtor to Old Bank. Subsequently, Baker acquires a new item of inventory. Who has priority in the new item of inventory—Old Bank or New Bank?

The 1972 Code did not have a provision directly on point. Under the 1999 Code at § 9-508, Old Bank's financing statement is effective to perfect a security interest in the new item of inventory in which Baker has rights. However, 1999 § 9-326(a) gives priority to New Bank regardless of whether New Bank filed its financing statement before Old Bank filed its financing statement. See Comment 1 to 1999 § 9-326, Example 2.

CHAPTER 8

BANKRUPTCY OR
INSOLVENCY OF DEBTOR

§ 1. General Effect of Insolvency

In some instances, the debtor in a secured transaction may become insolvent. Under § 1-201(23), a person is "insolvent" who "either has ceased to pay his debts in the ordinary course of business or cannot pay his debts as they become due or is insolvent within the meaning of the federal bankruptcy law." In many instances, when a debtor becomes insolvent, some form of "insolvency proceedings" may ensue. That term is defined in § 1-201(22) as including "any assignment for the benefit of creditors or other proceedings intended to liquidate or rehabilitate the estate of the person involved."

Insolvency proceedings may be instituted by or against an insolvent debtor under either state law or under the federal Bankruptcy Code. Normally, federal bankruptcy procedures will be utilized. However, where state law is utilized, there may be

an informal arrangement between the debtor and
creditors, including a composition with creditors or
an extension of time of payment, or both.   The
debtor may also make an assignment for the benefit
of creditors or the court may appoint a receiver to
manage the debtor's assets on behalf of his creditors.
Note that Uniform Commercial Code 1972 § 9-
301(3) and 1999 § 9-102(a)(52) declare that an
assignee for the benefit of creditors is a lien creditor
from the time of assignment and a receiver in equity
is a lien creditor from the time of appointment.
Such a representative of creditors has lien creditor
status even though the creditors represented are
general creditors and not lien creditors.

It follows that an assignee for the benefit of
creditors or a receiver has priority as a lien creditor
over an unperfected security interest under 1972 § 9-
301(1)(b) and 1999 § 9-317(a)(2). See Chapter 7,
§ 2a.

Conversely, a security interest which has been
perfected at the time an assignment for the benefit of
creditors is made or at the time a receiver is appointed has priority over the subsequent lien of the
assignee or receiver. Note, however, that there is a
possibility of attacking a perfected security interest
as a fraudulent transfer under state law where the
value of the collateral is substantially dispropor-

tionate to the debt secured or where there are other facts indicating that the interest is taken in fraud of other creditors of the debtor. See Uniform Fraudulent Transfer Act § 4.

§ 2. A Brief Summary of Federal Bankruptcy Law

a. The Statute

Some knowledge of federal bankruptcy law is necessary when considering the impact of bankruptcy on a secured transaction. The summary here is necessarily brief; other sources should be consulted for general discussion of bankruptcy law. Among such sources, see Epstein, Nickles, and White, BANKRUPTCY. For other discussion of the effect of bankruptcy on secured transactions, see White & Summers, 4th ed., Chapter 23.

The law of bankruptcy is federal law under U.S. Constitution Art. 1, § 8, cl. 4. Bankruptcy statutes have often referred to state law or permitted the use of state law for particular purposes, such as UCC Article 9. For many years, bankruptcy and certain proceedings directed toward rehabilitation of a debtor in financial straits were governed by the Bankruptcy Act of 1898, referred to in this Nutshell as the "1898 Act." In 1978, Congress enacted a new statute known as the "Bankruptcy Reform Act of 1978." The new act is referred to in this Nutshell as the "Bankruptcy Code." References to the "Code" are to the Uniform Commercial Code. The Bankruptcy Code completely replaced the 1898 Act and applies to bankruptcy proceedings commenced on or after October 1, 1979. The substantive provisions of the Bankruptcy Code are in Title I, codified in revised Title 11 U.S.C.A. Congress has amended the Bankruptcy Code in 1984, 1986, 1988, 1990, 1992 and 1994. Congress is contemplating further amendments to the Bankruptcy Code at the time of writing this Nutshell. References in this Nutshell to sections of the Bankruptcy Code as amended are to those sections as codified in 11 U.S.C.A. For example, a reference to Bankruptcy Code § 547 is to 11 U.S.C.A. § 547.

One of the reasons a creditor obtains a security interest in the debtor's property is to better the creditor's prospects of collection if the debtor ends up in bankruptcy. However, it may be said that the lot of the secured party in an Article 9 transaction is not always a particularly happy one, where the debtor files bankruptcy or an involuntary bankruptcy proceeding is filed by creditors against a debtor under the Bankruptcy Code. Bankruptcy has far-reaching effects on an Article 9 security interest. At the worst, the security interest may be set aside or rendered ineffective, with the secured party relegated to the position of an unsecured general creditor of the insolvent debtor. Even at best, as where the security interest is "impregnably" perfected, the secured party is usually subject to the jurisdiction of the bankruptcy court and sometimes to the whims of the debtor's trustee in bankruptcy in dealing with the collateral. In short, the remedies of the secured party under Uniform Commercial Code 1972 § 9-501 et seq. and 1999 § 9-601 et seq. are considerably curtailed as against a bankrupt debtor. Various problems of bankruptcy as affecting secured transactions are discussed in detail in the balance of this chapter of the Nutshell.

b. *The General Nature of Bankruptcy*

The traditional aim of bankruptcy has been to enable an impecunious debtor to "get a new start in life" at least in a financial sense. The Bankruptcy Code contemplates that a bankrupt individual debtor may obtain, in most instances, a discharge of most (though not necessarily all) debts owed. A "discharge" means that the debtor need not pay his debts except to the extent required in the bankruptcy proceeding. See Bankruptcy Code § 727. This is usually accomplished through the appointment of a trustee who gathers together and converts into cash the debtor's non-exempt assets for ratable distribution to creditors in accordance with a statutory scheme of priorities. It follows that most bankruptcy cases are *liquidation* proceedings (or "straight bankruptcy" cases under the former law) governed by Bankruptcy Code Chapter 7, § 701 et seq.

In some instances, *rehabilitation* of the debtor is the objective, rather than liquidation and distribution to creditors of the debtor's non-exempt assets. The creditors look more to future earnings of the debtor to satisfy claims in whole or in part. Bankruptcy Code Chapter 11, § 1101 et seq., deals with rehabilitation or reorganization of a business debtor, who may be an individual or an entity such as a corporation or partnership.

Rehabilitation is also the objective in a proceeding under Bankruptcy Code Chapter 13, § 1301 et seq., which provides for adjustment of the debts of an individual with "regular income" and obligations of fixed unsecured debts of less than $269,250 and of fixed secured debts of less than $807,750.

A third rehabilitation procedure is provided for at Bankruptcy Code Chapter 12, § 1201 et seq. It provides for adjustment of debts of a family farmer with regular income and will not be considered in this Nutshell. Chapter 12 is in large part patterned after Bankruptcy Code Chapter 13.

General provisions of the Bankruptcy Code, Chapters 1, 3 and 5, §§ 101 et seq., 301 et seq. and 501 et seq., apply to liquidation cases under Chapter 7 and rehabilitation cases under Chapters 11 or 13 unless otherwise specified. There is also a Bankruptcy Code Chapter 9, § 901 et seq. dealing with adjustment of debts of a municipality, which should rarely if ever affect secured transactions under Uniform Commercial Code Article 9. Note that 1972 § 9-104(e) specifically excludes from Article 9 transfers by a government or governmental subdivision or agency. Under 1999 § 9-109(c)(2) and (3), UCC Article 9 applies to security interests created by a State, foreign country, or a governmental unit of either, except to the extent that another statute governs the issue in question.

Bankruptcy and rehabilitation cases are heard in *bankruptcy courts* which exist in each federal judicial district. A bankruptcy court has broad jurisdiction over all of the property, wherever located, of the debtor, as of the time of commencement of the case. The court has broad powers covering virtually all aspects of bankruptcy or rehabilitation. The judge of such a court is called a *bankruptcy judge*. The powers of a bankruptcy judge are somewhat limited under the Bankruptcy Code.

Most Bankruptcy Code cases start with filing by the debtor of a *voluntary petition* under Chapter 7 or, in some instances, Chapter 11, 12 or 13. See Bankruptcy Code § 301. In certain instances, creditors of a debtor may file an *involuntary petition* against a debtor under Chapter 7 or Chapter 11, but not under Chapter 12 or 13. See Bankruptcy Code § 303. The petition is filed in the bankruptcy court and the case is then commenced. *The time of filing of the petition is the time of the bankruptcy.*

The next event after the filing of a petition is a meeting of creditors under Bankruptcy Code § 341. This meeting usually results in election by the creditors of a *trustee*, if the proceeding is a liquidation case. See Bankruptcy Code § 702.

The trustee is essentially a creature of federal law acting as a representative of general creditors, and having various statutory duties and powers. In a liquidation proceeding, the general duties of the trustee are to "collect and reduce to money the property of the state for which such trustee serves, and close such estate as expeditiously as is compatible with the best interests of parties in interest." Bankruptcy Code § 704(1). In this connection, "property of the estate" is described in seven numbered subparagraphs of Bankruptcy Code § 541 (a). This includes, under Bankruptcy Code § 541(a)(1), "all legal or equitable interests of the debtor in property as of the commencement of the case." Thus, it is clear that property of the estate includes the debtor's property subject to a security interest, even if the interest is perfected. Whether the debtor or secured party has "title" to the collateral is irrelevant. In this connection, see Uniform Commercial Code 1972 § 9-202 and 1999 § 9-202.

In a Chapter 11 proceeding, the debtor ordinarily remains in possession of the property of the estate and assumes most of the powers of the trustee. See Bankruptcy Code § 1107. Although no trustee is appointed in most instances, one may be appointed; and where no trustee is appointed, an examiner with somewhat limited powers may be appointed. See Bankruptcy Code § 1104.

In a Chapter 13 case, the court appoints the trustee and there may be a "standing trustee" named by the court to handle Chapter 13 cases in the judicial district. See Bankruptcy Code § 1302.

Although liquidation under Chapter 7 ordinarily

results in disposition of collateral subject to a security interest (see § 3d of this chapter of the Nutshell), the debtor in a Chapter 11, 12 or 13 proceeding is often allowed to retain and use the collateral, even where the secured obligation is in default. The reason is that such a rehabilitation proceeding often takes the form of extension of the time of payment and perhaps scaling down the indebtedness. Continued use of the collateral by the debtor is often necessary to permit the carrying out of the rehabilitation plan. Even in a Chapter 7 liquidation, there may be instances where it is advantageous to permit continued use of the collateral on behalf of the debtor's estate for a limited period.

§ 3.   General Effect on Secured Transactions

a. *Stay of Enforcement of Security Interest*

Bankruptcy Code § 362(a) provides for an "automatic stay." It is effective upon the filing of a bankruptcy petition. This is very broad in scope and bars virtually all collection efforts against the debtor. *Thus, any act which a secured party might take against a debtor or the debtor's property is automatically suspended or barred, upon the filing of a petition under Bankruptcy Code Chapters 7, 11, 12 or 13.* A secured party may not collect the debt, obtain or enforce a judgment, make a setoff, repossess the collateral or perfect a security interest (except as indicated below).

Bankruptcy Code § 362(b) sets forth some exceptions to the automatic stay. This includes the right of a secured party to perfect a security interest if such perfection would, under state law, be retroactive to a date before the filing of the petition. Bankruptcy Code §§ 362(b)(3) and 546(b). This means that a security interest may be perfected by filing within 10 days under the 1972 Code and within 20 days under the 1999 Code after the debtor receives possession of the collateral even if such perfection by filing takes place after the filing of the petition under the Bankruptcy Code. Thus, the Bankruptcy Code substantially adopts the 10-day rule of Uniform Commercial Code 1972 § 9-301(2) and the 20-day rule of 1999 § 9-317(e) applicable to purchase-money security interests. Note that if a state with the 1972 Code provides for a non-uniform grace period such as 20 days, the 20-day period would be applicable.

Example. Debtor gives a purchase-money security interest, receives possession of the collateral on May 1 and files a bankruptcy petition on May 6. Secured party may effectively file a financing statement on or before May 10, even with knowledge of the bankruptcy filing, assuming that the uniform 10-day grace period of 1972 § 9-301(2) or 20-day grace period of 1999 § 9-317(e) is enacted in the applicable state.

Provision is made in Bankruptcy Code § 362(d)-(g) for relief under certain circumstances from the automatic stay. A secured party may request such relief as a "party in interest" and the court shall grant it for cause, including the lack of "adequate protection" of the security interest. See Bankruptcy Code § 362(d)(1). The issue of "adequate protection" is covered in Bankruptcy Code § 361. This permits protection of a secured party's interest by such means as periodic cash payments to the extent of a decrease in value of the collateral, an additional or replacement lien, or other relief (except allowance of compensation as an "administrative expense") as will result in the realization of the "indubitable equivalent" of the interest in the property. The meaning of "indubitable equivalent" is not clear and it is the function of the bankruptcy court to decide what is an "indubitable equivalent" in a particular case.

Relief may also be granted from the automatic stay if "the debtor does not have an equity" in the collateral, as where the secured debt exceeds the value of the collateral, and the property "is not necessary to an effective reorganization." Bankruptcy Code § 362(d)(2). A stay is terminated 30 days after the request is made unless the court takes other action. Provision is made for a preliminary hearing and a final hearing by the court and for a continuation of the stay or early relief from the stay under certain circumstances. Bankruptcy Code § 362(e) and (f).

The party requesting relief from the stay "has the burden of proof on the issue of the debtor's equity in property; and the party opposing such relief has the burden of proof on all other issues." Bankruptcy Code § 362(g).

b. *Turnover of Collateral by Secured Party*

Bankruptcy Code § 542(a) basically requires the turnover of the property of the debtor's estate to the trustee. This means that a secured party in possession, whether by original pledge or by repossession under Uniform Commercial Code 1972 § 9-503 or 1999 § 9-609, must deliver the collateral to the trustee, unless excused by the court. This is so, even if the security interest has been perfected and is immune from attack under the Bankruptcy Code, although such a perfected interest ordinarily retains that status under the Bankruptcy Code. In some instances, particularly in a Chapter 7 case, the secured party in possession may be permitted to retain possession.

c. *Abandonment by the Trustee*

The trustee is permitted, after notice and a hearing, to "abandon any property of the estate that is burdensome to the estate or that is of inconsequential value and benefit to the estate." Bankruptcy Code § 554(a). The court may also order abandonment at the request "of a party in interest." Bankruptcy Code § 554(b). This should permit abandonment by the trustee of collateral that is valued at less than the secured debt and allow the secured party to take and dispose of such collateral under Uniform Commercial Code 1972 § 9–501 et seq. and 1999 § 9–601 et seq. The provisions for abandonment are in addition to the provision for relief from the automatic stay, discussed in § 3a of this chapter of the Nutshell.

d. *Sale or Disposition of Collateral*

Bankruptcy Code § 363 provides for sale of the collateral by the trustee. In most instances, the sale must either be authorized by the secured party or authorized by the bankruptcy court. Provision is made for "adequate protection" of the interest of the secured party when the trustee sells the collateral (see discussion of "adequate protection" in § 3d of this chapter of the Nutshell). In most instances, the sale is free and clear of the security interest or any other interest; but the "adequate protection" given the secured party substitutes for the collateral now sold. Bankruptcy Code § 363 also authorizes use or lease of the collateral by the estate.

In certain instances, a trustee may borrow on the collateral on behalf of the debtor's estate. Although a lender to the trustee will generally occupy a status inferior to that of a secured party with a perfected interest in the collateral, Bankruptcy Code § 364(d) permits borrowing by the trustee and the granting to the new lender of superpriority over the secured party with respect to the collateral. However, where such superpriority is allowed, there must be "adequate protection" to the secured party. (See discussion of "adequate protection" in § 3d of this chapter of the Nutshell.)

Generally, borrowing will take place only where the trustee (or debtor in possession) continues to operate the debtor's business, and such borrowing must be approved by the bankruptcy court. This will normally occur in a Chapter 11 proceeding, and is rather unlikely in a Chapter 7 or Chapter 13 proceeding.

e. *Status of Secured Party*

Bankruptcy Code § 506 deals with the determination of secured status. The court may allow a claim "secured by a lien on property in which the estate has an interest." Where the secured party is unable to obtain relief from an automatic stay (see § 3a of this chapter of the Nutshell) or obtain abandonment of the collateral (see § 3c of this chapter of the Nutshell), it is often necessary for the secured party to participate in the bankruptcy case.

If the value of the collateral exceeds the secured debt, the secured party may claim in that status, assuming that the security interest was perfected prior to the debtor's bankruptcy and is not subject to attack as a preference or otherwise. The secured party is entitled after the sale of the collateral under Bankruptcy Code § 363 to full payment of the secured debt, plus interest, together with reasonable fees, costs or charges provided by the security agreement or other agreement. See Bankruptcy Code § 506(b). However, the trustee may also recover from the proceeds of the sale "reasonable, necessary costs and expenses of preserving, or disposing of, such property to the extent of any benefit" to the secured party. Bankruptcy Code § 506(c).

If the collateral is valued at less than the debt secured, the secured party may file proof of claim as an unsecured creditor to the extent of the debt exceeding the value of the collateral. Bankruptcy Code § 506(a). It should be noted that Bankruptcy Code §§ 501 and 502 cover the filing and allowance of claims generally against the debtor's estate.

It also should be noted that even though a bankruptcy discharges the debt, i.e. the debtor's personal liability is terminated, the lien resulting from the security interest is not so affected.

f. Unenforceable Security Interest

A security interest that is unenforceable against the debtor is equally unenforceable against the debtor's estate. This is made clear by Bankruptcy Code § 558, which gives the debtor's estate the benefit of any defense available to the debtor against a third person, "including statutes of limitations, statutes of frauds, usury, and other personal defenses." A waiver by the debtor after commencement of the case is ineffective.

This means that a security interest which does not attach under Uniform Commercial Code 1972 § 9-203(1) or 1999 § 9-203(b) is not enforceable in bankruptcy. As to the requirements of a writing or possession and other requirements for attachment, see Chapter 2 and Chapter 3, § 1 of this Nutshell.

Moreover, Bankruptcy Code § 558 should enable the trustee to set aside a secured transaction for any other reason that would have enabled the debtor to get out of the deal, such as unconscionability where applicable to a credit sale of goods under Uniform Commercial Code § 2-302, fraud, duress, undue influence, mutual mistake, or any defense available under a consumer-protective statute.

§ 4.   The "Strong-Arm" Provisions of the Bankruptcy Code

Bankruptcy Code § 544(a), like its predecessor of the 1898 Act, might sometimes (perhaps with some exaggeration) be referred to as the "strong-arm" clause. *It basically allows the trustee to set aside an unperfected security interest* and relegate the unperfected secured party to general creditor status. Thus, the collateral would now be sold and the proceeds applied to all unsecured claims, as opposed to being used to satisfy exclusively the unperfected secured party's claim. Bankruptcy Code § 544(a) enables the trustee to avoid any transfer of property that is voidable by (1) a creditor who obtains a judicial lien on the collateral, (2) a creditor who extends credit and then obtains an unsatisfied execution lien on the collateral, and (3) a bona fide purchaser of real property other than fixtures from the debtor against whom applicable law permits such transfer to be perfected.

The first two rules above are similar to rules of the 1898 Act. The latter rule (referring to a bona fide purchaser of real property) was not in the 1898 Act. Whether the strong-arm clause could also apply to set aside a security interest in a fixture which was perfected by a means other than by a fixture filing (see Chapter 7, § 7 of this Nutshell) was none too clear prior to the 1984 amendments to the Bankruptcy Code. The 1984 amendments clarify the rules as to fixtures and would give priority to a security interest in a fixture perfected by any means prior to bankruptcy.

It is important to note that the trustee is given the status of an ideal judgment creditor, execution creditor or real estate purchaser. Moreover, the "strong-arm" clause applies whether or not a judgment creditor, lien creditor or real estate purchaser actually exists. As such a creditor or real estate purchaser, the trustee may defeat the holder of a security interest which is unperfected at the time of filing of the petition.

The "strong-arm" clause is given full recognition in 1972 § 9-301(1)(b), (3) and 1999 §§ 9-317(a)(2), 9-102(a)(52) of the Uniform Commercial Code, which makes a security interest subordinate to the rights of a person who becomes a lien creditor before the security interest is perfected, and which explicitly recognizes a trustee in bankruptcy as such a lien creditor as of the date of filing of the petition. In other words, the trustee not only succeeds to the debtor's rights in the collateral, but is "promoted" to the status of a lien creditor and a bona fide purchaser of real property, even though the creditors represented are general creditors without a lien.

Although the trustee as a lien creditor under the "strong-arm" clause has priority over the rights of a secured party with an unperfected interest, the "strong-arm" clause has no application where the security interest is perfected before the time of bankruptcy (when the petition is filed), even if perfected only hours before bankruptcy. Note, however, that the trustee in bankruptcy is also armed with certain other legal weapons which may be used to defeat even a perfected security interest. See §§ 5 and 6 of this chapter of the Nutshell. See also § 3a of this chapter in this Nutshell that indicates a post-petition filing is allowed in some circumstances.

Example 1.   Secured Party took a security interest in certain equipment purchased by Debtor on February 1. Debtor went bankrupt (the petition was filed) on November 1. Secured Party filed and thereby perfected its security interest on November 2. The trustee in bankruptcy takes the equipment under the "strong-arm" clause.

Example 2.   Secured Party took a security interest in certain equipment purchased by Debtor on February 1. Secured Party filed and thereby perfected its security interest on October 31. Debtor went bankrupt (the petition was filed) on November 1. The trustee in bankruptcy may not take the collateral under the "strong-arm" clause (though he might have other grounds for attacking the security interest).

Note: The same result obtains in Example 2 if Secured Party, instead of filing, had taken possession of the collateral on October 31. Repossession of the collateral perfects an otherwise unperfected security interest as it operates like a pledge. See Chapter 4, § 4a of this Nutshell.

§ 5.   Preferential Transfers

a. The General Rule

Common law and the law of most states permit an insolvent debtor to treat some creditors more favorably than other creditors by paying the preferred creditors to the exclusion of the others. (A few states have enacted the Uniform Fraudulent Transfers Act which at § 5(b) makes some types of preferences avoidable). Moreover, a diligent creditor may obtain more favorable status against an insolvent debtor by getting a judgment or execution lien on property of the debtor under state law. On the other hand, federal bankruptcy law takes a different position as to preferential payments or voluntary or involuntary transfers by an insolvent debtor to certain favored creditors. The Bankruptcy Code permits a bankruptcy trustee to set aside so-called "preferential transfers" made within a relatively short time before the debtor's bankruptcy.

Under Bankruptcy Code § 547(b), five conditions must be met in order that a trustee may strike down a voluntary or involuntary transfer of property of an insolvent debtor to a particular creditor. The transfer of the debtor's property must be:

(1) to or for the benefit of a creditor;

(2) for or on account of an antecedent debt owed by the debtor before such transfer was made;

(3) made while the debtor was insolvent (it should be noted that Bankruptcy Code § 547(f) adds a rebuttable presumption that the debtor has been insolvent during the 90 days preceding the filing of the petition);

(4) made within 90 days before the filing of the petition (but a special one-year rule discussed below in § 5b of this chapter of the Nutshell governs a transfer to an "insider");

(5) a transfer that enables the creditor to receive more than he would have received had the transfer not been made and there had been a distribution to that creditor in a liquidation proceeding under Bankruptcy Code Chapter 7.

The Bankruptcy Code provision will apply to a secured transaction *if perfection is delayed and takes place within the 90-day period.* In general, Bankruptcy Code § 547(e) has the effect of fixing the time of transfer at the time of perfection of a security interest, rather than at an earlier time of attachment of the security interest. However, perfection within 10 days of attachment is deemed to relate back to the time of attachment. If the debt owed the secured creditor was incurred at that time, the transfer was not on account of an antecedent debt and is not avoidable as a preference. See Bankruptcy Code § 547(e)(2).

Example 1. On April 1, Debtor purchased and took delivery of widgets on credit and gave Seller a security interest for the unpaid price of $10,000. Seller filed a financing statement on May 15. Debtor filed a bankruptcy petition on August 1 (within 90 days of May 15). The delayed perfection by Seller can be set aside as a preferential transfer. Note, however, that if the widgets are consumer goods within the Code rule on perfection upon attachment alone (see Chapter 4, § 2a of this Nutshell), the filing on May 15 is not a preferential transfer.

Example 2. Assume the facts of Example 1 above, except that Seller, instead of filing, repossessed the collateral on May 15. The delayed perfection by repossession can be set aside as a preferential transfer if the widgets are not consumer goods.

Example 3. Assume the facts of Example 1 above, except that the bankruptcy petition was filed on September 1. Since perfection, although delayed, took place more than 90 days before the filing of the petition, there is no preferential transfer unless the secured party, Seller, is an "insider" (see discussion of the "insider" rules in § 5b of this chapter of the Nutshell).

Example 4. Assume that the credit purchase of Example 1 took place on April 1, the filing was on April 10 and the bankruptcy petition was filed on July 6. Since perfection, although within 90 days of the filing of the petition, was within 10 days after attachment of the security interest, there is no preferential transfer because the transfer is deemed to have occurred when the security interest attached at which time the debtor incurred the debt owed the secured party. Thus, the transfer was not on account of an antecedent debt and is not avoidable as a preference.

b. *"Insider" Transfers*

Special rules govern a preferential transfer to an "insider." The term "insider" has a lengthy definition in Bankruptcy Code § 101(31), which includes a number of personal or business relationship categories between the debtor and the creditor receiving the transfer. Among such "insider" categories of creditors are certain close relatives of an individual debtor, officers, directors or persons in control of a corporate debtor, or partners of a partnership debtor.

Where a transfer is made to an "insider," the transfer may be set aside not only within 90 days, as discussed above, but also between 90 days and one year before the date of filing of the petition.

"Insider" problems should not affect most secured transactions where problems of preferential transfer exist. But an "insider" problem might arise where there is a relationship between the debtor and secured party falling within the Bankruptcy Code § 101(31) definition. Thus, delayed perfection taking place more than 90 days but less than one year before the filing of a bankruptcy petition might be upset if the secured party is an "insider." A possible example of an "insider" secured party might include a controlling stockholder of a corporate debtor or a financer who has taken over the management of the debtor's business.

Although the possible time of the preferential transfer is extended where the creditor is an "insider," the rebuttable presumption of insolvency runs for but 90 days before the filing of the petition.

c. *Exceptions to the "Preference" Rules*

Eight exceptions to the basic "preferential transfer" rules of Bankruptcy Code § 547(b) are listed in Bankruptcy Code § 547(c):

(1) A "substantially contemporaneous" exchange for new value given to the debtor. This will protect cash sales where the seller is paid by check and waits several days to deposit and collect it. Similarly protected is a security interest for new value taken and promptly perfected (within 10 days).

(2) Ordinary-course payments of debts. this permits routine bill payments and should protect most sellers on open trade terms who are paid within a reasonable time after any sale.

(3) Purchase-money security interests which are perfected within 20 days after the debtor received possession of the collateral.

(4) Advances made by a creditor after a preferential transfer takes place. For example, if a debtor gives a creditor a security interest in certain collateral to secure an antecedent debt of $10,000, the security interest is delayed in perfection which takes place within 90 days of bankruptcy, but if the creditor then advances an additional $5,000, the amount of preferential transfer would be the value of the security interest less the $5,000.

(5) Certain perfected security interests covering after-acquired property. See the discussion that

follows in § 5d of this chapter of the Nutshell.

(6) Statutory liens that may not be avoided under Bankruptcy Code § 545. This should not affect a security interest, which is a consensual lien and not a statutory lien.

(7) Bona fide payments made to a spouse or child of a debtor in connection with a separation agreement or divorce decree. This exception should not affect a security interest.

(8) Regarding consumer debts, where the aggregate value of the property transferred is less than $600, such a transfer will not be avoided as a preference. Thus, acquisition of a security interest in property of a value less than $600 to secure a consumer debt would not be voidable as a preference.

d. *Where Security Interest Covers After-Acquired Property*

Probably the most troublesome area of litigation involving the effect of the 1898 Act on a Uniform Commercial Code security interest was an effort to apply the "preference" provisions of the 1898 Act to a security interest covering not only property then owned by the debtor but also property subsequently acquired. Generally, as to after-acquired property as collateral, see Chapter 2, § 7b of this Nutshell. Such "floating liens" are frequently used in financing inventory or accounts which normally "turn over" in the ordinary course of the debtor's business. Under 1972 § 9-204(1) or 1999 § 9-204(a), a security agreement may provide that after-acquired property (except for consumer goods in most instances) will serve as security for the debtor's obligations. Moreover, under 1972 § 9-205 or 1999 § 9-205, the security agreement may give the debtor the power to use or dispose of the collateral at will, without accounting to the secured party. Thus, if a security agreement covering inventory or accounts contains an after-acquired property clause and is properly perfected, the debtor may use the collateral as business needs dictate.

In some instances under the 1898 Act, a trustee in bankruptcy sought to set aside as a preferential transfer security interests in property acquired by the debtor within four months of bankruptcy (the preference period under the 1898 Act) under a security agreement covering after-acquired property, where filing took place more than four months before bankruptcy. The trustee would have argued that the time a "transfer" occurred was at the time the security interest was perfected, and that the security interest in after-acquired collateral was perfected only when the debtor acquired rights in the collateral, as prior to then the security interest was unattached. Thus the trustee would have argued the "transfer" occurred when the debtor acquired the after-acquired collateral and that the transfer was on account of an antecedent debt, the loan to the debtor having been made previously. The 1898 Act had no clear provision addressed to this problem, but most decided cases rejected the trustee's argument and upheld the security interest covering the after-acquired collateral, as against a claim of preferential transfer.

The Bankruptcy Code in § 547(c)(5) attempts a statutory solution by declaring in effect that a perfected security interest "in inventory or a receivable or the proceeds of either" is subject to attack as a preference to the extent that the secured party improves his position during the 90-day (or one-year in the case of the "insider") period preceding the filing of the petition "to the prejudice of other creditors holding unsecured claims."

Two measuring points are used: 90 days before the petition is filed and the date of the filing of the petition. Where the "insider" rule applies, the measuring points are one year before the filing of the petition and the date of filing. (An alternative rule substituting the date on which "new value was first given" for either the 90-day or one year date applies if new value is first given after such 90-day or one-year date.) In essence, if the secured party has improved his position with respect to the value of the collateral as against the secured debt at the time the petition is filed over the earlier measuring date (usually 90 days), the extent of improvement may be attacked as a preferential transfer.

Example. Debtor files a bankruptcy petition on May 1. Creditor has a valid security interest and floating lien on Debtor's inventory, entered into 15 months earlier at which time Creditor filed a financing statement proper in all respects. 90 days before May 1, the inventory had a value of $90,000 but the debt was $150,000. On May 1, the changing inventory had a value of $110,000 but the debt was $120,000. The debt in excess of the collateral was $60,000 90 days before May 1, but was only $10,000 on May 1. Thus, $50,000 of the interest in the inventory is a preferential transfer, and the secured party may claim only $60,000 of the $110,000 value of inventory at the time of bankruptcy.

It should be noted that Bankruptcy Code § 547(c)(5) only speaks in terms of "inventory or a receivable or the proceeds of either." Thus, a security interest in after-acquired equipment ac-

quired within 90 days of the filing of the petition
would likely be subject to attack as a preferential
transfer.

In short, the secured party with a perfected
security interest covering after-acquired property is
often not in as good a position under the Bankruptcy
Code as under case law arising under the 1898 Act.

Moreover, the Bankruptcy Code rule apparently
vitiates the effectiveness of Uniform Commercial
Code 1972 § 9-108 in an bankruptcy proceeding.
That Code provision purports to protect a security
interest in after-acquired property by declaring that
it is taken for new value and not as security for an
antecedent debt in the typical "floating lien" situation. The 1999 Code does not include a provision
like 1972 § 9-108.

It should be noted that a security interest covering
after-acquired property is generally limited as to
property acquired by the debtor or the estate after
bankruptcy. See § 7 of this chapter of the Nutshell.

§ 6. Fraudulent Transfers

Bankruptcy Code § 548 permits the trustee to set
aside any transfer by, or obligation incurred by, the
debtor within one year before the filing of the

petition, if the transfer or obligation was intended to hinder, delay or defraud any creditor, or if less than reasonably equivalent value was received and the debtor was insolvent or became insolvent as a result of the transfer or obligation, or where certain other like circumstances exist. This Bankruptcy Code provision is based on the Uniform Fraudulent Transfer Act.

Although fraudulent transfer problems should rarely exist in connection with secured transactions, it is conceivable that a security interest might be attacked under Bankruptcy Code § 548 if it is taken for grossly inadequate consideration or otherwise taken with intent to hinder, delay or defraud other creditors. As is the case with Bankruptcy Code § 547 preferences, a transfer is deemed to occur when it is perfected. See, Bankruptcy Code § 548(d).

State fraudulent transfer laws might also be utilized under Bankruptcy Code § 544(b) which permits the trustee to "avoid any transfer of an interest of the debtor in property or any obligation incurred by the debtor that is voidable under applicable law by a creditor holding an unsecured claim that is allowable * * *." Thus, if an unsecured creditor could avoid a transfer by the debtor, the trustee may step into the shoes of that creditor and completely avoid the transfer.

Bankruptcy Code § 544(b) should rarely apply in a secured transaction situation except to attack the acquisition of a security interest as a fraudulent conveyance. The reason is that it permits the trustee to act only if an *unsecured creditor* could act. Thus, the trustee could not step into the shoes of a creditor with a lien superior to a security interest, where there is delayed perfection.

Example. On February 1, Debtor gave Secured Party a security interest in widgets for a debt of $5,000. On March 1, Creditor levied on the widgets for an unsatisfied judgment of $100. On April 1, Secured Party filed a financing statement. On October 1, Debtor filed a bankruptcy petition. The trustee may not attack the security interest under Bankruptcy Code § 544(b) because Creditor had a lien and was not an unsecured creditor.

Probably the only possible application of Bankruptcy Code § 544(b) to set aside a security interest might be where an unsecured creditor could set the interest aside as a fraudulent transfer under state law. Note that the trustee could utilize Bankruptcy Code § 544(b) to attack a fraudulent transfer not subject to attack under Bankruptcy Code § 548 because it took place more than one year prior to bankruptcy.

§ 7.   Property Acquired After Bankruptcy

Problems of preferential transfers affecting after-acquired property are discussed above (§ 5d of this chapter of the Nutshell). In addition, the rights of a secured party to certain after-acquired collateral of a debtor are further restricted under Bankruptcy Code § 552. A security interest is ineffective with respect to property acquired by the estate or by the debtor after the commencement of the case, even though a security agreement entered into before the commencement of the case covers such property. See Bankruptcy Code § 552(a).

There is an exception to the above exclusionary rule. Proceeds, products, offspring, rents or profits from property subject to a perfected security interest, received after the commencement of the case, may be subject to the security interest if the security agreement extends to such property. However, the court "after notice and a hearing and based on the equities of the case" may order otherwise. See Bankruptcy Code § 552(b). Thus, if inventory subject to a perfected security interest is sold by the debtor prior to the filing of the petition and payment is received after such filing, the payment as proceeds would ordinarily go to the secured party.

§ 8. Security Interest in Exempt Property

Certain property of a debtor is exempt and is not distributed to creditors. Under Bankruptcy Code § 522, an individual debtor is entitled to claim exemptions allowed under state law or, alternatively, to take certain specified Bankruptcy Code exemptions. A state by legislation may limit the debtor to "state law" exemptions, which has occurred in many states.

Usually, a security interest which is otherwise valid in bankruptcy applies to exempt property to the extent permitted by state law. But certain security interests in exempt property are invalidated in bankruptcy. Bankruptcy Code § 522(f) permits the debtor to avoid a "nonpossessory, nonpurchase-money security interest" in various described household or similar consumer goods, implements or tools of the trade or health aids. Moreover, Bankruptcy Code § 522(e) makes ineffective a waiver by the debtor of the right to avoid such a nonpossessory and nonpurchase-money security interest.

A right of the debtor to redeem exempt property from a security interest is also given in Bankruptcy Code § 722. An individual debtor whose estate is in liquidation under Bankruptcy Code Chapter 7 may redeem "tangible personal property intended primarily for personal, family or household use from a lien securing a dischargeable consumer debt," if such property is exempted under Bankruptcy Code § 522 or has been abandoned by the trustee under Bankruptcy Code § 554, "by paying the holder of the secured claim the amount of the secured claim of such holder that is secured by such lien." The allowed secured claim is equal to the amount of the debt or value of the collateral, whichever is less. This rule applies whether or not the debtor has waived the right of redemption. See Bankruptcy Code § 722.

Example. Debtor, prior to filing bankruptcy, granted creditor a UCC Article 9 purchase money security interest in household furniture that is exempt under Bankruptcy Code § 522. Debtor files bankruptcy and owes creditor $5,000. The furniture has a value of $100. Debtor may redeem the furniture by payment of $100. To redeem outside of bankruptcy, the full amount of the debt must be paid. See Chapter 9, § 9 of this Nutshell and UCC 1972 § 9-506 and 1999 § 9-623.

§ 9. Right to Proceeds Upon Debtor's Insolvency

1972 § 9-306(4) deals with the extent to which a

secured party with a perfected security interest in proceeds may reach such proceeds upon the debtor's insolvency. This provision applies when *insolvency proceedings* are instituted by or against a debtor. That term refers to proceedings instituted under state law or under federal bankruptcy law. See § 1 of this chapter of this Nutshell.

It should be noted that the 1999 Code has no equivalent to 1972 § 9-306(4). According to the Code Comments, the debtor's entering into bankruptcy does not affect a secured party's right to proceeds. See Comment 8 to 1999 § 9-315.

It should be recognized that 1972 § 9-306(2) provides that a security interest in collateral which is sold or otherwise disposed of continues in "any identifiable proceeds including collections received by the debtor." Perfection of a security interest in proceeds is dealt with in 1972 § 9-306(3). (The 1972 Code in this regard generally makes perfection as to proceeds automatic when a security interest is perfected in the collateral giving rise to the proceeds.) For discussion of perfection as to proceeds, see Chapter 4, § 8 of this Nutshell.

Even where a security interest in proceeds is perfected, an obvious problem of identification or tracing exists, which may present a real problem when the debtor becomes insolvent. The approach taken in 1972 § 9-306(4) is to permit a secured party with a perfected security interest in proceeds to reach identifiable proceeds which have not been commingled. In addition, a limited right amounting to a "rule of thumb" is given to reach proceeds which have been commingled with other assets.

The approach taken in 1972 § 9-306(4) is outlined as follows:

a. Rules are given by the 1972 Code permitting the secured party to reach identifiable cash or non-cash proceeds. (For definitions, see Chapter 1, § 7d of this Nutshell.)

(1) Identifiable non-cash proceeds (such as traded-in goods) may be reached. The 1972 Code also has a provision permitting separate deposit accounts containing only proceeds to be reached. (This would permit the secured party to obtain a cash collateral account where all proceeds as collected are deposited.)

(2) Identifiable cash proceeds may be reached if they consist of money which is neither commingled with other money nor deposited in a deposit account prior to the insolvency proceedings.

(3) Identifiable cash proceeds may be reached if

they consist of checks and the like which are not deposited in a deposit account prior to the insolvency proceedings.

b. Rules are also given by the 1972 Code for reaching cash and deposit accounts of the debtor where proceeds are commingled with other funds. Such commingled cash or accounts may be reached under the following rules:

(1) They are subject to a right of set off (e.g., where the bank in which an account is deposited makes a set off).

(2) The amount which the secured party may reach is limited to the amount of cash proceeds received by the debtor within ten days before the institution of the insolvency proceedings, but less:

(a) payments to the secured party on account of cash proceeds received by the debtor during the ten-day period, and

(b) the cash proceeds received by the debtor during the ten-day period which are identifiable as money, checks or the like, or deposit accounts containing proceeds.

The effect of the Bankruptcy Code on the rules of Uniform Commercial Code 1972 § 9-306(4)(d) on cash or deposit accounts of the debtor in which proceeds have been commingled with other funds is not clear. However, some cases reach the conclusion that the secured party must actually trace proceeds into the debtor's bank account notwithstanding 1972 § 9-306(4)(d), declaring that 1972 provision to either be attackable as producing a preference under Bankruptcy Code § 547 or as a voidable statutory lien under Bankruptcy Code § 545. Thus, under this case law a secured creditor could only reach proceeds in the debtor's bank account that are traceable from the original collateral. The exception to the "preference" provision for after-acquired inventory, receivables and proceeds of either in Bankruptcy Code § 547(c)(5), discussed in § 5d of this chapter of the Nutshell, does not expressly refer to commingled proceeds as covered in 1972 § 9-306(4)(d). It is possible that the rule of 1972 § 9-306(4)(d) might apply in bankruptcy under Bankruptcy Code § 546(b) or § 552(b), but that is not clear.

It should be noted once again that the 1999 Code has no equivalent to 1972 § 9-306(4).

§ 10. Reclamation Rights of Unpaid Sellers

Priorities affecting an unpaid seller of goods and a secured party with a security interest in such goods given by the buyer are discussed in Chapter 7, § 5 of this Nutshell. However, the right of an unpaid seller in a cash sale under Uniform Commercial Code § 2-507(2) or § 2-511(3) or an unpaid seller in a credit sale under § 2-702(2) and (3) to reclaim when the buyer becomes bankrupt was somewhat questionable in case law under the 1898 Act.

Bankruptcy Code § 546 has the effect of permitting a limited right of reclamation by an unpaid seller. The seller has to make a written demand for reclamation "before ten days after receipt of such goods by the debtor." The court is empowered to deny reclamation if it either grants the seller an "administrative expense" priority in the bankruptcy proceedings or "secures such claim by a lien."

It should be noted that Bankruptcy Code § 546(c) permits reclamation by the unpaid seller within the 10-day period both in a "cash sale" situation under Code §§ 2-507(2) and 2-511(3) and in a "credit sale" situation under Code § 2-702(2). But the § 2-702(2) language doing away with the 10-day limitation when there is a written misrepresentation of solvency by the buyer does not apply in a proceeding under the Bankruptcy Code. In other words, the unpaid seller has to make a written demand for the goods within 10 days of receipt by the buyer. Moreover, the court may deny reclamation and instead grant an "administrative expense" priority to the seller or give a lien on other property. Such action might be taken where the debtor-buyer's business is to be continued in a Bankruptcy Code Chapter 11 proceeding or temporarily continued under Bankruptcy Code Chapter 7.

CHAPTER 9

DEFAULT AND ENFORCEMENT
OF SECURITY INTEREST

§ 1. What Constitutes Default

UCC Article 9 has no provision defining the term "default" or specifying what constitutes a "default." Thus, contract law generally governs the issue of whether a default has occurred. See UCC § 1-103. From this, it follows that a breach by the debtor of any of the terms of the security agreement will constitute a default. The most typical default is failure to make a payment when due, but the security agreement may, and often does, specify acts on the part of the debtor other than nonpayment which are also events of default. For a discussion of events of default in a security agreement, see Chapter 2, § 8e.

Security agreements frequently also provide that upon the occurrence of an event of default, the secured party may accelerate payment. Sometimes, a security agreement may even permit acceleration at will, or when the secured party deems himself insecure. When acceleration takes place, failure of the debtor to make the total of all payments due will be a default. For a discussion of acceleration clauses in a security agreement, see Chapter 2, § 7d. It should be noted that consumer protection legislation and regulatory law separate from UCC Article 9 may prohibit acceleration under some circumstances.

Upon the happening of one of more events of default specified in the security agreement, the secured party may resort to the "default" provisions of Article 9 (1972 §§ 9-501 through 9-507 and 1999 §§ 9-601 through 9-628). However, the secured party may not take "default" action in the absence of an event of default set forth in the security agreement. The taking of such "default" action in the absence of default may subject the secured party to possible liability to the debtor.

Example. Debtor gave Creditor a security interest in his inventory to secure a debt calling for monthly payments. Immediately after making a monthly payment, Debtor died. No payments were in arrears at that time and no other event of default had occurred. The security agreement had no provision making Debtor's death an event of default. Nevertheless, Creditor takes immediate action to repossess the collateral. The repossession is improper and Creditor may be held liable to

Debtor's executor, administrator or heirs for losses sustained upon such repossession, and possibly also for punitive damages.

Note: It should be kept in mind that the rights of the secured party upon default by the debtor are limited where the debtor is in a bankruptcy under federal law. See Chapter 8 for general discussion of the effect of bankruptcy.

The 1999 Code has a special provision regarding default in connection with an agricultural lien. Agricultural liens fall within the scope of the 1999 Code. 1999 § 9-109(a)(2). A default occurs in connection with an agricultural lien at the time the secured party becomes entitled to enforce the lien in accordance with the statute under which the lien was created. 1999 § 9-606. Once such a default occurs, the holder of the agricultural lien has available the enforcement remedies of a secured party generally. See Comment 2 to 1999 § 9-606.

Even when a default occurs, the secured party cannot enforce the security interest when the secured party waives the right to do so. A "waiver" occurs when the secured party knowingly relinquishes its right to enforce a security interest. For example, according to some case law, if the debtor has failed repeatedly to make timely payments contrary to the terms of a security agreement, or has repeatedly sold collateral contrary to the terms of a security agreement, without objection of the secured party, the right to enforce the security agreement upon recurrence of such events of default may have been waived. Under such circumstances, to reinstate the secured party's right to enforce the security interest in the event of waiver, the secured party must notify the debtor that in the future strict compliance with the terms of the security agreement will be required.

§ 2. Rights of Secured Party Generally

When the debtor is in default, the rights and obligations of the secured party and the rights of the debtor are set forth in Part 5 of 1972 Article 9, §§ 9-501 through 9-507 and Part 6 of 1999 Article 9, §§ 9-601 through 9-628. The rights of the secured party in the collateral after the debtor's default are of the essence of a secured transaction. They are the rights which distinguish the secured from the unsecured lender.

The secured party is given a broad choice of legal weapons with which to enforce his rights. These are somewhat indexed in 1972 § 9-501(1) and 1999 § 9-601(a). In this regard, the secured party has the rights and remedies provided in 1972 §§ 9-501 through 9-507 and 1999 §§ 9-601 through 9-628 and (with some limitations which may not be waived at least before default) the rights provided in the security agreement. Under 1972 § 9-501(1) and 1999 § 9-601(a), the secured party also has the following rights:

(a) to reduce his claim to judgment;

(b) to foreclose or otherwise enforce the security interest by any available judicial procedure;

(c) if the collateral is documents, to proceed either as to the documents or as to the goods covered thereby.

When the secured party is in possession, he has all the rights, remedies and duties prescribed in 1972 § 9-207 and 1999 § 9-207.   See 1972 § 9-501(2) and 1999 § 9-601(b). As to such rights and duties, see Chapter 3, § 4.

The above rights and remedies are stated to be cumulative. 1972 § 9-501(1) and 1999 § 9-601(c). In other words, the secured party may elect one of the above courses of action without being barred from taking some other course in order to enforce the security interest. For example, the secured party may obtain a judgment for the amount of the debt and then attempt to collect it by any legal means (such as by execution on other property of the debtor, by garnishment of a debt due the debtor from a third person or by pursuing other creditor's remedies). Such action does not prevent the secured party from realizing on the collateral under the "default" procedures of Article 9.

Certain rights are also given the secured party under the other "default" provisions of Article 9. These are summarized here and discussed in detail in later sections of this chapter. Among such rights are:

(a) the right to repossess the collateral, under 1972 § 9-503 and 1999 § 9-609;

(b) the right to make direct collection from any account debtor or obligor on an instrument and to take control of any proceeds to which the secured party is entitled, under 1972 § 9-502 and 1999 §§ 9-607, 9-608.

(c) the right to sell or otherwise dispose of the collateral, under 1972 § 9-504 and 1999 §§ 9-610, 9-611, 9-615, 9-617, 9-618 and 9-624;

(d) the right to propose to take the collateral in satisfaction of the debt (the right of strict foreclosure), under circumstances outlined at 1972 § 9-505(2) and 1999 §§ 9-620 through 9-622, 9-624.

When the security agreement covers both real and personal property, the secured party may proceed under the default procedures of Article 9 with respect to the personal property or may proceed exclusively under real estate law with respect to both real and personal property. See 1972 § 9-501(4) and 1999 § 9-604.

§ 3.   Judicial Foreclosure and Sale

Upon default, the secured party may reduce his claim to judgment, foreclose or otherwise enforce the security interest by any judicial procedure. 1972 § 9-501(1) and 1999 § 9-601(a)(1). Note that under the 1999 Code agricultural liens can be enforced in the same manner. While in probably the majority of instances, the secured party will repossess the collateral and sell it without resort to judicial process, there may be instances when it may be desirable to utilize the courts, obtain a judgment against the debtor and execute on the debtor's property, including the collateral securing the debt. In such a case, 1972 § 9-501(5) provides that the lien of any levy on the collateral by virtue of execution based upon the judgment shall relate back to the date of perfection of the security interest. Similarly, under 1999 § 9-601(e) the lien relates back to the earliest of the date of perfection of the security interest or agricultural lien, the date of filing a financing statement, or any date specified in a statute under which the agricultural lien was created.

In other words, if it is necessary for the secured party to execute on the collateral, but the security interest was earlier perfected by a still-effective filing, the time of execution relates back to the time of filing. Thus, if the debtor becomes bankrupt within 90 days of the time of execution, but if filing took place more than 90 days before bankruptcy, the trustee cannot attack the execution as a preferential transfer under the Bankruptcy Code. See Chapter 8, § 5 for discussion of preferential transfers.

Where the collateral is sold by a judicial sale following execution, this is considered a foreclosure of the security interest by judicial procedure. The secured party is permitted to purchase the collateral at such a judicial sale and hold it free of other requirements of Article 9. See 1972 § 9-501(5) and 1999 § 9-601(f).

Moreover, where there is a sale approved in a judicial proceeding, the sale is conclusively deemed to have been commercially reasonable. See 1972 § 9-507(2) and 1999 § 9-627(c). However, this does not mean that a judicial sale is necessary or that a nonjudicial sale is necessarily commercially unreasonable.

§ 4. Debtor's Protective Rights

After default, the debtor has the rights and remedies provided in the "default" provisions of 1972 Article 9 §§ 9-501 through 9-507 and 1999 Article 9 §§ 9-601 through 9-628, those provided in the security agreement, and those provided in 1972 § 9-207 and 1999 § 9-207 dealing with rights and duties when the secured party has possession. See 1972 § 9-501(2) and 1999 § 9-601(d). It should be noted that 1972 § 9-207 and 1999 § 9-207 apply not only to the situation where the secured party is in possession before default as a pledgee, but also where the secured party is in possession after default. Nevertheless, the relations of the parties have been changed under default and 1972 § 9-207 and 1999 § 9-207 as they apply after default must be read together with the default provisions of Article 9. In particular, agreements permitted under 1972 § 9-207 and 1999 § 9-207 cannot waive or modify certain rights of the debtor following default. See Comment 3 to 1972 § 9-501 and, similarly, Comment 4 to 1999 § 9-607. As to rights and duties when the secured party is in possession, see Chapter 3, § 4.

1972 § 9-501(3) sets forth certain rights of the debtor following default which may not be waived or varied by agreement (i.e., the security agreement) *in advance of default* (although written waiver following default is permitted). Under the 1972 Code, these include the following:

a. The duty of the secured party to account for surplus proceeds after sale of the collateral pursuant to 1972 § 9-504(2), or to account for surplus proceeds when collection of assigned accounts, general intangibles, instruments or chattel paper is undertaken on a "recourse" basis by the secured party under 1972 § 9-502(2).

b. The right to enforce compulsory disposition of consumer goods collateral in certain circumstances under 1972 § 9-505(1) and to require that certain steps be taken by the secured party in connection with disposition of the collateral under 1972 § 9-504(3).

c. The right of the debtor to object to the secured party taking the collateral in satisfaction of the debt under 1972 § 9-505(2). But the debtor may waive this right after default by failure to object to such disposition.

d. The debtor's right of redemption under 1972 § 9-506.

e. The secured party's liability under 1972 § 9-507(1) for failure to comply with the default provisions of Article 9.   However, presumably, the debtor may waive this right *after default* by a written waiver or renunciation signed by the debtor, under UCC § 1-107.

1999 § 9-602 also sets forth certain rights of the debtor following default which may not be waived or varied by agreement (i.e., the security agreement) except as permitted by 1999 § 9-624.   Under the 1999 Code these include essentially the same rights as listed above as non-waiveable prior to default under the 1972 Code plus a few of the rights not listed as non-waiveable prior to default by the 1972 Code.   The rights that are listed as non-waiveable prior to default under the 1999 Code include the following:

a. Rights under 1999 § 9-207(b)(4)(C), which deals with use and operation of the collateral by the secured party.

b. Rights under 1999 § 9-210, which deals with requests for an accounting and requests concerning a list of collateral and statement of account.

c. Rights under 1999 § 9-607(c) which deals with collection and enforcement of collateral.

d. Rights under 1999 §§ 9-608(a) and 9-615(c) to the extent that they deal with application or payment of noncash proceeds of collection, enforcement, or disposition.

e. Rights under 1999 §§ 9-608(a) and 9-615(d) to the extent that they require accounting for or payment of surplus proceeds of collateral.

f. Rights under 1999 § 9-609 to the extent that it imposes upon a secured party that takes possession of collateral without judicial process the duty to do so without breach of the peace.

g. Rights under 1999 §§ 9-610(b), 9-611, 9-613, and 9-614, which deal with disposition of collateral.

h. Rights under 1999 § 9-615(f), which deals with calculation of a deficiency or surplus when a disposition is made to the secured party, a person related to the secured party, or a secondary obligor.

i. Rights under 1999 § 9-616, which deals with explanation of the calculation of a surplus or deficiency.

j Rights under 1999 §§ 9-620, 9-621, 9-622, which deal with acceptance of collateral in satisfaction of obligation.

k. Rights under 1999 § 9-623, which deals with

redemption of collateral.

l.   Rights under 1999 § 9-624, which deals with permissible waivers.

m.   Rights under §§ 9-625 and 9-626, which deal with the secured party's liability for failure to comply with this article.

Under the 1999 Code, certain debtor rights are waiveable by an agreement entered into and authenticated after default. 1999 § 9-624. Those rights include the right to notification of disposition of collateral under 1999 § 9-611, the right to require disposition of collateral under 1999 § 9-620(e), and except in consumer transactions, the right to redeem collateral under 1999 § 9-623.

The reason for not permitting waiver of the foregoing rules in the security agreement or otherwise before default is explained in Comment 4 to 1972 § 9-501. That Comment states in part:

"In the area of rights after default our legal system has traditionally looked with suspicion on agreements designed to cut down the debtor's rights and free the secured party of his duties: no mortgage clause has ever been allowed to clog the equity of redemption. the default situation offers great scope for overreaching; the suspicious attitude of the courts has been grounded in common sense."

Although there is no such Comment to the 1999 Code, it is clear the same policy sentiment underlies the non-waiver provisions of the 1999 Code above described.

However, 1972 § 9-501(3) and 1999 § 9-603 do permit the parties by agreement to determine the standards by which the fulfillment of these rights and duties is to be measured if such standards are not manifestly unreasonable. See also the similar provision of § 1-102(3). For example, the security agreement might conceivably contain some provision relating to the method of disposition of the collateral after default, such as the place of sale, if such provision is not "manifestly unreasonable." On the other hand, the 1999 Code invalidates such agreements to the extent they relate to the duty not to breach the peace when a secured party repossesses collateral extrajudicially. 1999 § 9-603(b).

CAVEAT. While Article 9 generally permits waiver by the debtor of his rights after default, statutes outside the Code such as consumer credit laws and retail installment sales laws may contain more restrictive provisions relating to consumer goods as collateral than those in Article 9. Such other statutes control in the event of conflict with Article 9.

§ 5.   Collection Rights for Accounts, Instruments or Chattel Paper

a. *Generally*

The secured party is entitled to notify an account debtor (the person who is obligated on an account, chattel paper or general intangible) or the obligor of an instrument (such as the maker of a promissory note taken as collateral for an obligation of the payee) to make payment to him (the secured party). This may be done whether or not the assignor (debtor) was previously making his own collections on the collateral. See 1972 § 9-502(1) and 1999 § 9-607(a)(1).

Example. Seller-Assignor sells goods on open account to various account debtors. Seller-Assignor assigns the accounts to Secured Party. The assignments are on a "non-notification" basis permitting Seller-Assignor to make his own collections from the account debtors (permitted under 1972 §9-205 and 1999 § 9-205). Upon default by Seller-Assignor, Secured Party notifies account debtors to make payments to him (Secured Party). Account debtors must thereafter pay Secured Party as assignee under 1972 § 9-318(3) and 1999 § 9-406(a).

The secured party is also entitled to take control of any proceeds to which he is entitled under 1972 § 9-306 and 1999 § 9-315. See 1972 § 9-502(1) and 1999 § 9-607(a). For discussion of the right to proceeds upon the debtor's insolvency, see Chapter 8, § 9.

b. *Duties of Secured Party; Right to Surplus or Liability for Deficiency*

In some instances, a secured party taking an assignment of an account, chattel paper or general intangible or taking a note or other instrument as security may be entitled to charge back uncollected collateral against the debtor-assignor or may be otherwise entitled to full or limited recourse against the debtor-assignor. In such a case, 1972 § 9-502(2) and 1999 § 9-607(c) require that the secured party proceed in a commercially reasonable manner in making the collection, but he is entitled to deduct his reasonable expenses of realization from the collection. If the security agreement secures an indebtedness, the secured party must account to the debtor-assignor for any surplus and, unless otherwise agreed, the debtor-assignor is liable for any deficiency.

This means that where the assignee does not assume the full credit risk and retains a right of full or limited recourse or charge back for uncollectible accounts, both the debtor-assignor and other creditors have a right that the assignee not "dump the accounts" if the result will be to increase a possible deficiency claim or to reduce a possible surplus. In other words, the assignee must liquidate the accounts in a commercially reasonable manner. See Comments 2 and 3 to 1972 § 9-502 and Comment 9 to 1999 § 9-607.

On the other hand, if the underlying transaction is a sale of accounts or chattel paper [which is within Article 9 under 1972 § 9-102(1)(b) and 1999 § 9-109(a)(3)] and there is no right of recourse or charge back if the account or chattel paper is uncollectible, the assignee assumes the credit risk completely. In such circumstances, the debtor is not entitled to any surplus, nor is liable for any deficiency, unless the security agreement so provides. See 1972 § 9-502(2) and Comment 2, and 1999 § 9-608(b) and Comment 3.

§ 6. Secured Party's Right of Repossession

a. *Generally*

Unless otherwise agreed a secured party has on default the right to take possession of the collateral. In taking possession a secured party may proceed without judicial process if this can be done without breach of the peace. 1972 § 9-503 and 1999 § 9-609(a), (b). Those Code provisions also permit the secured party to proceed by "action" to take possession of the collateral. Presumably, this would permit repossession by replevin or a claim and delivery action.

These provisions permit "peaceable" self-help repossession by the secured party without having to resort to the courts. A number of decisions have considered whether self-help repossession is peaceable or not under particular circumstances; in this connection, pre-Code decisions are also in point. Generally, the courts define a "breach of the peace" to be a disturbance of public order by an act of violence, or by any act likely to produce violence, or which by causing consternation and alarm, disturbs the peace and quiet of the community. While an exhaustive list of circumstances involving "peaceable" repossession or repossession constituting a "breach of the peace" is beyond the scope of this

Nutshell, a few rules may be set forth here.

The following acts are likely to be considered as "peaceable" in connection with repossession.

(1) Removal of collateral such as an automobile from a street or parking lot without the knowledge or objection of the debtor. It is likely that even removal by "jump-starting" a car without using the ignition key will be unobjectionable. It is also probable that removal from the debtor's open premises such as a driveway is unobjectionable.

(2) Removal of collateral with the debtor's consent, or even with the debtor's knowledge in the absence of express objection by the debtor.

(3) Removal of collateral from the premises of a third person in the absence of knowledge or objection by the debtor or the third person.

On the other hand, the following acts are likely to be considered as involving a "breach of the peace" and therefore improper in connection with repossession:

(1) Removal of collateral over the express objection of the debtor, even in the absence of physical violence. The same is probably true where the removal is over the express objection of a third person.

(2) Entry into the debtor's home, garage or other building without consent for the purpose of removal. In other words, where there is a technical "breaking and entering" of premises, removal of the collateral is improper.

(3) Removal of the collateral after threatening or appearing to threaten violence to the debtor or a third person present, whether or not violence takes place.

(4) Removal of collateral by posing as a policeman or law enforcement officer or by obtaining the aid of a policeman or law enforcement officer who is acting beyond the scope of his official authority.

b. *Constitutional Problems*

Two constitutional problems may arise in connection with repossession under 1972 § 9-503 and 1999 § 9-609. The first involves the constitutionality of repossession under a writ of attachment or replevin. The second involves the possible constitutionality of 1972 § 9-503 and 1999 § 9-609 themselves as permitting self-help repossession.

Supreme Court decisions have invalidated in some instances state statutes allowing pre-judgment remedies by a creditor against a debtor. In one case, the Supreme Court held unconstitutional several state statutes permitting pre-judgment replevin of property on the ground that the statutory procedures deprived debtors of their property without due process insofar as they deny a right to a prior opportunity to be heard before chattels are taken from their possessors. On the other hand, it has been indicated that replevin or a similar pre-judgment proceeding may be constitutional where the writ is issued by a judge (instead of more perfunctorily by a court clerk) even though there is no hearing prior to the issuance of the writ where the debtor might have a chance to object. However, the Supreme Court has indicated that a state law permitting garnishment through a writ issued by a court clerk without notice or opportunity for an early hearing and without participation by a judicial officer will not be upheld.

In other words, the use of replevin or similar process in some circumstances may be unconstitutional. In determining the constitutionality of replevin following default in a secured transaction, the particular state statute should be examined. The statute might well have been amended in an attempt to meet the constitutional objections.

There has also been considerable litigation over the constitutionality of the provision of 1972 § 9-

503 permitting self-help repossession. Such litigation involves issues that will also be associated with self-help repossession under 1999 § 9-609. The challenges have been based on the requirements under the United States Constitution that there be no deprivation of property without due process of law and on the prohibition of unreasonable seizures. However, the difficulty to challenges in these instances is that these constitutional limitations apply only to *state action*. Such *state action* takes place when there is prejudgment replevin or the like; the writ is issued by a judge or clerk of court and a sheriff or similar official seizes the property. On the other hand, it is difficult to find the existence of *state action* when collateral of a debtor is merely repossessed privately with self-help methods by a secured party.

While the Supreme Court has not (as of the time of this writing) considered a direct constitutional challenge to the self-help repossession feature of 1972 § 9-503 or 1999 § 9-609, most other federal and state courts that have considered the matter have upheld 1972 § 9-503 on the ground that it does not involve *state action*. Thus, it would seem that the self-help feature of 1972 § 9-503 and 1999 § 9-609 is constitutionally valid, in the light of a preponderance of decisions to date.

It should be noted that some state constitutions have "due process" provisions that apply even when the state is not involved in the taking of property. Thus, one must also consult the relevant state constitution when analyzing the constitutionality of a repossession.

c. Steps Permitted in Lieu of Repossession

1972 § 9-503 and 1999 § 9-609 not only permit "self-help" repossession or repossession with the aid of the courts, but also have several provisions which may aid the secured party in instances where repossession is not physically feasible.

If the security agreement so provides, the secured party may require the debtor to assemble the collateral and make it available to the secured party at a place to be designated by the secured party which is reasonably convenient to both parties. 1972 § 9-503 and 1999 § 9-609(c). This would permit the secured party to utilize judicial help in requiring a debtor in possession of collateral spread at a number of locations to gather the collateral at one convenient place after default. However, the security agreement must permit this. Presumably, this would be useful in cases where the debtor has collateral such as mobile equipment scattered in a number of places and even in a number of states.

In the case of collateral such as heavy equipment, the physical removal from the debtor's plant and the storage of the equipment pending resale may be exceedingly expensive and in some cases impractical. Accordingly, the Code permits the secured party, without removal, to render equipment unusable and to dispose of collateral on the debtor's premises. See 1972 § 9-503 and 1999 § 9-609(a)(2). Any action in this regard by the secured party must be "commercially reasonable." See Comment to 1972 § 9-503 and Comment 6 to 1999 § 9-609.

d. Removal of Fixtures and Accessions

When the secured party has priority over all owners and encumbrancers of the real estate with respect to collateral which is a fixture, he may on default (subject to the "default" provisions of Article 9) remove his collateral from the real estate. He must reimburse any encumbrancer or owner of the real estate who is not the debtor and who has not otherwise agreed for the cost of repair of any physical injury, but not for any diminution in value of the real estate caused by the absence of the goods removed or by any necessity of replacing them. A person entitled to reimbursement may refuse permission to remove the fixture until the secured party gives adequate security for the performance of this obligation. 1972 § 9-313(8) and 1999 § 9-604(c), (d).

This provision abandons the "material injury to the freehold" rule of some pre-Code cases and permits removal of a fixture by a secured party having priority, subject only to a duty to reimburse any real estate claimant other than the debtor for the physical injury caused by the removal. The real estate claimant may refuse permission to remove in the absence of security or indemnity for such physical injury. See Comment 9 to 1972 § 9-313 and Comment 3 to 1999 § 9-604.

Example. Secured Party has a priority interest in a furnace over a mortgagee of the real estate. Upon default by the debtor, Secured Party may remove the furnace, and need only reimburse the mortgagee for any physical injury to the building caused by the removal, but not for the loss of value of the real estate caused by the absence of a furnace.

For discussion of priority with respect to fixtures between a secured party and real estate interests, see Chapter 7, § 7.

A similar provision exists with respect to accessions under 1972 § 9-314(4) and 1999 § 9-335(e), (f). When a secured party has an interest in accessions which has priority over the claims of all persons who have interests in the whole, he may on default (subject to the "default" provisions of Article 9) remove his collateral from the whole. He must reimburse any encumbrancer or owner of the whole who is not the debtor and who has not otherwise agreed for the cost of repair of any physical injury, but not for any diminution in value of the whole caused by the absence of the goods removed or by any necessity for replacing them. A person entitled to reimbursement may refuse permission to remove the accession until the secured party gives adequate security for the performance of this obligation.

For discussion of priority with respect to an accession between a secured party and an interest in the whole of the goods, see Chapter 7, § 8.

§ 7.   Taking the Collateral for the Debt

After the secured party has repossessed the collateral, two possible alternatives exist on behalf of the secured party. One of the alternatives is to sell or dispose of the collateral and apply the sales proceeds to the unpaid debt. The other alternative is for the secured party to propose to retain the collateral in satisfaction of the entire debt (or, under the

1999 Code, the secured party also may propose to retain the collateral in satisfaction of some portion of the debt). Such retention of collateral for the debt has been referred to as "strict foreclosure." Under the 1972 Code the secured party must be in possession of the collateral in order to propose strict foreclosure; the 1999 Code does not require the secured party to be in possession. See Comment 7 to 1999 § 9-620.

In many instances, strict foreclosure is preferable. The parties are often better off without going through the rigmarole of a sale, application of the sales proceeds and either accounting to the debtor for a surplus or (as happens much more frequently) attempting to collect a deficiency from the debtor.

Generally, except in the case of consumer goods when a substantial percentage of the debt is already paid before default, a secured party in possession (under the 1999 Code the secured party need not be in possession) may after default propose to retain the collateral in satisfaction of the obligation under 1972 § 9-505 and 1999 §§ 9-620 through 9-622, and 9-624(b). There are some significant differences between the 1972 and 1999 Codes regarding strict foreclosure.

a. 1972 Code Strict Foreclosure

Under the 1972 Code, the secured party may so retain the collateral in the following circumstances:

(1) He must send written notice of his proposal to the debtor to keep the collateral in satisfaction of the entire debt, unless the debtor has after default signed a statement renouncing or modifying his rights under 1972 § 9-505(2).

(2) Where the collateral is consumer goods, no other notice need be given. In other cases notice must be sent to any other secured party from whom the secured party has received (before sending his notice to the debtor or before the debtor's renunciation of his rights) written notice of a claim in the collateral.

(3) The secured party may retain the collateral in the absence of receiving written objection from a person entitled to receive notification (including the debtor who has not previously renounced his rights) within 21 days after the notice was sent. If the secured party receives such written objection, he must then dispose of the collateral under 1972 § 9-504.

(4) If no objection is received, the entire debt is extinguished and the secured party loses his right to

a deficiency judgment while the debtor loses his right to any surplus should the collateral be later sold by the secured party.

(5) If the secured party receives written objection from a person entitled to receive notification within the 21-day period prescribed in 1972 § 9-505(2), the secured party may not take the collateral for the debt, but must dispose of it under 1972 § 9-504.

(6) The secured party is also required to make compulsory disposition of the collateral under 1972 § 9-504 in certain instances where consumer goods are the collateral. If the debtor has paid (a) 60 percent of the cash price in the case of a purchase money security interest in consumer goods or (b) 60 percent of the loan in the case of another security interest in consumer goods (and has not signed *after default* a statement renouncing or modifying his rights to require disposition of the collateral), a secured party who has taken possession must dispose of it under 1972 § 9-504. If he fails to do so within 90 days after he takes possession, the debtor at his option may recover in conversion or under 1972 § 9-507(1) dealing with the secured party's liability. The reason for the latter rule is that a debtor who has paid 60 percent of the cash price or the loan has built up equity in the goods and a

properly-conducted resale might result in a surplus (although this is not always the case). However, the debtor may expressly sign away his right to demand a resale if he does so after default.

b. *1999 Code Strict Foreclosure*

Under the 1999 Code, the secured party may accept the collateral in partial or full satisfaction of the debt in the following circumstances (see 1999 § 9-620):

(1) The debtor must consent to the acceptance of the collateral. A debtor consents to a partial satisfaction of the debt only if the debtor agrees to the terms of the acceptance in a record authenticated after default. A debtor consents to a full satisfaction of the debt only if the debtor agrees to the terms of acceptance in a record authenticated after default or the secured party sends a notice of proposal to accept the collateral in full satisfaction of the debt and does not receive notice of objection from the debtor within 20 days after the proposal is sent. Such a notice must be sent to other parties in addition to the debtor under some circumstances. See 1999 § 9-621. If objection is received, the secured party must sell the collateral.

(2) The 1999 Code limits use of strict foreclosure in consumer transactions, that is, when the collateral is consumer goods. Where 60 percent of the cash price has been paid in the case of a purchase money security interest or 60 percent of the principal amount of the secured obligation has been paid, the secured party must sell the collateral within 90 days unless the secured party and the debtor otherwise agree. Additionally, in a consumer transaction, a secured party may not accept collateral in partial satisfaction of the debt it secures.

(3) Should strict foreclosure occur, the 1999 Code provides that the obligation secured is discharged to the extent consented to by the debtor (full or partial). 1999 § 9-622. Unless otherwise agreed, the debtor loses its right to any surplus and remains liable for any deficiency only in the case of acceptance of the collateral in partial satisfaction of the debt. See Comment 2 to 1999 § 9-622.

(4) A debtor may waive his right to require the secured party to dispose of the collateral. However, such a waiver is effective only if made by an authenticated agreement after default. 1999 § 9-624(b).

§ 8. Sale or Other Disposition of Collateral

a. *Generally; Application of Proceeds*

Under 1972 § 9-504(1) and 1999 § 9-610(a), a secured party after default may sell, lease or otherwise dispose of the collateral in its then condition or following any commercially reasonable preparation or processing. The 1972 Code indicates that any sale of goods is subject to Article 2 of the Code dealing with Sales. There is no equivalent provision within the 1999 Article 9, although it would seem Article 2 would still apply unless pre-empted by some contrary provision in 1999 Article 9.

While in many instances, it is optional on the part of the secured party to sell or otherwise dispose of the collateral, the secured party *must* dispose of the collateral under 1972 § 9-504 and 1999 § 9-610(a) and cannot use strict foreclosure under the circumstances considered in § 7 of this chapter, above (as where the secured party receives written objection to retaining the collateral in satisfaction or partial satisfaction of the debt or where the collateral is consumer goods and substantial payments of the debt or price have been made).

When the collateral is disposed of under 1972 § 9-504(1) and 1999 § 9-610(a), the proceeds are required to be applied in the following order as dictated by 1972 § 9-504(1) and 1999 § 9-615(a):

(1) To paying the reasonable expenses of retaking and disposing of the collateral (and to paying reasonable attorneys' fees and legal expenses if provided for in the security agreement and not prohibited by law).

(2) To the satisfaction of the debt owed the secured party. This should include principal, interest or finance charges and any other lawful unpaid charges provided for in the security agreement.

(3) To pay over the remaining proceeds to the extent necessary to satisfy the holder of any junior security interest in the same collateral if the holder of the junior interest has made a written demand and furnished on request reasonable proof of his security interest. Senior interests do not receive distribution as their claims in the collateral are unaffected by the sale.

(4) Under the 1999 Code, to a secured party that is a consignor if the secured party receives demand for distribution of proceeds from the consignor.

Note: For an example illustrating the application of proceeds, see the immediately following discussion.

b. *Right to Surplus or Liability for Deficiency*

If the security interest secures an indebtedness, the secured party must account to the debtor for any surplus and, unless otherwise agreed, the debtor is liable for any deficiency. 1972 § 9-504(2) and 1999 § 9-615(d). If the owner of the collateral is not the debtor, the owner is entitled to the surplus, if any, but is not liable for any deficiency. See 1972 § 9-112. [Note that there is no specific equivalent provision in the 1999 Code, but the outcome is the same. See 1999 § 9-102(a)(28).] Under the 1999 Code, in a consumer-goods transaction, the secured party must provide the debtor or obligor with an explanation of how the deficiency or surplus was calculated. 1999 § 9-616. For a discussion of rights when the secured party knows that a third person owns the collateral, see Chapter 3, § 5.

Example. Debtor owes SP-1 $10,000 and is in default. SP-1 repossesses and resells the collateral. The sale (properly conducted) brings $15,000. Before the proceeds are distributed, SP-1 receives written notice from SP-2 of a junior security interest of $2,000. The expenses of the sale are $200 and the fee due the attorney for SP-1 is $500. The proceeds of the sale are applied as follows: (1) $200 to expenses and $500 to attorneys' fees, (2) $10,000 to pay the claim of SP-1, (3) $2,000 to pay the claim of SP-2, and (4) the surplus of $2,300 to Debtor. Note that if the sale (properly conducted) had brought only $8,000, the proceeds would have been applied $200 to expenses and $500 to attorneys' fees and $7,300 to apply against the debt due SP-1. That would leave Debtor liable for a $2,700 deficiency to SP-1 and the full $2,000 due SP-2.

In probably the majority of cases, a deficiency will result following the sale of collateral because such sales often do not bring favorable prices even when properly conducted and because some of the proceeds will be applied to expenses, attorneys' fees and like items.

CAVEAT. A number of states by statute outside the Code have restricted the right of a creditor with a security interest in consumer goods to repossess or sell the collateral and then collect a deficiency judgment. In some instances (particularly when the debt is under a certain amount) the secured party must elect between obtaining a judgment and attempting to collect the full debt, *or* repossessing and reselling the collateral but abandoning any claim to a deficiency judgment. Such statutes when in conflict with the Code override the provision of 1972 § 9-504(2) and 1999 § 9-615(d) permitting deficiency judgments.

Where the underlying transaction is a sale of accounts or chattel paper [which is within Article 9 under 1972 § 9-102(1)(b) and 1999 § 9-109(a)(3)], the debtor is entitled to any surplus or is liable for any deficiency only if the security agreement so provides. See 1972 § 9-504(2). See the similar provision in 1972 § 9-502(2). The same rules apply under the 1999 Code. See 1999 §§ 9-615(e) and 9-608(b).

c. *Method of Disposition: Public or Private Sale*

A secured party after default may sell or otherwise dispose of the collateral, under 1972 § 9-504(1) and 1999 § 9-610(a). The method of disposition is governed by 1972 § 9-504(3) and 1999 §§ 9-610, 9-611 and 9-624(a). This provides that disposition (sale) of the collateral may be by public or private proceedings and may be by one or more contracts. The reference to "public proceeding" is to a sale by auction. The reference to "private proceeding" is to a sale in some other way, such as one through commercial channels (e.g., a sale to a dealer who is in the business of selling goods of that kind).

Although public sales are recognized by the Code, it is hoped that private sales will be encouraged where, as is frequently the case, private sales through commercial channels will result in higher realization on collateral for the benefit of all parties. In this regard, the Code departs from certain pre-Code statutes which required public sales. See Comment 1 to 1972 § 9-504 and Comment 2 to 1999 § 9-610.

The sale or other disposition may be as a unit or in parcels and at any time and place and on any terms, but every aspect of the disposition must be commercially reasonable, under 1972 § 9-504(3) and 1999 § 9-610(b). The collateral may be disposed of on the debtor's premises if such method of disposition is reasonable. See 1972 § 9-503 and Comment, and 1999 § 9-609 and Comment 6.

d. Requirement That Sale Be "Commercially Reasonable"

Every aspect of the sale or other disposition of the collateral "including the method, manner, time, place and terms must be commercially reasonable." 1972 § 9-504(3) and 1999 § 9-610(b). The term "commercially reasonable" is not defined in the Code, but certain rules are set forth below to assist in determining whether disposition in a particular case is commercially reasonable. These rules are taken from 1972 § 9-507(2) and 1999 § 9-627.

(1) The fact that a better price could have been obtained by a sale at a different time or in a different method from that selected by the secured party is not of itself sufficient to establish that the sale was not made in a commercially reasonable manner. In other words, a low price received on the sale is not itself always determinative of lack of commercial reasonableness. However, there are indications from case law that a disposition shown to be at a price substantially under what might well have been received is not commercially reasonable. In particular, if the sale of the collateral is followed by a second sale at a substantially greater price, the first sale may be deemed not to have been commercially reasonable. Also, if the secured party is shown not to have exerted reasonable efforts (as by failure to contact a large number of prospective buyers) the sale may be held not commercially reasonable.

Example. Debtor bought a car from Dealer at a price of $1,395. Dealer assigned Debtor's chattel paper to Finance Company. Upon default, Finance Company repossessed the car and sold it back to Dealer for $348. Dealer made repairs costing $402 and then resold the car for $1,050. The sale by Finance Company to Dealer was not commercially reasonable.

(2) If the secured party either (a) sells the collat-

eral in the usual manner in any recognized market therefor, or (b) if he sells at a price current in such market at the time of his sale, or (c) if he has otherwise sold in conformity with reasonable commercial practices among dealers in the type of property sold, he has sold in a commercially reasonable manner. In this connection, it is recognized that a sale to or through a dealer is a method which in the long run may realize better average returns. See Comment 2 to 1972 § 9-507. The 1999 Code does not have an equivalent Comment, but it would appear the same policy is followed. See 1999 § 9-627(b)(3).

(3) The principles stated in points (1) and (2) above also apply as may be appropriate to other types of disposition (e.g., leasing of the collateral).

(4) A disposition which has been approved in any judicial proceeding or by any bona fide creditors' committee or representative of creditors shall conclusively be deemed to be commercially reasonable.

(5) None of the methods of disposition set forth above is to be regarded as either required or exclusive in determining if the disposition is commercially reasonable. See Comment 2 to 1972 § 9-507. The 1999 Code does not have an equivalent Comment, but it would appear the same rule would

continue to apply. See generally, 1999 § 9-627.

Unlike some former statutes, the Code sets forth no period within which disposition of the collateral must be made, except in the case of consumer goods, which under 1972 § 9-505(1) and 1999 § 9-620(e), (f) must in certain instances (if the debtor has paid over 60 percent of the price or loan) be sold within 90 days after the secured party has taken possession. The failure to prescribe a statutory period during which disposition must be made is in line with the policy adopted in Article 9 to encourage disposition by private sale through regular commercial channels. It may, for example, be wise not to dispose of goods when the market has collapsed, or to sell a large inventory in parcels over a period of time instead of in bulk. Note, however, that under 1972 § 9-504(3) and 1999 § 9-610(b), every aspect of the sale or other disposition of the collateral must be commercially reasonable; this specifically includes method, manner, time, place and terms. Accordingly, a secured party who has held collateral a long time without disposing of it, thus running up large storage charges against the debtor, where no reason existed for not making a prompt sale, might be found not to have acted in a "commercially reasonable" manner. See Comment 6 to 1972 § 9-504 and Comment 3 to 1999 § 9-610.

Note further the obligation of good faith required under § 1-203.

e. 1972 Code Requirement of Notice of Sale

Some pre-Code statutes had a required waiting period after repossession and before sale or required the giving of notice of the sale to the debtor in a specified manner (as by use of registered mail).

The 1972 Code departs from the more detailed requirements of some earlier statutes by merely requiring reasonable notification of the time and place of any public sale or reasonable notification of the time after which any private sale or other intended disposition is to be made. 1972 § 9-504(3).

Under the 1972 Code, the following additional requirements exist as to the giving of notification of sale:

(1) The notice must be sent to the debtor. The notice need not be given if the debtor has signed *after default* a statement renouncing or modifying his right to notification of sale.

(2) In the case of consumer goods, no notice need be given except to the debtor.

(3) In cases other than where the collateral is

consumer goods, the 1972 Code requires that reasonable notification be sent to any other secured party from whom the secured party has received (before sending his notification to the debtor or before the debtor's renunciation of his rights) written notice of a claim of an interest in the collateral.

(4) The requirement is merely that the notification be *sent* to the debtor (and in some instances to another secured party). The term "reasonable notification" is not defined in Article 9. At a minimum, the notification must be sent in such time that persons entitled to receive it will have sufficient time to take appropriate steps to protect their interests by taking part in the sale or other disposition if they so desire. See Comment 5 to 1972 § 9-504.

(5) Notification of impending disposition is not required where the collateral is (a) perishable, or (b) threatens to decline speedily in value, or (c) is of a type customarily sold on a recognized market. Examples of the latter category might be commodities or corporate stock traded on an exchange. However, used cars are not considered as items customarily sold in a recognized market.

Some decisions have construed the requirement of notice of sale under 1972 § 9-504(3). In this connection, it should be kept in mind that the requirement is merely that the notice be *sent*, not that it be received. It should be sent early enough so that debtor has time to act upon it if it is received in normal circumstances. However, there is no requirement that registered or certified mail be used; ordinary mail is sufficient if properly addressed and accompanied by proper postage.

Example 1. Secured Party, intending to sell the repossessed collateral privately one week later, sent a letter by certified mail to Debtor. Debtor, who lived on a rural mail route, received a notice that the piece of mail was being held for him at the post office. Debtor did not pick up the letter for two weeks. The collateral had been sold by that time. The notice was held sufficient.

Example 2. Secured Party orally notified Debtor of the impending sale of the collateral but failed to send written notice. The oral notice was held insufficient, in view of the requirement of 1972 § 9-504(3) that notification be *sent* and the definition of "send" in § 1-201(38) as indicating that the word apply only to a written communication.

Example 3. On June 6, Secured Party sent notice of public sale to be held on June 8. The notice was not received by Debtor until June 10. The notice was held insufficient.

In some instances, the contents of the notice may be relevant. The Code provision requires that the notice give the time and place of any public sale or the time after which any private sale or other intended disposition is to be made.

Example 4. The notice sent to the debtor merely stated that unless arrangements to pay were promptly made, the repossessed collateral would be sold. Such notice was held insufficient.

f. 1999 Code Requirement of Notice of Sale

Although the 1999 Code requirement of notice of sale is similar to the 1972 Code, there are some significant differences. In general, the 1999 Code notice requirement is more specific and detailed while requiring in most instances a pre-sale notice much like the 1972 Code. Thus, a secured party that disposes of collateral under 1999 § 9-610 must send to the debtor (and possibly other parties as discussed below) a reasonable authenticated notification of disposition. 1999 § 9-611(b).

(1) 1999 § 9-611(c) specifies the persons to whom notice of disposition must be sent. These persons include the debtor [1999 § 9-102(a)(28)], a secondary obligor [1999 § 9-102(a)(71)], any person

who has given the foreclosing secured party notice of a claim of interest, and generally, any other secured party that holds a perfected security interest in the collateral to be sold. 1999 § 9-611(c), (e). The notice need not be given the debtor or a secondary obligor if they have waived the requirement by an agreement to that effect entered into and authenticated after default. 1999 § 9-624(a).

(2) In the case of consumer goods, notice need be given only to the debtor and any secondary obligors. 1999 § 9-611(c)

(3) The notification must be sent within a reasonable time which is a question of fact. 1999 §§ 9-611(b), 9-612(a). However, unlike the 1972 Code, the 1999 Code specifies that in a non-consumer transaction a notice of disposition is reasonable if sent after default and 10 days or more before the earliest time of disposition set forth in the notice. 1999 § 9-612(b).

(4) Notice of the impending disposition is not required if the collateral is (a) perishable, or (b) threatens to decline speedily in value, or (c) is of a type customarily sold on a recognized market. 1999 § 9-611(d).

(5) The required form and content of the notice of disposition is described in detail in 1999 §§ 9-

613, 9-614. A "model form" is set out in 1999 § 9-613(5). Although a particular phrasing of the notice is not required [1999 § 9-613(4)] and other information may be included [1999 § 9-613(3)(A)], and minor errors are tolerated [1999 § 9-613(3)(B)], the required contents otherwise include: a description of the debtor and secured party; a description of the collateral subject to the disposition; a statement of the method of intended disposition; a statement that the debtor is entitled to an accounting of the unpaid surplus; and a statement of the time and place of a public sale or the time after which any other disposition is to be made. 1999 § 9-613(1). Additional information is required in a consumer-goods transaction: a description of any liability for a deficiency of the person to which the notice is sent; a telephone number from which the amount that must be paid to the secured party to redeem is available; and a telephone number or mailing address from which additional information concerning the disposition and the obligation secured is available. 1999 § 9-614(1). A "model form" for consumer goods transactions is set out in 1999 § 9-614(3).

g. *Rights of Buyer of Collateral*

When collateral is disposed of by the secured

party after default, the disposition (1) transfers to a purchaser for value all of the debtor's rights in the collateral; (2) discharges the security interest under which the disposition is made; and (3) discharges any subordinate or junior security interest or lien. 1972 § 9-504(4) and 1999 § 9-617(a).

Example. D gives a security interest in widgets to SP-1 to secure a loan (D then owning the widgets free and clear). SP-1 files. D then gives a security interest in the widgets to SP-2 to secure another loan. SP-2 also files but has an interest subordinate to SP-1 who filed first. Later, LC gets a judgment against D and levies on the widgets. D then defaults in payment to SP-1, who repossesses the widgets and sells them to P. P gets title to the goods free of the rights of D, SP-1, SP-2 and LC. (Note: If the repossession and sale had been conducted by SP-2 instead of SP-1, P would take the widgets free of the rights of D, SP-2 and LC, but subject to the senior security interest of SP-1).

Under 1972 § 9-504(4) and 1999 § 9-617(b), the purchaser takes free of all the above rights and interests (those of the debtor, secured party and junior security interests or liens although senior interests survive) even though the secured party has failed to comply with the default procedure requirements of 1972 §§ 9-501 through 9-507 and 1999

§§ 9-601 through 9-628, or of any judicial proceedings, if (1) in the case of a public sale, the purchaser has no knowledge of any defects in the sale and does not buy in collusion with any person connected with the sale; or (2) in any other case, if the purchaser acts in good faith. See 1972 § 9-504(4) and 1999 § 9-617(b).

In other words, the usual result is that the purchaser of the collateral after repossession and sale by the secured party takes good title to the collateral, even if the secured party has not complied with the default procedures (as by failing to give the debtor notice of the sale, selling in a commercially unreasonable manner, or the like), so long as the purchaser is acting in good faith. Note that a sale at an excessively low price might be an indication of lack of good faith.

The 1999 Code also provides that warranties that would run to a purchaser in a voluntary disposition also run to the purchaser in an Article 9 disposition. The secured party may disclaim those warranties. See 1999 § 9-610(d) through (f). The 1999 Code also provides for a procedure by which title is formally transferred of record to the buyer. 1999 § 9-619.

h. *Right of Secured Party to Buy Collateral*

In any instance where the secured party sells the collateral under 1972 § 9-504 or 1999 § 9-610, he may purchase (buy-in) the collateral himself. It is flatly provided in 1972 § 9-504(3) and 1999 § 9-610(c)(1) that the secured party may buy the collateral at any public sale. On the other hand, the right of the secured party to buy-in the collateral at a private sale is severely restricted; he may do so only if the collateral "is of a type customarily sold in a recognized market or is of a type which is the subject of widely distributed standard price quotations." 1972 § 9-504(3) and 1999 § 9-610(c)(2).

A secured party also has the right to purchase the collateral at a judicial sale and thereafter hold it free of any other requirements of the Code. This right is unqualified (except by the requirement of good faith) and exists whether the judicial sale is public or private. See 1972 § 9-501(5) and 1999 § 9-601(f).

The restriction on the right of the secured party to buy-in the collateral at a private, non-judicial sale recognizes that creditors have been known to overreach by conducting a sham sale, buying-in the collateral at an excessively low price, and then holding the debtor for a sizeable deficiency. However, that evil is less likely to exist where there is a private sale of goods sold on a market or subject to standard price quotations at the market or quoted price to the secured party. With the requirement of commercial reasonableness in 1972 § 9-504(3) and 1999 § 9-610(b), the very limited right of the secured party to buy-in at a private sale is unlikely to produce the abuses that have sometimes existed in the past. The same is true where a commercially reasonable public sale is made or where a sale is conducted under judicial supervision.

In any event, it would seem that the action of a secured party buying-in the collateral will be the subject of close scrutiny if challenged by the debtor. This should be particularly so if the secured party later sells the collateral at a price substantially above what he bought it for at his own sale.

i. *Effect of Payment by Guarantor or Like Person*

"A person who is liable to a secured party under a guaranty, indorsement, repurchase agreement or the like and who receives a transfer of collateral from the secured party or is subrogated to his rights has thereafter the rights and duties of the secured party. Such a transfer of collateral is not a sale or disposition of the collateral under [Article 9]." 1972 § 9-504(5). A nearly identical provision is found at

1999 § 9-618.

This provision is intended to preserve the common-law right of subrogation of a surety or guarantor in a secured transaction. If such a surety or guarantor has to pay the debt and acquires the collateral, he becomes the secured party and the security interest against the original debtor remains. Moreover, such a payment by the surety or guarantor is not a sale or disposition of the collateral following default, and is not governed by 1972 § 9-504(3) or 1999 § 9-618(b).

Example. Dealer sold a car and transferred the buyer's installment contract to Finance Company. When the buyer defaulted, Dealer repurchased the contract from Finance Company. The repurchase is not a private sale of the collateral under 1972 § 9-504(3) or 1999 § 9-610(b).

§ 9. Right of Redemption

Redemption (a term not defined in the Code) means the right to free the collateral from any lien or encumbrance and regain absolute title by payment of the amount due. Under 1972 § 9-506, the debtor or any other secured party may redeem the collateral by tendering fulfillment of all obligations secured by the collateral, as well as certain expenses, and (if provided in the security agreement and not prohibited by law) reasonable attorneys' fees and legal expenses. 1999 § 9-623 similarly permits a debtor, secondary obligor or any other secured party or lienholder to redeem.

If the agreement contains a clause accelerating the entire balance due on default in one installment, the entire balance would have to be tendered. See Comment to 1972 § 9-506 and Comment 2 to 1999 § 9-623. However, local consumer statutes should be consulted to determine if consumer debtors will be allowed simply to bring current the outstanding debt.

The right of redemption must be exercised before (1) the secured party has disposed of the collateral or entered into a contract for its disposition under 1972 § 9-504 or 1999 § 9-610, or (2) before the obligation has been discharged under 1972 § 9-505(2) and 1999 § 9-622 by the secured party taking the steps to retain the collateral in satisfaction of the debt. See 1972 § 9-506 and 1999 § 9-623(c) (this 1999 provision adds that redemption must occur prior to the time the secured party has accepted the collateral under 1999 § 9-622). These provisions depart from some real estate law and pre-Code secured transactions law by not setting forth a fixed period of time after foreclosure or sale within which redemption is permitted.

Under 1972 § 9-501(3)(d) and 1999 § 9-624(c), the debtor may not waive his right of redemption in the security agreement or otherwise *before default*. This recognizes the fundamental rule that "no mortgage clause has ever been allowed to clog the equity of redemption." Comment 4 to 1972 § 9-501. On the other hand, the debtor may waive his right of redemption *after default* by an agreement in writing under the 1972 Code or by an agreement to that effect entered into and authenticated after default under the 1999 Code. See 1972 § 9-506 and 1999 § 9-624(c), which includes an exception in a consumer goods transaction.

It should be noted that where a third person puts up the collateral for the debtor and that fact is known to the secured party, the third person has the right of redemption. See 1972 § 9-112(c) and 1999 §§ 9-102(a)(28), 9-623(a).

§ 10. Liability for Noncompliance With "Default" Provisions Under the 1972 Code

a. *Generally*

If it is established before disposition that the

secured party is not proceeding in accordance with the "default" provisions of 1972 §§ 9-501 through 9-507, disposition may be ordered or restrained on appropriate terms and conditions. 1972 § 9-507(1). In particular, if the debtor is under the jurisdiction of a bankruptcy court, there is inherent power in that court to restrain disposition, regardless of the reasonableness of the secured party's action. See Comment 1 to 1972 § 9-507.

If the disposition has already occurred, a purchaser for value will take free of the claims of the debtor, secured party and junior interests, under 1972 § 9-504(4). But, under 1972 § 9-507(1), the debtor (or any person entitled to notification or whose security interest has been made known to the secured party prior to the disposition) has a right to recover from the secured party any loss caused by a failure to comply with the "default" provisions of 1972 §§ 9-501 through 9-507.

The right to hold the secured party liable under 1972 § 9-507(1) also extends to a third person who has put up the collateral, where this is known to the secured party, under 1972 § 9-112(d).

A special rule in 1972 § 9-507(1) permits the debtor to recover a minimum of the credit service charge plus 10 percent of the principal amount of the debt or the time price differential plus 10 percent of the cash price, where the collateral is consumer goods and the secured party has failed to comply with the "default" provisions of 1972 §§ 9-501 through 9-507. This is a minimum but does not prevent the debtor recovering actual losses if any exceeding such minimal amounts.

Note that this rule does not bar recovery by the debtor under any consumer credit or similar law allowing a greater recovery, such as one in the nature of a civil penalty.

Example: Debtor borrowed $2,000 on an automobile financed at $6 per $100 over a period of three years. Under the special rule of 1972 § 9-507(1), Debtor may recover a minimum of $200 (10 percent of the principal amount) plus $360 (the credit service charge of $6 times 20 hundreds times 3 years) or a total of $560.

b. *Application of Rule of Liability*

Most of the cases where the debtor has attempted to hold the secured party liable for noncompliance with one or more of the "default" provisions of 1972 §§ 9-501 through 9-507 have involved such problems as:

(1) Improper repossession (as by repossessing the collateral prior to default or in breach of the peace or otherwise improperly), under 1972 § 9-503;

(2) Failure to give the debtor notice of the sale of the collateral under 1972 § 9-504(3);

(3) Resale at an excessively low price or otherwise under circumstances which are not commercially reasonable, under 1972 § 9-504(3).

Where the minimum recovery rule is not applied in the case of consumer goods (and sometimes where it is applied), there has been a tendency on the part of a number of courts to deny the secured party a deficiency judgment although there is conflicting authority. This is perhaps taking the easy way out, since it is often difficult for a debtor to show the damage or loss sustained by noncompliance. In particular, it would seem difficult for a debtor to show what loss was sustained by failure of the secured party to send notice of the sale of the collateral, unless the debtor cold also show that the giving of such notice would have enabled him to take some beneficial action.

Where the resale is found to be at an excessively low price and not conducted under commercially reasonable circumstances, some courts have indicated that the proper damages would be the difference between the fair market value of the collateral and the resale price, and this could be used to offset a deficiency judgment. Some other courts have also declined to disallow a deficiency judgment but have indicated the debtor could offset any loss shown against such deficiency judgment.

In several instances, improper repossession has subjected a secured party to a possible granting of punitive damages. This has occurred where the repossession has taken place unjustifiably in blatant disregard of the rights of the debtor or even of third persons (as where a secured party repossessed from a buyer in ordinary course of business who took free of the security interest or repossessed from a debtor who was not in default). There have also been several cases indicating other non-Code liability where repossession of property not subject to the security interest took place (as where a secured party repossessing a car failed to check the glove compartment in which valuables had been stored).

§ 11. Liability for Noncompliance With "Default" Provisions Under the 1999 Code

The 1999 Code provisions that determine the liability of a secured party for noncompliance with the default provisions of the 1999 Code [§§ 9-601 through 9-624] are set forth in 1999 §§ 9-625 through 9-628. Although these provisions are similar to the 1972 Code, there are some significant differences. In general, the 1999 Code provisions are more specific and detailed.

As is the case under the 1972 Code, if the secured party is not proceeding in accordance with the default provisions of the 1999 Code, a court may order or restrain continued enforcement of the security interest as appropriate to ensure compliance. 1999 § 9-625(a). Additionally, the secured party will be liable for damages in the amount of any loss caused by his failure to comply with the 1999 Code default provisions [1999 § 9-625(a)], including loss resulting from the secured party's failure to provide requested information under 1999 § 9-210 [1999 § 9-625(b)]. As to 1999 § 9-210, see discussion in Chapter 3, § 6.

The 1999 Code specifies who may recover damages. It includes the following persons: the debtor; an obligor; and a person who holds a security interest in or other lien on the collateral. 1999 § 9-625(c)(1). If the collateral is consumer goods, a debtor or secondary obligor may recover in any event an amount not less than the credit service charge plus 10 percent of the principal amount of the obligation or the time-price differential plus 10 percent of the cash price. 1999 § 9-625(c)(2).

If damages recoverable eliminate any deficiency, a debtor may recover damages for loss of surplus, but otherwise may not recover damages under previously discussed 1999 § 9-625(b) caused by the secured party's failure to comply with the default provisions of the 1999 Code. 1999 § 9-625(d).

Statutory damages are recoverable in addition to damages recoverable under 1999 § 9-625(b). The debtor, consumer obligor, or a person named as a debtor in a filed record may recover $500 in each case that a person violates various provisions of the 1999 Code including those found in 1999 §§ 9-208, 9-209, 9-509(a), 9-513(a) or (c), 9-616(b)(1), and 9-616(b)(2). Similarly, a debtor or consumer obligor may recovery $500 in addition to § 9-625(b) damages for violation of § 9-210.

The 1999 Code devotes 1999 § 9-626 to rules applicable to an action in which deficiency or surplus is an issue. In non-consumer transactions, the secured party need not prove compliance with the default provisions of the 1999 Code unless his compliance is placed in issue, in which case, the secured party does have the burden of proving his compliance. If the secured party fails to prove compliance, his recovery of a deficiency judgment is limited to an amount by which the sum of the secured obligation, expenses and attorneys' fees exceed the greater of the proceeds of collection (including disposition of the collateral) or the amount of proceeds that would have been realized had the secured party complied with the default provisions of the 1999 Code which amount is presumed to be equal to the secured obligation and related expenses unless the secured party proves otherwise. 1999 § 9-626(a)(3). If the commercial reasonableness of the conduct of the secured party is at issue, 1999 § 9-627 applies to provide guidance as to whether the conduct was commercially reasonable.

With regard to the effect of violations of the 1999 Code default provisions on the secured party's ability to obtain a deficiency judgment against a consumer debtor, the 1999 Code expressly leaves the matter to the courts. See 1999 § 9-626(b).

The 1999 Code does provide some secured parties with protection from liability described above in this section of the Nutshell. 1999 § 9-628 is an exculpatory provision designed to protect secured parties from liability that would otherwise result to unknown persons and under circumstances that would not allow a secured party to protect itself. See Comment 2 to 1999 § 9-628 and 1999 § 9-605.

Additionally, if a secured party acts under the reasonable belief that the transaction is not a consumer transaction, the transaction will be treated as a non-consumer transaction for most purposes associated with liability of the secured party. However, the basis for the reasonable belief must involve a debtor's or obligor's representation. 1999 § 9-628(c). See also, Comment 2 to 1999 § 9-628.

INDEX

References are to Chapters (Ch.)
and Sections (§)

INDEX

References are to Chapters (Ch.) and Sections (§)

PRIORITIES

See also Priorities, Buyers of Collateral;
Priorities Between Secured Parties

PRIORITIES, BUYERS OF COLLATERAL

See also Priorities; Priorities Between
Secured Parties